CHALLENGES AND NEW DIRECTIONS IN JOURNALISM EDUCATION

Drawing on original and innovative contributions from educators, practitioners and students, *Challenges and New Directions in Journalism Education* captures and informs our understanding of journalism pedagogy in the context of ongoing shifts in journalism practice.

Journalism is once again facing challenges, accused of elitism and often branded as too far removed from the reality of people's lives. The post-truth context has engendered a crisis of trust, and journalism is portrayed as core to the problem, rather than the solution. Citizen journalism and societal shifts have provoked a move away from 'top-down' reporting, towards greater interactivity with audiences, but inclusivity remains an issue with news organisations and industry councils intensifying protocols in a bid to create more diverse newsrooms. This poses multiple questions for journalism educators: How is journalism education engaging with these imperatives in the 'post-pandemic' context? How can student perspectives inform our response? What journalism should we teach? Against this landscape, and in response to these questions, this book engages with a series of key themes and objectives related to challenges and new directions in journalism education. These include discussions around safeguarding, sustainability, journalism's 'democratic deficit', integrating media literacy and the 'post-pandemic' context. Each chapter draws on primary data, case studies and examples to describe and unpack the topic, and concludes with practical suggestions for journalism educators.

Challenges and New Directions in Journalism Education is key reading for anyone teaching or training to become a teacher of journalism.

Karen Fowler-Watt is Associate Professor of Journalism and research theme lead for the Journalism Education Research Group in Bournemouth University's Centre for Excellence in Media Practice, UK. She is a former BBC journalist who worked in Radio 4 News and Current Affairs as an output editor and as a field producer in the Middle East and the United States.

CHALLENGES AND NEW DIRECTIONS IN JOURNALISM EDUCATION

Edited by Karen Fowler-Watt

LONDON AND NEW YORK

Designed cover image: © filo/DigitalVision Vectors via Getty Images

First published 2023
by Routledge
4 Park Square, Milton Park, Abingdon, Oxon OX14 4RN

and by Routledge
605 Third Avenue, New York, NY 10158

Routledge is an imprint of the Taylor & Francis Group, an informa business

© 2023 selection and editorial matter, Karen Fowler-Watt; individual chapters, the contributors

The right of Karen Fowler-Watt to be identified as the author of the editorial material, and of the authors for their individual chapters, has been asserted in accordance with sections 77 and 78 of the Copyright, Designs and Patents Act 1988.

All rights reserved. No part of this book may be reprinted or reproduced or utilised in any form or by any electronic, mechanical, or other means, now known or hereafter invented, including photocopying and recording, or in any information storage or retrieval system, without permission in writing from the publishers.

Trademark notice: Product or corporate names may be trademarks or registered trademarks, and are used only for identification and explanation without intent to infringe.

British Library Cataloguing-in-Publication Data
A catalogue record for this book is available from the British Library

ISBN: 9781032293226 (hbk)
ISBN: 9781032293189 (pbk)
ISBN: 9781003301028 (ebk)

DOI: 10.4324/9781003301028

Typeset in Bembo
by Newgen Publishing UK

CONTENTS

List of illustrations   vii
List of contributors   viii

Introduction   1

PART I
Challenges in journalism education   9

1. A changed landscape: Re-imagining journalism education 'post-pandemic'   11
   Karen Fowler-Watt

2. Broadening horizons: How student perspectives can help meet journalism's challenges   23
   Andrew Bissell

3. A "hotchpotch of conflicting schools": The problems plaguing journalism education in the 2020s   36
   Graham Majin

4. Sports journalism's dilemma: All about celebrating the spectacle?   48
   Max Mauro

5. Why politics and public affairs still matter   62
   David Brine

6 Media literacy and/in journalism education: Learning from
   (media) action   70
   Julian McDougall

PART II
New directions in journalism education   **87**

7 Inclusive approaches to news   89
   Daniel Henry and De-Graft Mensah

8 Integrating journalism education and the sustainability agenda 100
   Fiona Cownie and Michael Sunderland

9 From skillset to mindset: The re-conceptualisation of
   entrepreneurial journalism in higher education   115
   Jo Royle

10 My story: Journalism for and by young people to prevent
   the recruitment of children and teenagers by non-state armed
   groups in Colombia   130
   Mathew Charles

11 Better safe than sorry: Preparing journalism students for a
   dangerous world   146
   Jaron Murphy

   Reflections   161

Index   *175*

ILLUSTRATIONS

Figures

6.1	Theory of change	74
8.1	Framework for sustainability within journalism education	112

Tables

1.1	WJEC panel recommendations	18
6.1	Mapping organisational strategy to the theory of change	76

CONTRIBUTORS

Andrew Bissell has spent 30 years as a newspaper and online journalist. Before joining the academy in 2013, he was employed as a news reporter, features and news editor. He is the author of two social history books that record memories of London's East End and Southampton during the 1920s, 1930s and Blitz years. A fully qualified NCTJ journalist and Doctor of Education, Andrew's research focuses on student perspectives of their experiences of journalism education. He is currently Deputy Head of the Communication and Journalism Department at Bournemouth University.

David Brine is a highly experienced news and features editor, working in the regional press. He is a fully qualified NCTJ journalist and is now a Lecturer in Journalism at Bournemouth University, who works to deliver the NCTJ/Facebook Community Reporter training programme. David's research interests focus on the teaching of politics and public affairs.

Mathew Charles is Principal Professor in the Faculty of International Political and Urban Studies at Del Rosario University, Bogota, Colombia. He is interested in creative and participatory peace building. His research focuses on organised crime in Latin America and the participation of children and teenagers in gangs and non-state armed groups in particular.

Fiona Cownie is Associate Professor with a background in marketing and a track record of leadership in Higher Education, with a focus on relational, collaborative and co-created strategy. Fiona works within a cross-disciplinary (academic/professional services) team to advance the Sustainability strategy at Bournemouth University, including the recently approved Climate and Ecological Crisis Action Plan. Her research interests focus on the academic/student relationship.

Karen Fowler-Watt is Associate Professor of Journalism and Global Narratives and research theme lead for the Journalism Education Research Group in Bournemouth University's Centre for Excellence in Media Practice, UK. She is a former BBC journalist and a Fellow of the Salzburg Academy on Media & Global Change. Karen is editor (with Stephen Jukes) of *New Journalisms: Rethinking Practice, Theory and Pedagogy* (Routledge, 2020) and (with Julian McDougall) *The Palgrave Handbook of Media Misinformation* (Palgrave Macmillan, 2022). Her research focuses on reporting trauma and conflict, marginalised voices and re-imagining journalism education.

Daniel Henry is a TV journalist and documentary maker, with over a decade of experience in news. Prior to his recent move to ITV London, he was a reporter/producer for the flagship BBC World TV bulletin, Focus on Africa. His latest film follows the Black Lives Matter protests across the UK, sparked by the killing of George Floyd in Minneapolis. 'Fighting the Power – Britain After George Floyd' was commissioned by BBC Three. Previously, Daniel worked for BBC London, ITV News, Sky News and Channel 4 News, as well as *The Independent* and *The Daily Telegraph*.

Graham Majin has more than 20 years' experience working in TV news, factual filmmaking and media production. He has been an on-screen reporter, news editor and senior producer – including working for 14 years at BBC News, during which time he regularly edited the evening news for London and the South East. He also produced 'See Hear', the BBC's magazine for the Deaf community, and directed documentaries for BBC2. Graham researches fake news and how the concept of truth is understood differently by audiences, journalists and academics. His research is inter-disciplinary and draws on media theory, cognitive psychology, philosophy, narrative theory and intellectual history.

Max Mauro has worked for ten years as a journalist and writer in Italy, Germany and Venezuela. In 2014, he was awarded FIFA Research Scholarship to conduct a study on migrant youth, football and belonging, which led to the publication of *The Balotelli Generation. Issues of inclusion and belonging in Italian football and society* (Peter Lang, 2016). In 2019, he completed a follow-up to his PhD research and published the book *Youth sport, migration and culture. Two football teams and the changing face of Ireland* (Routledge, 2019). Max's research interests encompass sport and processes of racialisation; mass media and national identity; journalism and ethnographic writing.

Julian McDougall is Professor in Media and Education, Head of the Centre for Excellence in Media Practice and Principal Fellow of Advance HE. He runs the Professional Doctorate (EdD) in Creative and Media Education at Bournemouth University and convenes the annual International Media Education Summit. He is the author of a range of over 100 books, articles, chapters and research reports and has provided numerous research projects for research councils, media industry, charities and non-profit organisations. These include the European Union and European Commission, British Council, Arts and Humanities Research Council, ESRC and EPSRC, Samsung, the United Kingdom Literacy Association, UK Government DCMS, US Embassy, ITV and BBC.

De-Graft Mensah is the presenter of BBC *Newsround* and the podcast, 'If You Don't Know'. He is a broadcast journalist with an interest in producing news for young audience and brining as many voices as possible into news storytelling. De-Graft's experience ranges from working in television news to online news and he has also been involved in finding innovative ways to use social media to engage audiences.

Jaron Murphy has extensive international experience in journalism encompassing print and digital news, mostly in senior editorial/production and management roles, including staff trainings. An award-winning journalist, he appeared in 2018 on the NCTJ list of most respected journalists following research which asked journalists working in the UK and Ireland 'which living journalist they felt most embodies the values of journalism that they respect and adhere to'. He is Principal Academic in Communication, Journalism and Literature at Bournemouth University, UK, and holds a DPhil from the University of Oxford.

Jo Royle is Head of the School of Creative and Cultural Business at Robert Gordon University, Aberdeen. Jo has a sustained track record in leadership within Higher Education. Her research interests span creative and cultural education, media management, media strategy, electronic publishing and e-books. Her doctoral thesis examined the challenges of teaching entrepreneurship to journalism students in HEIs.

Michael Sunderland is a former Sky News journalist who has spent much of his career in Africa, as a journalist and working for Save the Children. He is a Programme Leader for MA Multimedia Journalism at Bournemouth University and a PhD candidate with research interests in humanitarian communications, campaigning and media and sustainability. Mike is currently working on a research and capacity building project aiming to strengthen disaster preparedness among crisis communicators in Sierra Leone.

INTRODUCTION

Challenges and New Directions in Journalism Education was produced in the early stages of what is now tentatively referred to as the 'post-pandemic' era. Two years after the coronavirus disease 2019 (Covid-19) first hit the headlines in early 2020, we are experiencing a heightened sense of precarity characterised by economic crisis and social dissonance: Russia's invasion of Ukraine in February 2022 has been a key destabilising factor, as evidence of genocide rapidly emerged, with the conflict exacerbating the cost-of-living crisis on a global scale and intensifying the impact of coronavirus by displacing millions of people who were fleeing for their lives. In the early months of the pandemic, Black Lives Matter protests following the murder of George Floyd in the United States had shone a spotlight on persistent issues of race and social justice. As we entered the third decade of the 21st century it felt as though any advances towards more inclusive, tolerant and civically engaged societies had been inadequate, or too slow to have an impact and were now under threat in the wake of pandemic, protest and conflict.

'Covid times' were dark times, captured by Britain's poet laureate Simon Armitage, describing the endless lockdowns as a period in which "The sky stretched thin over the frame of day",[1] when time seemed to stand still, lives flattening out into linear existence, without the anchor of events or memories. Every day was quiet, following the same pattern, and often viewed through a window. Journalists, reporting on events never seen before in their lifetime, faced challenges, which were not even experienced when reporting war – they were living the story that they were reporting on, rather than just bearing witness. Journalists too were watching through windows, often delivering the news from their own bedrooms. It could be said that the global pandemic brought trauma to their own doorstep (Jukes et al, 2021). As journalists and journalism educators we faced these new challenges in a context already toxified by mis- and dis-information, dominated by populist and/ or opportunistic narratives, where holding power to account was often deemed

DOI: 10.4324/9781003301028-1

'unpatriotic' rather than an act of civic responsibility. In the UK, a YouGov poll of 1,652 people conducted in April 2020 for Sky News found that two-thirds of the pubic were untrusting of TV journalists (a pre-existing issue, not a result of coronavirus), but the public was generally supportive of the government and its policies in "rallying around the flag" (Jennings et al, 2020). In the heart of the pandemic, across the world people turned to the media for information, with many journalists finding their voice, but media freedom was also often challenged, particularly when regimes used the threat of the virus as a reason to close down debate or protest (Selva, 2020).

The idea for a book that explores how journalism education can make a positive contribution to debates about the future shape and form of media 'post-pandemic' evolved against this backdrop: the product of conversations within the Journalism Education Research Group (JERG) – a group that includes alumni and colleagues in industry and the academy – based in our research centre, the Centre for Excellence in Media Practice (CEMP) at Bournemouth University in the UK. As a collective, we share an interest in student perspectives and innovative thinking around journalism pedagogy with a focus on voice, inclusivity and civic impact. We aim to make a contribution to the wider academic community, through our interest in journalism's role within wider media ecologies, putting research at the forefront of journalism education. Hence, *Challenges and New Directions in Journalism Education* aims to inform our understanding of journalism education in the context of shifts in journalism practice. It hopes to start a conversation.

The importance of listening

The emphasis is on listening, not telling. It seems we face multiple questions as journalism educators: How is journalism education engaging with the imperatives of the 'post-pandemic' context? How can student perspectives inform our response? What journalism should we teach? How do we navigate the inherent tensions between skills delivery and critique of practice? In response to such questions, we seek to engage actively and critically with a range of themes related to challenges and new directions in journalism education:

- Listening to journalism educators in a changed landscape
- Broadening horizons through journalism students' perspectives
- Reflecting on shifts in journalism's normative values
- Evaluating critical challenges in sports journalism
- Integrating media literacy in journalism pedagogy
- Including a diverse range of voices in news and newsrooms
- Engaging journalism students in sustainability issues
- Tackling journalism's democratic deficit
- Re-conceptualising entrepreneurial journalism
- Introducing participatory journalism to marginalised youth
- Safeguarding journalists

The active form of verbs here is important – the book presents a snapshot captured in the midst of tumult, but we see this as opportunity rather than threat: a chance to reimagine journalism education. We are, however, actively engaged in tussling with these issues and do not propose easy answers, rather we seek to spark further debate about a range of topics that present challenges, invite new ideas and to offer some tentative thoughts about new directions, in journalism education, including our manifesto for change, which we hope will add to the conversation (see: Final Reflections).

Challenges and new directions

The challenges facing journalism in today's turbulent media landscape are well documented; its normative practices and risks to the profession, along with disruption of its traditional business model, are regularly scrutinised, as noted elsewhere (Fowler-Watt et al, 2020). This edited collection aims to offer a study of the ways in which journalism and media educators are engaging with current challenges within these difficult contexts through making interventions and offering responses, as well as driving and leading change. The chapters therefore seek to capture their self-reflexive accounts anchored in the experience of pedagogic practice.

Each chapter describes a challenge or new direction in journalism education and unpacks it, drawing on original material, case studies, examples and lived experiences and concludes with either questions to debate further, practical suggestions for journalism educators and/or calls to action. The final chapter represents a semi-structured conversation between several of the chapter authors, in which we share our reflections on the process of writing up our ideas, the challenges that we have engaged with throughout the book and thoughts about the future shape and form of journalism, both practice and pedagogy. Inspired by Freirian[2] ideas of the potential for transformation inherent within dialogue, we hope that in representing this dialogic forum, readers will be encouraged to engage in their own process of reflection – and discussion. Given the current period of disbelief in information and a serious decline in trust – now becoming endemic in the contemporary media landscape – we also hope that this book will make a contribution to wider socio-political debates about the role of journalism education in civic society.

Part I: Challenges in journalism education

In Chapter 1, 'A Changed Landscape: Re-imagining Journalism Education Post-pandemic', as editor, I aim to set the scene for the rest of the book, taking as a starting point this dramatically changed landscape within which we all live and work. In assessing the impact of the Covid-19 crisis on journalism students' lived experiences, and on educators, seeking to design responsive, agile pedagogies, this chapter considers what approaches could be used to achieve and support resilience – for educators and students – in 'post-pandemic' journalism education.

Student perspectives play a vital role in the debate about what journalism could and should be. In Chapter 2, 'Broadening Horizons: Can Student Perspectives Help Meet Journalism's Challenges?' Andrew Bissell draws on the philosophy of Hans-Georg Gadamer (2004) to employ the metaphor of horizon to capture students' thoughts on how journalism education can better equip them to address the issues pertinent to them. He seeks to produce a practical, co-produced approach to journalism pedagogy, enriched by student interpretation, due to its relevance to young people and their lives.

The question 'What journalism should we teach?' runs like a red thread through Chapter 3: 'A "Hotchpotch of Conflicting Schools": The Problems Plaguing Journalism Education in the 2020s'. Graham Majin assesses the challenges presented to the dominant approach of Boomer Journalism by Unofficial Journalism – two journalisms that, he argues, are mutually incompatible and hostile – so which should be taught? How can we teach journalism if we are unsure exactly what it is? The chapter presents a provocation to encourage educators to reflect on the wider picture as they design curricula that recognises the needs of students in changing educational and social contexts.

Historically, sports journalism has often been considered the 'toy department' of a media outlet. The challenges this presents are examined by Max Mauro in Chapter 4, 'Sports Journalism's Dilemma: All about Celebrating the Spectacle?' Students enrolling on sports journalism courses will be dealing with issues beyond a match report – issues ranging from *sportswashing* to racism – and the list is growing. This presents a critical challenge: the need to equip future sports journalists with multiple practical skills and the appropriate critical lens through which to comprehend the complexity of their specialism – a combination of skills that is essential to guarantee the credibility of sports journalism.

Chapter 5 focuses on another area of specialism – politics – and is presented in the form of an essay, written from the perspective of a former newspaper editor and now educator, training future journalists in the UK for the professional diploma of the National Council for the Training of Journalists (NCTJ). In 'Why Politics and Public Affairs Still Matter', David Brine draws on the teaching of Public Affairs – what he calls the "Cinderella subject" – to present a case study of the challenges of teaching public interest journalism to students who manifest decreasing levels of knowledge, understanding and interest in politics. The essay concludes that it is incumbent on journalism educators to find inspiring ways for trainee journalists to translate theory to practice in order to engage in the public sphere.

The final chapter in this part pivots towards new approaches to journalism education, whilst engaging with the challenges presented by media literacy (ML). As a media literacy researcher, Julian McDougall shares his experience of working with BBC Media Action to develop a strategy for the charity to combine the training of journalists in media literacy with increasing the media literacies of audiences. 'Media Literacy and/in Journalism Education – Learning from (Media) Action' argues that the task of both raising media literacy levels and situating a broadcaster as a conduit for ML can work only in a "third space" between the everyday practices of people and the need to raise awareness about the value of public interest media. The author reflects on the process and looks ahead to present a theory of change, concluding with a set of recommendations for journalism education practice.

Part II: New directions in journalism education

The second part of the book aims to explore the new directions for journalism education, against the backdrop of challenges set out in Part I. Inclusivity continues to present major challenges within journalism – both in practice and pedagogy. Chapter 7: 'Inclusive Approaches to News' brings two young black journalists together in conversation to discuss issues of lack of diversity in newsrooms, systemic racism and the persistence of an attainment gap. BBC *Newsround* presenter and podcaster, De-Graft Mensah focuses on young people and news, how we engage them in key issues around class and race, making complex stories such as Black Lives Matter accessible and inclusive. Daniel Henry is a TV journalist and documentary maker, who has taken his own experiences out into journalism schools to share with students the mental health impacts of systemic racism. In this conversation, they discuss their own backgrounds and lived experiences of working in news and they urge calls to action for journalism educators to help lead and accelerate change.

Chapter 8, 'Integrating Journalism Education and the Sustainability Agenda' offers critical perspectives on teaching sustainability to journalists. Media researcher Fiona Cownie and journalism educator Michael Sunderland share good practice, and using two case studies from undergraduate and postgraduate journalism teaching, they highlight challenges faced by journalism education in addressing the sustainability agenda – notably the UN's Sustainable Development Goals (SDGs) – and suggest action moving forward. The ultimate aim is to equip future journalists to contribute to ethically responsible societies.

Entrepreneurial skills have long been vaunted as a route to employability for journalism students and trainees, but Chapter 9 acknowledges that it is no longer possible to merely impart a skills toolkit as preparation for a career in journalism. In 'From Skillset to Mindset: The Re-conceptualisation of Entrepreneurial Journalism in Higher Education', Jo Royle shares the fieldwork for her doctoral research carried out in four higher education institutions in the UK and US. This chapter proposes that newsroom-based approaches to journalism education restrict whose voices are heard and that journalists must be able to exhibit an entrepreneurial mindset that makes them more relevant in participatory, digital culture.

The transformative potential of journalism education for marginalised young people is the focus of Chapter 10, which features the participatory news project *Mi Historia*. In 'My Story: News for and by Teenagers Preventing the Recruitment of Youngsters by Non-state Armed Groups through Participatory Journalism in Colombia', journalist, documentary maker and educator Mathew Charles – who is based in Bogotá in Colombia – discusses the project and its potential for enhancing positive self-efficacy amongst at-risk teenagers by building their capacity to claim a greater voice within their communities and changing their perceptions of life within an armed group.

Part II concludes with a chapter that pulls together the themes of building resilience and educating journalism students for challenging environments. On average, every five days a journalist is killed for their reporting, according to UNESCO. The threats to journalists are not just physical, they are also mental and virtual, with online violence described in a recent report as "the new frontline in journalism safety" (UNESCO, 2020). In Chapter 11, 'Better Safe than Sorry: Preparing Journalism Students for a Dangerous World', former investigative journalist Jaron Murphy considers how journalism educators can prepare their students to face these challenges, dangers and threats. Drawing on case studies and interviews with industry experts and NGOs, who aim to support journalists through training in self-care, the chapter offers practical advice on how we can best prepare students to speak truth to power whilst staying safe in an increasingly dangerous world.

As already described, in the final section, 'Reflections' of several of the authors on the process of writing for this book are captured in a conversation that pulls together collective themes to consider transformative approaches to journalism education and hopes to inspire further dialogue through a 'manifesto for change'.

I would like to thank my colleagues in the Journalism Education Research Group (JERG) in the Centre for Excellence in Media Practice (CEMP), our colleagues who are alumni, journalists in industry and academics based in HE elsewhere in the UK and overseas and all those who contributed to this book. It is the result of many conversations shared in all sorts of spaces and places – but mainly virtual in recent times! Thank you for your support, interest and commitment in bringing those dialogues to the page as the book took shape through the immediate 'post-pandemic' period when we were still living in the story that we were teaching students to report on. Many of us faced significant challenges through this time, but relished an opportunity to reflect on our practice and to discuss with our peers the shifting shape of journalism education. We shared those initial reflections as an intervention in an online journal article (Fowler-Watt et al, 2020) which gave us a *modus operandi* as we developed the design of *Challenges and New Directions in Journalism Education*. It has been a positive and energising experience. I appreciate hugely the care, time and work that each contributor has put in. My thanks to Andrew Bissell, David Brine, Mathew Charles, Fiona Cownie, Daniel Henry, Max Mauro, Graham Majin, Julian McDougall, De-Graft Mensah, Jaron Murphy, Jo Royle and Michael Sunderland. I would also like to thank the Salzburg Academy for Media and Global Change, for maintaining a constant focus on the importance of transformative media pedagogies, and for their support for me as a Fellow of the Academy. Thanks also go to Bournemouth University, particularly the Centre for Excellence in Media Practice and, at Routledge to Hannah McKeating.

Karen Fowler-Watt
September 2022

Notes

1 Simon Armitage has been Britain's poet laureate since 2019. He wrote a series of lockdown poems, and this is a line from 'The Sky Stretched Thin'. You can read the full poem here: www.theguardian.com/books/2021/may/08/windows-on-the-world-pandemic-poems-by-simon-armitage-hollie-mcnish-kae-tempest-and-more
2 Paolo Freire (1921–1997) was a Brazilian educator and philosopher who advocated critical pedagogy. Freire emphasised the role of dialogue in effecting transformation and enabling freedom.

References

Fowler-Watt, K., Majin, G., Sunderland, M., Phillips, M., Brine, D., Bissell, A., and Murphy, J. (2020). 'Reflections on the shifting shape of journalism education in the Covid-19 pandemic'. *Digital Culture and Education*, 22 June 2020. Available at: www.digitalcultureandeducation.com/reflections-on-covid19/journalism-education

Gadamer, H-G. (2004). *Truth and Method*. London: Continuum.

Jennings, W., and Curtis, C. (2020). 'No trust in the media has not collapsed because of coronavirus'. YouGov, 29 April 2020. Available at: https://yougov.co.uk/topics/entertainment/articles-reports/2020/04/29/no-trust-media-has-not-collapsed-because-coronavir

Jukes, S., Fowler-Watt, K., and Rees, G. (2021). 'Reporting the Covid-19 pandemic: Trauma on our own doorstep'. *Digital Journalism*, 12 September 2021. Available at: www.tandfonline.com/doi/full/10.1080/21670811.2021.1965489

Selva, M. (2020). 'Healing words: How press freedom is being threatened by the coronavirus pandemic'. Reuters Institute for the Study of Journalism, 7 April 2020. Available at: https://reutersinstitute.politics.ox.ac.uk/news/healing-words-how-press-freedom-being-threatened-coronavirus-pandemic

UNESCO (2020). *Safety of Journalists Covering Protests: Preserving Freedom of the Press During Times of Turmoil*. Available at: https://unesdoc.unesco.org/ark:/48223/pf0000374206, accessed 18 September 2022.

PART I
Challenges in journalism education

1
A CHANGED LANDSCAPE

Re-imagining journalism education 'post-pandemic'

Karen Fowler-Watt

Introduction

We live and work within a dramatically changed landscape. The coronavirus disease 2019 (Covid-19) crisis presented journalists with the unique challenge of living in the story that they were also reporting (Jukes et al, 2021); in the heart of the pandemic, the Black Lives Matter protests in the spring of 2020 shone a spotlight on issues of voice and marginality and as the world started to emerge from lockdown early in 2022, Russia's invasion of Ukraine exacerbated a global sense of precarity. In a briefing note on the impact of the global pandemic on different groups of workers for the Resolution Foundation, Gustafsson and McCurdy (2020) placed young people at the epicentre of the crisis. In assessing the impact of the Covid-19 crisis on journalism students' lived experiences, and on educators, seeking to design responsive, agile pedagogies, this chapter considers what approaches could be used to achieve and support resilience in 'post-pandemic' journalism education. As journalism educators, responding and adapting to crisis, we have also discovered – through the work of our students in the virtual space – new ways of teaching journalism and innovative approaches to storytelling as we grapple together with the shifting shapes of journalism practice and journalism education (Fowler-Watt et al, 2020).

Re-imagining journalism education in an era of change

At the end of 2021, I was invited to produce a report on the impact of the Covid-19 pandemic on journalism education, to scope out the context for a panel discussion of this topic at the World Journalism Education Council's online conference, 'Reimagining journalism education in the age of change' which took place on 30 June 2022. The report was circulated to the panel chair, Pascal Guénée,

DOI: 10.4324/9781003301028-3

director of the Institute of Practical Journalism at Paris Dauphine University and to the participants, ten journalism educators from the Philippines, South Africa, Chile, Georgia, Russia, Brazil, UK, Jammu, Egypt and UAE, forming a basis for discussion at the live streamed global event.[1] The panel was founded on the idea that the pandemic had a particular impact on journalism schools and on journalism practice, with journalism education having to adapt in real time and newsrooms having to adapt due to lockdowns. Teaching and work in the field had to respond instantly. Journalism education and journalism practice continue to adapt and appear to have changed permanently as a result of their response to crisis.

Journalists usually report on crisis. The pandemic placed journalists, like everyone else, in the crisis, thus presenting a unique challenge to journalism, its normative values and to journalism educators. Drawing from the report I produced for World Journalism Education Congress (WJEC), the presentations and discussions amongst the international group of journalism educators in the conference stream, and the observations of practising journalists, in this chapter I consider how journalism education has responded and continues to adapt, over two years later, engaging with the core themes defined by the conference panel. It will then assess whether journalism education is permanently modified and share the conclusions drawn from the WJEC panel discussions. Finally, it will add to the mix, the work of students and faculty at the 2022 Salzburg Academy for Media and Global Change,[2] with its theme of 'Transformative Media After Pandemic', to consider what lessons can be learned when journalism education is placed in the wider context of transformative media pedagogies.

'Red flags' raised

Prior to the pandemic, journalists and journalism educators already faced significant challenges. Journalism is accused of elitism and often branded as too far removed from the reality of people's lives (McGill, 2016; Snow, 2017). The post-truth context has engendered a crisis of trust, and journalism is often portrayed as contributing to the problem, rather than offering solutions. In her McTaggart lecture, at the Edinburgh TV Festival in August 2022, former BBC journalist and presenter Emily Maitlis acknowledged the dangers presented to journalism by the current climate, which she discerned to be characterised by journalists "becoming anesthetised to the rising temperature in which facts are getting lost, constitutional norms trashed, claims frequently unchallenged" (Maitlis, 2022).

Despite a brief reprieve in the heart of the pandemic, when trust levels improved worldwide, journalism remains seriously fractured, some would say, broken. For some time now, citizen journalism and societal shifts have engendered a move away from 'top-down' reporting, towards greater interactivity with audiences, but inclusivity remains an issue: news organisations are grappling with initiatives to create more diverse newsrooms, but there is still a long way to go.

The pandemic raised more 'red flags' for journalism, according to a survey conducted by the International Center for Journalists (ICFJ) and the Tow Center for Digital Journalism at Columbia University (Posetti et al, 2020), which gathered responses from 1,400 English speaking journalists in 125 countries: 70% rated the psychological and emotional impacts of dealing with the Covid-19 crisis as the most difficult aspect of their work; 81% were working in a context where mis/disinformation presented key issues. The 'info-demic', defined by the World Health Organisation as "an overabundance of information, both online and offline", has created a toxic environment

> It includes deliberate attempts to disseminate wrong information to undermine the public health response and advance alternative agendas of groups or individuals. Mis- and disinformation can be harmful to people's physical and mental health.
>
> *(WHO, 23 September 2020)*

Many journalists felt the weight of responsibility and a heightened sense of mission to disseminate accurate, reliable information about coronavirus, often whilst struggling to assess risk and make decisions for their own households (Jukes et al, 2021). This presents a difficult landscape within which to teach the journalists of tomorrow. The pandemic exacerbated some of the challenges facing journalism, whilst providing opportunity for innovation and change.

Over two years on from the start of the pandemic, this was the context within which the WJEC conference stream debated four key areas:

- Teaching and assessment methods
- Relationship with industry
- Well-being and duty of care
- Future directions

Teaching and assessment methods

Rapid response was required at the outset of the pandemic. The move to teaching online, generally over Zoom, presented challenges for a discipline that flourishes in face-to-face, newsroom environments and usually with a shoulder-to-shoulder apprenticeship model style of pedagogy. Social distancing and mask-wearing compromised this model. Teaching online thus required tutors of practical skills to respond with creativity, whilst ensuring equity in terms of students' access to technology (Ndzinisa and Diamini, 2021), a reliable broadband connection and the requisite capabilities with remote, rather than hands-on, technical support. Issues of access, equity and inclusivity were sharpened by the move online. At the WJEC conference, journalism educators from the Philippines and South Africa presented samples of the impact of this inequity; for example, students from Filipino provinces who lacked stable internet connection became more reliant on asynchronous materials, which they could access when they could connect; in South Africa, journalism educators faced regular power cuts or 'load shedding' (an issue prior to the pandemic), presenting a challenge to the attempts of one educator in Durban working on a collaborative project with a university in the US. Hierarchies can become flattened in the virtual space, but access to that space needs to be universally available; the pandemic highlighted socio-economic inequity within and across national boundaries. In 2020, a World Economic Forum report described the pandemic as "an economic wrecking ball with intragenerational consequences" (Goldin et al, 2020). Its 'Covid Action' platform monitored key areas where inequality was most keenly felt, such as income, gender, minority populations and issues of access to healthcare, jobs, green spaces and the digital divide (World Economic Forum report, August 2020).

Journalism educators worldwide devised innovative approaches to attempt to mitigate inequity: from publication of detailed documents providing information, of free virtual technical tools (e.g., see the work at Concordia University, Montreal, 2020) to allowing students to conduct interviews over the phone or via video conference call, as one of the WJEC panellists from the former Soviet republic of Georgia observed, mobile phones could be used to make video packages, but it is important to ensure that all students have the digital competencies to do so. New formats for storytelling evolved: for example, inspired by the rise in lockdown-style video diaries (Estefania, 2020; Toniolo, 2020), educators in the UK adapted industry-accredited television journalism teaching to a mobile journalism "survivor video" alternative (Fowler-Watt et al, 2020). In sub-Saharan Africa, the pandemic accelerated experimentation with online tools for teaching journalists (Reuters Institute report, 2021). In other areas, the flipped classroom model of pedagogy already employed in some J-Schools (such as the Indian Institute of Journalism and New Media, Bangalore), gave institutions a head start in the move online. However, according to research conducted in 15 journalism J-schools in Russia, shared at the WJEC panel, new practices in online teaching were often imported from off-line methods, and not always fit for purpose in terms of inspiring interactivity. This indicates that a restructure of journalism education is required to make it more compatible with the mix of face-to-face and online delivery.

When hybridity was introduced and some teaching took place back on campus, or students could report in the community again, seminar groups had to shrink in size to accommodate social distancing, perhaps half the student number would be online, the other half in the newsroom – which led students and teachers to develop their communication skills, experimenting with channels like Slack and Teams to build digital communities – often mimicking newsroom workflows in the process. Original modes of storytelling such as mobile videos also moved from temporary fix to become baked into journalism pedagogic practice. Similarly, experimentation with different social media platforms such as Tik Tok developed apace. Covid-19 is redrawing the boundaries of the journalistic field breaking down objectivity and amplifying subjectivity, as human stories, often with auto/biographical elements, were employed to engage audiences with relatable information – for journalism students, family often provided the most accessible interview material for their storytelling.

Modes of assessment also had to change quickly and equitably: presentations were recorded or conducted live online, group news days were flipped into portfolios, peer assessment was developed and innovative modes such as photo diaries, self-reflections, vlogs and blogs integrated into assessment schedules. In the UK, the leading industry council, the National Council for the Training of Journalists (NCTJ)[3], devised online strategies for all of its professional diploma exams. Journalists are known for their flexibility and adaptability; troubleshooting and finding workarounds became part of the daily routine for journalism educators and journalists alike (Leonard, 2020). This was reflected by all of the journalism educators on the WJEC panel: from the need to devise grading systems that were neither too severe, nor too lax, whilst striving to maintain standards (Philippines) to designing assessments that effectively examine distance learning (Egypt and UAE). The importance of formative feedback was also enhanced, so that students could chart their progress and draw on the advice of their tutors – usually via online tutorials and/or written feedback – to improve their performance in the final assignment.

Relationship with industry

Work placement, internships and industry experience are integral to practice-orientated journalism programmes worldwide. The pandemic closed down these opportunities for students, with some news organisations moving mentoring and internships online, others seizing the chance to review their structures and workflows, at worst downsizing and reducing workforce numbers. In the 'post-pandemic' context news organisations are recovering from temporary lay-offs and furlough, with many making the decision not to return to full-time office working (see, Poynter Institute, 2022; Mayhew and Turvill, 2020). This has knock-on effects for journalism students and underlines the sense of precarity experienced by journalists in the pandemic (Posetti et al, 2020). As one of the WJEC panellists from the UK noted, graduates entering the newsroom are less likely to benefit from the opportunity to learn osmotically from senior colleagues. This presents a challenge to journalism educators in the 'post-pandemic' world, who may need to integrate into curricula training in online platforms such as Slack that encourage collaborative working in remote environments. Journalism educators supporting students also need to be innovative and flexible over work placement, whilst conforming to industry and accreditation body requirements (notably in the US and UK).

Most J-Schools benefit from part-time and/or freelance staff who work in industry, but come into the academy to share their skills and expertise; in the heart of the pandemic, it has been of great benefit to map this expertise onto changing delivery patterns, as newsrooms experienced the same challenges. These are some of the key areas where this has been evident:

- mobile journalism
- human interest stories that are often 'auto/biographical'

- interviewing with social distancing measures in place
- ethics – compassionate and humane reporting of crisis
- risk assessment
- fact-checking and verification of social media and UGC, news sources
- specialist journalism, notably data journalism and science/health journalism
- critical reflection
- trauma training and self-care

The relationship between J-Schools and industry has arguably become closer in the pandemic; it will be interesting to see whether these benefits can be captured to drive and lead change as we enter the 'post-pandemic' era, if the pandemic is seen to be a 'critical moment for journalism' (Quandt et al, 2021; Jukes et al, 2021; Perreault et al, 2021).

Well-being and duty of care

Student well-being in Higher Education was a serious matter of concern before the pandemic (Hubble and Bolton, 2020; Crawford, 2018), but global crisis witnessed heightened student anxiety and concerns for educators. Pascal Guénée, chair of the WJEC panel, felt that journalism educators were "overwhelmed by it" as they were dealing with the issue of student well-being on such a massive scale, and "it is still a huge issue for us after the pandemic". Journalists are often depicted as resilient, but, the pandemic was a unique event, which, as we have already established, journalists were living *in* and reporting *on*. This presented unique challenges to journalism educators striving to ensure safeguarding and student well-being. As Bissell (2020) notes,

> There is a sense that belonging to the same dreadful story has fostered a need to belong together. Nonetheless, the virtual sphere can also accentuate a sense of human distance and estrangement.

Journalism is fundamentally a human activity; 'post pandemic', educators have observed a loss of confidence, a disinclination for group working, with poor student attendance and engagement noted as HE sector-wide problems. As one panellist from South Africa noted, the mood in the classroom has changed significantly. Some observers have adopted a psycho-social approach, seeking to understand student well-being issues in the pandemic (e.g., in the UK, Burns et al, 2020; in Europe and Russia, Plakhotnik et al, 2021). WJEC Panellists adopted a range of approaches and responses: dividing students into groups on Zoom to mitigate their aversion for group working with student-led group activities and quizzes to foster social interaction (Chile), collaborative online journalism projects based in the community (Brazil), creating engaging and interactive teaching materials to overcome confidence issues (Egypt and UAE) and timetabling mental health breaks (Philippines).

We are only just beginning to assess the effects of the pandemic on young people's mental health (Deeker, 2022), but within J-Schools, a renewed focus on the need for trauma training is evident, with some institutions drawing from the excellent work of the Dart Center for Journalism and Trauma, for example, and evident in the newly formed international Journalism Education and Trauma Research Group (JETREG),[4] also organisations like the Headlines network, which focus on improving mental health in the media. One educator from Jumma told the WJEC panel that the region of south-east Asia – the most populous in the world – still had a long way to go, with students educators and journalists ill-prepared to deal with trauma. This highlights another area where synergies between the academy and industry can be observed and utilised to focus on building resilience in journalists. However, it can be more challenging to prioritise care and compassion in pedagogy within environments where precarity is endemic, such as Southern Africa, Latin America, the MENA region. In Lebanon, for example, which is already in the throes of an economic and political crisis, coronavirus intensified deep socio-economic fissures, exacerbated by a return to partisan and politicised media coverage (Melki et al, 2020.

Future directions

In April 2020, in the heart of the pandemic, the World Innovation Summit for Education, organised by the Qatar Foundation and Salzburg Global Seminar, considered the impact of Covid-19 on education and how it could be re-imagined in the wake of disruption. The virtual gathering concluded that, although 'post-pandemic' education could not go back to business as usual, its central ethos remained that "education is about forming personas. It is about integral, responsible citizens who ... are committed to their community and with a broad perspective on what happens in the world" (Marmalejo, 2020).

This provides food for thought for journalism educators. Society needs resilient journalism to function effectively: robust, effective and accurate communication and media are fundamental to trust in institutions, to informing publics, to encouraging ethical and empathic behaviours and to the mitigation of risk. The 'info-demic' of misinformation about coronavirus combined with the precarity of journalism and journalists (emotional and socio-economic) arguably presents a significant threat to the resilience of the post-pandemic world. Journalism education can be at the forefront in helping to address these challenges if we, as educators, can integrate the lessons learned during the pandemic into pedagogic design and delivery going forwards. The call and response will vary according to the media ecology within which journalism education is located – for example, in some contexts, such as in South Africa (see, Open Society Foundation report, 2021), Latin America (see UNESCO report, 2021), Lebanon (Melki et al, 2020), Covid-19 may have accelerated factors that already exist; fragility has been present for a long time, both within journalism and society. However, there is evidence – discernible when media educators have taken the opportunity to discuss best practice – for example, at the conference and symposia hosted by AEJMC, AJE, WJEC, MES[5] – and in institutional initiatives (e.g., 'Journalism in the Time of Crisis' hosted by Carleton School of Journalism and Communication in 2020) – of a shared ambition in the academy and industry to look ahead to more resilient, trustworthy, inclusive and trauma-informed journalism practice and pedagogy.

The WJEC panel, with its broad international composition, concluded with a set of recommendations (Table 1.1) for journalism educators, with building resilience as the overarching theme.

Finally, there was a shared sense of opportunity arising from those very real challenges of being 'always on' within a digital media environment and for students not being able to learn within the 'normal' environments and spaces, just as journalists have been unable to work within the physical newsroom – so they have had to adapt. Looking forwards, within journalism education we may need to consider that the design of newsrooms does not always mean a physical space and that some of those tools developed as responses in the pandemic – if designed carefully – could equip students to engage with this changed working world effectively, so building resilience within the next generation of journalists.

TABLE 1.1 WJEC panel recommendations

Recommendation	*Suggested approaches*
Equity, inclusivity, accessibility	Upgrading competencies so that everyone has an equal experience, wherever they are based, particularly in remote communities where there is poor internet connection.
Collaboration and community building	Intercultural. Freirian engagement in 'dialogue with a moment of crisis' as a way of awakening students to their own lived experience. Links with community (local and global) as potentially a route to building resilience and mutual understanding.
Training in specialist journalism	Health, science, media literacy – integrate into curricula and potential to build resilience as invests confidence in the journalist's ability to navigate dis/mis information and to disseminate accurate information.
Develop teaching and assessment in the context of pandemic experience	Blended learning. Hybrid approaches. Promote autonomous learning through asynchronous materials. Focus on student well-being and support progress, build confidence, understanding and resilience, through, e.g., formative feedback.
Renewed focus on trauma literacy to build resilience	Trauma training as integral to journalism education to instil duty of care that we have as educators and students have to themselves and to others through trauma literacy.

Conclusions and reflections

Whilst writing this chapter, the immediate global context remains challenging and the media landscape is turbulent, but there appears to be strong potential for journalism education to make a positive contribution to the 'post-pandemic' world. I was aware of this opportunity as I travelled to Salzburg in Austria in late July 2022 to take part in the Salzburg Academy for Media and Global Change with its theme of 'Re-imagining media after the pandemic' (2022). More than 70 students and faculty from 15 different universities around the world gathered[6] to deliberate how media organisations can re-imagine their roles and responsibilities in contemporary societies. The focus was on advancing equitable and just civic futures, and activities ranged from workshops, lectures and seminars to interactive and experiential sessions. At the end of the two-week academy, the student groups produced five different projects focused on creating transformative media learning experiences under the banner *re-Connect,* incorporating the elements of care, transformation and agency to explore new routes to supporting stronger and more inclusive media in the post-pandemic world:

- Escaping Stereotypes: An interactive experience based on the escape room format to address the cultural misconceptions and stereotypes about refugees.
- Global ECHO: To provide unheard voices a platform to connect with other countries and cultures that they originally would not have been exposed to.
- Truth or Consequences: An immersive gaming experience for young individuals to enhance their understanding of issues associated with misinformation and fake news across social media platforms.
- The Weight of Words: A workshop for journalists and laypeople to learn effective methods for more accurate, accessible and inclusive reporting on public health issues.
- One Planet: An interactive experience that aims to help children exercise their agency by having pivotal conversations and dialogue around climate change as an activist navigating the virtual world.

(Taken from the Salzburg Academy for Media and Global Change website: www.salzburgglobal.org/news/latest-news/article/reimagining-media-after-the-pandemic)

One of the students articulated how 'libraries of knowledge' are ultimately the lived experience of people. In debating with and learning from each other, the participants at the Academy, like the panel of journalism educators at the WJEC conference a month earlier, were actively searching for routes through a changed landscape that, as we have established, was challenging enough prior to the pandemic. Both gatherings were founded on a commitment to transformative approaches to pedagogy with a focus on improving civic agency and engagement, whilst caring for ourselves and each other.

The initial discussions shared in this chapter indicate that for journalism education to play an important role in the future may require a long-term commitment to flexible, innovative approaches to teaching and learning strategies, a critical mindset that actively interrogates journalism's normative values and professional boundaries, a focus on the pedagogy of compassion. The call to action? To draw on the lessons of reporting *on* and living *in* the pandemic to lead change and build resilience in journalism pedagogy and practice.

Notes

1 The recording of the stream 'Covid-19 and journalism education' can be viewed here: https://wjec.net/2022-online-conference/
2 The Salzburg Academy for Media and Global Change met for the first time since 2019 in July/August 2022, to reflect on the impact of the pandemic and to imagine 'more robust and inclusive communities and to become agents for positive social change after the pandemic'. See more here: www.salzburgglobal.org/news/latest-news/article/reimagining-media-after-the-pandemic
3 National Council for the Training of Journalists is the main industry accreditation body in the UK: www.nctj.com
4 Journalism Education and Trauma Research Group (JETREG) was founded in 2020 to promote trauma literacy in journalism education: https://jetreg.blogs.lincoln.ac.uk
5 AEJMC = Association for Education in Journalism and Mass Communication; AJE = Association of Journalism Education; MES = Media Education Summit.
6 After a two-year absence, the Academy convened face-to-face with participants from Argentina, Austria, Japan, South Korea, Philippines, Thailand, Turkey, India, Lebanon, Mexico, UK and US.

References

Bissell, A. (2020). 'Reflections on the shifting shape of journalism education in the Covid-19 pandemic'. *Digital Culture and Education,* 22 June 2020. Available at: www.digitalcultureandeducation.com/reflections-on-covid19/journalism-education

Burns, D., Dagnall, N., and Holt M. (2020). 'Assessing the impact of the Covid-19 pandemic on student wellbeing at universities in the United Kingdom: A conceptual analysis'. *Frontiers in Education,* 14 October 2020. Available at: www.frontiersin.org/articles/10.3389/feduc.2020.582882/full

Carleton University, School of Journalism and Communication (2020). Journalism in the Time of Crisis Symposium, 7–9 October 2020. Available at: https://medium.com/journalism-in-the-time-of-crisis/tagged/carleton-university

Concordia University (2020). 'How to teach – and learn – about journalism during a global pandemic'. Available at: www.concordia.ca/cunews/main/stories/2020/04/08/how-to-teach-and-learn-about-journalism-during-a-global-pandemic.html

Crawford, M. (2018). 'A mental health crisis is the true cost of university marketization'. *Red Pepper.* Available at: www.redpepper.org.uk/a-mental-health-crisis-is-the-true-cost-of-university-marketization/].

Deeker, W. (2022). 'The Covid generation: The effects of the pandemic on youth mental health'. https://ec.europa.eu/research-and-innovation/en/horizon-magazine/covid-generation-effects-pandemic-youth-mental-health

Estefania, R. (2020). 'Coronavirus: A diary of self-isolation under Covid-19 lockdown'. BBC News, 22 March 2020. Available at: www.youtube.com/watch?v=Cwaf0CrPUXE&feature=emb_title].

Fowler-Watt, K., Majin, G., Sunderland, M., Phillips, M., Brine, D., Bissell, A., and Murphy, J. (2020). 'Reflections on the shifting shape of journalism education in the Covid-19 pandemic'. *Digital Culture and Education,* 22 June 2020. Available at: www.digitalcultureandeducation.com/reflections-on-covid19/journalism-education

Goldin, I., and Muggah, R. (2020). 'Covid-19 is increasing all kinds of inequality: Here's what we can do about it'. World Economic Forum Report, 9 October 2020. Available at: www.weforum.org/agenda/2020/10/covid-19-is-increasing-multiple-kinds-of-inequality-here-s-what-we-can-do-about-it/

Gustafsson, M., and McCurdy, C. (2020). 'Risky business: Economic impacts of the coronavirus crisis on different groups of workers'. Resolution Foundation, 28 April 2020. Available at: www.resolutionfoundation.org/publications/risky-business/

Hubble, S., and Bolton, P. (2020). 'Support for students with mental health issues in higher education in England'. *UK Parliament Briefing Paper.* Available at: https://commonslibrary.parliament.uk/research-briefings/cbp-8593/

Jukes, S., Fowler-Watt, K., and Rees, G. (2021). 'Reporting the Covid-19 pandemic: Trauma on our own doorstep'. *Digital Journalism,* 12 September 2021. Available at: www.tandfonline.com/doi/full/10.1080/21670811.2021.1965489

Leonard, C. (2020). 'Teaching journalism in the time of Covid-19: "We can absolutely do this!"'. *Cronkite News*, Arizona State University. Available at: https://thewholestory.solutionsjournalism.org/teaching-journalism-in-the-time-of-covid-19-4158e921dcf7

Maitlis, E. (2022). 'Boiling frog: Why we have to stop normalising the absurd'. James MacTaggart Memorial Lecture, Edinburgh TV Festival, 24 August 2022. Available at: www.youtube.com/watch?v=PzqezAV3x_8

Marmalejo, F. (2020). 'Education cannot go back to business as usual after Covid-19'. *Education Disrupted, Education Reimagined,* World Innovation Summit for Education (online), organised by Qatar Foundation and Salzburg Global Seminar, 15–16 April 2020. Available at: www.wise-qatar.org/education-cannot-just-go-back-to-business-as-usual-after-covid-19-qf-educator/

Mayhew, F., and Turvill, W. (2020). 'More than 2,000 newspaper jobs hit as hundreds of publications across UK face Covid-19 cuts'. *Press Gazette,* 16 April 2020.

McGill, A. (2016). 'US media's real elitism problem'. *The Atlantic,* 19 November 2016.

Melki, J., Zeid, M.A., and El Takach, A. (2020). 'Lebanon: Coronavirus and the media'. *European Journalism Observatory,* 17 June 2020. Available at: https://en.ejo.ch/ethics-quality/lebanon-coronavirus-and-the-media

Ndzinisa, N., and Dlamini, R. (2021). 'Responsiveness vs. accessibility: Pandemic-driven shift to remote teaching and online learning'. *Higher Education Research & Development.* DOI: 10.1080/07294360.2021.2019199. Available at: www.tandfonline.com/doi/full/10.1080/07294360.2021.2019199

Open Society Foundation for South Africa (2021). 'Thinking globally, acting locally: Reviving and sustaining South African journalism in a post-Covid world'. Digital Journalism Research Project, March 2021.

Perreault, M., and Perreault, G.P. (2021). 'Journalists on Covid-19 journalism: Communication ecology of pandemic reporting'. *American Behavioral Scientist,* 65(7): 976–991. Available at: https://journals.sagepub.com/doi/full/10.1177/0002764221992813

Plakhotnik, M.S., Volkova, N.V., Jiang, C., Yahiaoui, D., Pheiffer, G., McKay, K., Newman, S., and Reißig-Thust, S. (2021). 'The perceived impact of COVID-19 on student well-being and the mediating role of the university support: Evidence from France, Germany,

Russia, and the UK'. *Frontiers in Psychology,* 12. Available at: www.frontiersin.org/articles/10.3389/fpsyg.2021.642689/full

Posetti, J., Bell, E., and Brown, P. (2020). 'Journalism and the pandemic: A global snapshot of impacts'. Accessed 7 May 2020. Available at: https://towcenter.columbia.edu/content/journalism-and-pandemic-global-snapshot-impacts

Poynter Institute (2022). 'Monitoring of job losses in US newsrooms'. Available at: www.poynter.org/business-work/2022/here-are-the-newsroom-layoffs-furloughs-and-closures-caused-by-the-coronavirus/

Quandt, T., and Wahl-Jorgensen, K. (2021). 'The coronavirus pandemic as a critical moment for digital journalism'. *Digital Journalism,* 9(9): 1199–1207. Available at: www.tandfonline.com/doi/full/10.1080/21670811.2021.1996253

Reuters Institute Report (2021). 'How journalism training is changing (and flourishing in sub-Saharan Africa'. 15 February 2021. Available at: https://reutersinstitute.politics.ox.ac.uk/news/how-journalism-training-changing-and-flourishing-sub-saharan-africa

Salzburg Academy for Media and Global Change (2022). 'Re-imagining media after the pandemic'. 18 July 2022–1 August 2022. Available at: www.salzburgglobal.org/news/latest-news/article/reimagining-media-after-the-pandemic

Snow, J. (2017). The MacTaggart Lecture 2017 at the Edinburgh TV Festival, 23 August 2017.

Toniolo, M. (2020). *Inside Italy's coronavirus 'red zone'*. *The Guardian,* 25 February 2020. Available at: www.youtube.com/watch?v=sPkZZkU6jvg&feature=emb_title]

UNESCO (2021). 'Impact of the COVID-19 pandemic on media sustainability in Latin America: Changes and transformations in the production models, sources of income, and products of Latin American media'. Available at: https://unesdoc.unesco.org/ark:/48223/pf0000377631_eng

World Economic Forum (2020). '5 things Covid-19 has taught us about inequality'. 18 August 2020. Available at: www.weforum.org/agenda/2020/08/5-things-covid-19-has-taught-us-about-inequality/

World Health Organisation (2020). 'Managing the Covid-19 info-demic: Promoting healthy behaviours and mitigating the harm from misinformation and disinformation'. Joint statement by WHO, UN, UNICEF, UNDP, UNESCO, UNAIDS, ITU, UN Global Pulse, and IFRC, 23 September 2020. Available at: www.who.int/news/item/23-09-2020-managing-the-covid-19-infodemic-promoting-healthy-behaviours-and-mitigating-the-harm-from-misinformation-and-disinformation

2
BROADENING HORIZONS
How student perspectives can help meet journalism's challenges

Andrew Bissell

Future storytelling: introducing an unlikely guidebook

A philosopher's *magnum opus* appears to be an odd book recommendation for students studying journalism. A cursory glance at the Contents Page – one referencing ontology, aesthetics and hermeneutics – certainly seems to confirm initial suspicions of the work's irrelevance. Little reassurance follows in the Translators' Preface where the challenging complexity of the work is readily acknowledged. To top it all, the book does not include a single mention of journalism. Yet *Truth and Method* by Hans-Georg Gadamer merits closer inspection. Gadamer's masterly study of art, human sciences and language can speak to journalists. It is, after all, a deep dive into the meaning of truth, conceptions of objectivity and the ways in which we interpret and understand our experiences of others. Six decades have slipped away since Gadamer wrote his magisterial tome in 1960. Yet *Truth and Method's* penetrative genius is that it does not simply transcend the passage of time as such; the book appears to grow in contemporary resonance and significance as a result of it. Consequently, its essential ethos may help journalists story the past, present and future.

Truth and Method is preoccupied with understanding history and interpreting the texts that belong to it. However, Gadamer's ideas claim a wider legitimacy that extends to the understanding to be found in the myriad of ways that we connect and interact with others (Barthold, n.d.). For fellow philosopher Charles Taylor, "the great challenge of the coming century, both for politics and for social science, is that of understanding the other" (2002, p. 126). This, I believe, is also the fundamental challenge facing journalism. Although journalism's existential focus remains securement of financial sustainability (House of Lords 2020; Cairncross 2019), reaching the unreached remains a disingenuous ambition unless a deeper understanding is sought of those encountered. Drawing upon key Gadamerian tenets and concepts, I will propose that this pursuit of understanding can begin in the journalism classroom. Teachers can commence a cross-examination of their sedimented understandings by first reflecting upon their students' societal and journalistic viewpoints. In turn, students can then be encouraged to consider how their confident opinions, comforting perspectives and silent prejudices may shape their approach to others and alternative standpoints. Together, staff and students begin to understand others differently.

Truth and Method emerges as an unlikely guide with which to engage with these challenges. It has the potential to lead the reader to a contemplative place where deepened self-understanding can occur. It's a place where personal horizons may be broadened – and better storytelling awaits. A brief overview of Gadamer's world now follows before *Truth and Method* enters the journalism classroom. The chapter goes on to build the case for a Gadamer-inspired humanist approach that can inform journalism education and practice. This approach is duly termed 'Horizon Journalism'.

A world of stories: Gadamer, the interpretive guide

The last sentence of Gadamer's treatise is perhaps the best place to start. In Gadamer's final summarising utterance, the momentum of the previous 483 pages assumes a critical mass that suddenly reduces and detonates with atomic power. As the dust clears, the moorings of our scientific and methodological truth appear to be less secure. What comes into view is "a discipline that guarantees truth", one "achieved by a discipline of questioning and inquiring" (Gadamer 2004, p. 484). What is this 'truth' and how could it inform journalists?

Entry to Gadamer's world requires storytellers to see themselves as interpreters and accept that all understanding entails interpretation. His realm is governed by 'hermeneutics' – "the theory that everything is a matter of interpretation" (Caputo 2018, p. 4). Gadamer's hermeneutic domain of interpretation and questioning also features 'horizons'. Horizon "refers to one's standpoint or situatedness (in time, place, culture, gender, ethnicity etc.) and the standpoint or situatedness of that which one is trying to understand" (Scott and Usher 2011, p. 33). Broadening one's horizon requires work: the task commences with reflexive connection with the historically handed-down prejudices and pre-understandings that constitute one's current horizon. Although prejudices and pre-understandings present obstacles to objectivity, they become conditions of interpretation and understanding for Gadamer. Indeed, they provide the essential ground from which one can begin to comprehend. Without these frames of prior reference, it would be impossible to interpret anything at all. It's the shock, puzzlement and surprise provoked by difference that can alert us to our prejudices and pre-understandings during engagement with text or conversation. Similarity can also help us "recognise ourselves and know ourselves better" (Grondin 2011, p. 15). It is this attunement and sensitivity to the alien and familiar through "openness to the other" (Gadamer 2004, p. 355) that enables our prejudices and pre-understandings to be revealed, reassessed and reviewed. We can then take on board more fully the perspectives of others, play them off our own views and better accommodate and assimilate what is said. Another's viewpoint is better accessed and a deeper mutual comprehension reached. For Gadamer, "understanding is always the fusion of these horizons" (2004, p. 305) and this fusion "results from an understanding that is grounded in both standpoints" (Scott and Usher 2011, p. 33). The conversational speech partners have gone beyond the limits of their present horizons and deepened their understanding of each other. Horizons have been broadened through shared understanding.

With understanding grounded in language, a different form of truth-telling emerges. In the opening pages of *Truth and Method*, Gadamer states his intention to free the question of truth from narrow scientific and methodological conceptions (Grondin 2003). This has implications for truth anchored in 'objectivity'. Media theorists have long anguished over journalistic objectivity, a traditional normative standard that has been variously described as "authority in disguise" (Fiske 2011, p. 158), "historical invention" (Ward 2010, p. 137), a "firmly entrenched" myth (Knight and Cook 2013, p. 106) and a "long-running swindle" (Winston and Winston 2021, p. 11). With journalistic objectivity unable to deliver its own rhetoric, Gadamer's 'fusion of horizons' offers truth via intersubjective relationships where different and conflicting interpretations are played out and agreement sought; this constitutes a "standard of objectivity" that functions as an alternative to the objectivity of positivist, factual scientific method (Scott and Usher 2011, p. 33). Gadamer's truths emanate from the relational and dialogic encounters that this consensus seeking requires. While we share, communicate and live by these truths (Grondin 2003), they are gleaned through questioning, listening and hearing. Indeed, while Gadamer famously declared that "being that can be understood is language" (2004, p. 470), he essentially saw hermeneutics as the ability to listen to others in the belief that they could be right (Grondin 2003). For journalists, the 'inter' part of the 'interview' thus becomes a conversational event for intersubjective exchanges and truth seeking. Here cultural understanding derives from genuinely open discussion and resistance to "the standard ethnocentric temptation" to make sense of strangers in one's own terms (Taylor 2002, p. 138). Resulting Gadamerian truth can be seen as "a synonym for understanding at its best", one "in which the horizons of the interpreter and the interpreted are fused for a moment" (Matheson 2009, p. 711). Hermeneutic storytellers are therefore tasked to cautiously approach the scientific language of objectivity that continues to dominate journalism practice. Yet care is equally required when choosing the hermeneutic path of intersubjectivity. Objectivity is not discarded; it is rather re-described with pure objectivity or pure facts replaced "with the distinction between good interpretations and bad ones" (Caputo 2018, p. 9).

What follows is a personal reflection upon a hermeneutic exercise conducted with journalism undergraduates studying at a UK university. My aim was to explore the pedagogic potential of applying Gadamerian concepts to journalism teaching and practice. This necessitated the introduction of *Truth and Method* to students.

Exploring student horizons

Gadamer's book made its debut as part of a final year undergraduate capstone unit during which students were encouraged to reflect upon the challenges involved in journalism practice. *Truth and Method* featured during a workshop when 25 students were invited to re-imagine practice through interrogation of journalism's normative values.

During a preliminary discussion phase, debate ensued regarding core concepts such as fairness, impartiality and truthfulness. The workshop then took a distinctly philosophical turn with presentation of Gadamer's take on objectivity and the truth he believed could be found through openness to others and communication. Students were also introduced to horizons – current perspectives of understanding – and Gadamer's challenge to grow a little beyond the limits of one's present standpoints. Finally, students were invited to complete a questionnaire. The first section sought a deeper understanding of their current horizons – how they perceived the world and journalism. I hoped these responses would challenge my own thinking, my own interpretations and understandings – my own horizons. The second section then explored students' horizonal positions regarding 'truth', 'objectivity' and 'detachment'. It also encouraged them to reflect upon the challenges posed by their subjective presence in the stories they tell and the implications for interpreting and understanding others.

The resulting questionnaire transcripts were approached hermeneutically. I awaited the self-disturbance that might suggest my horizons were being questioned. In Gadamer's words, I wanted to be "pulled up short by the text" and alerted to meaning that was either incompatible with what I had expected or received with a comforting familiarity (Gadamer 2004, p. 270). The student horizons that materialised are now thematically presented.

Horizons of angst: Students' perceptions of societal problems

Truth and Method proposes that our understanding of the world is an 'effect' of history: the past shapes us ensuring understanding occurs within a particular horizon determined by our historical situatedness (Gadamer 2004). The situated voices of the workshop students echoed the historic failings of humankind: homophobia, racism, sexism and intolerance darkened their societal horizons. Additional concerns emanated from more recent times. Although climate change and Coronavirus predominated, students also lamented fake news circulating on social media and life that entailed "constant comparison to others" and "the threat of being publicly shamed or cancelled". Russia's military invasion of Ukraine had meanwhile commenced on 24 February 2022; students entered the workshop discussing a 40-mile column of Russian tanks and artillery heading for the capital, Kyiv.

Collective angst accordingly permeated their questionnaires. Some depicted horizons of uncertainty and despair – even fear – while others linked technology to a pervading sense of generational insularity. Personal horizons were becoming increasingly closed, limiting connections and possibilities of change. Ominous horizons became visible:

> People of my generation expect the worst to happen. What future could we possibly have?
>
> The recent attack on Ukraine has made me re-evaluate my position [after leaving university]. I have found myself paranoid and very low.
>
> Isolation from a range of views in favour of echo chambers via social media – either intentional or unintentional – limits our ability to be open minded. We have become so reinforced in our belief systems that we are immune to change and adaptation.
>
> I believe society is facing a struggle to connect with government institutions and is growing further away from being able to trust those in power. Technological changes are a big reason for this.
>
> I think society in general is changing for the worse. I am cautious of voicing opinions that may now be controversial because in today's society everyone seems to get offended over the slightest thing.

There is much for educators to ponder here, not least the raw emotionality that imbues personal horizons. Clearly, student horizons require sensitive exploration and careful handling. Their comments also confirm the pedagogic redundancy of "bank-clerk" education where information is deposited into passive students who are viewed to be in the world but not "with the world or others" (Freire 2005, p. 75). If students are to become "critical co-investigators in dialogue with the teacher" (Freire 2005, p. 81), their empowerment can commence with enhanced understanding of their perspectives and standpoints – their personal horizons. Educators need to be receptive to what students tell them and be prepared for their traditional stances and assumptions to be challenged. In turn, students can then be encouraged to question their own world views and standpoints. Essentially, Gadamerian teachers are required to see education as the questioning of acquired knowledge in order to open up new perspectives; they will see the process of learning as a fusion of horizons (Grondin 2011). For students, learning about others becomes crucially contingent on their desire to seek fused horizons.

Horizons of trust: Students' perceptions of journalism's challenges

A journalistic commitment to Gadamerian openness and understanding would fundamentally entail trust in storytelling – something that has long troubled the profession. While the UK media are less trusted by its citizens than the media in any other surveyed country in Europe (House of Lords 2020), there has been a worldwide erosion of trust in news (Toff et al. 2020; Edelman 2021). Although most of the workshop students largely trusted mainstream media – particularly the BBC – trust was nonetheless highlighted as the predominant challenge confronting journalism. It seemed many students anticipated distrust and alienation before even commencing their journalistic careers:

> [There is a] lack of trust between the reader and the journalist. Too many people now dismiss journalists or journalism as being fake news or against them.
>
> [The] rise in social media is creating a barrier to accurate journalism. People are not willing to speak to journalists and share their stories. And the need for instant news can put accuracy at risk.
>
> Given the invasion of Ukraine, the BLM marches and the pandemic, society is very sensitive and on edge. Journalism has become even more looked at and challenged. With the rise in citizen journalism, there is a fight for more established and trusted news outlets to maintain and bring in a new audience.

Alongside concerns over trust, some students felt journalism needed to be more representative of society; it had "left the small people behind" and continued to be mired in clickbait and "irrelevant journalism where newsworthiness can be questioned". Amid allied worries that journalism had failed to hold power to account, one student suggested that perhaps too much is expected:

> The world is so complex and there are so many variables to take into account that journalists often lack the necessary context and history of issues; instead [they] focus on more superficial understandings that are easier to digest for their audiences.

If journalism has succumbed to "superficial understandings", an appropriate Gadamerian response would entail the building of trust through a more concerted attempt to understand others. A renewed sensitivity during interviews may be required, one gained through tapping into personal prejudices to more clearly perceive the horizons of others. It comes down to the questions being asked. For Gadamer, enabling students to raise the right type of questions is a hallmark of humanist education (Grondin 2011). Indeed, teachers should encourage students to ask new questions that are capable of forming an "independent judgement about things" (Grondin 2011, p. 14). Those who have interrogated various perspectives and possess a broad horizon become educated (Grondin 2011). They are better equipped to understand others.

Horizons of truth: Students' views on objectivity and subjectivity

The students were next invited to consider a subject that lies at the beating heart of Gadamer's opus – the meaning of truth. While they wrestled with their personal convictions, their collective confliction appeared to reflect how journalism has made itself vulnerable to attack "through its own claims of virtue – of neutrality and objectivity and truthfulness" (Winston and Winston 2021, p. 3). Many endorsed the pursuit of an 'objective truth', one that was strongly linked to accuracy, fact-checking, trusted sources, validity, fairness, impartiality, integrity and 'laying out the facts'.

However, the intruding complexity of subjectivity and its negotiation were never far away:

> [There is a] lack of objective truth. We live in a society where we are told to "live your truth" meaning there isn't a universal truth. This leads to confusion and conflict between people.
>
> So many people and groups shout that they hold the truth that it becomes almost impossible to know who is truly right.
>
> Everyone's right and wrong is different – who decides?
>
> These days people are taking journalism into their own hands with their own truth meaning. If we are not careful, that will simply add to the problem rather than offer a solution.

Others ventured deeper into Gadamerian territory. They suggested truth might involve more than collecting facts or adopting correct techniques and approved methods. Truths could be communicated though they cannot be scientifically verified. These students maintained that truth "can be achieved through building relationships" and "truth comes from what people say". For one, truth starts with "being honest with yourself, first and foremost," a comment that could be adopted to promote the virtues of hermeneutic self-reflection. A fellow student added the following insight, reflecting that everyone's limited horizon is open to connection with other horizon perspectives (Scott and Usher 2011):

> Truth in conversations change depending on people. One truth is different from another but the collective truth – the similarities – is what should be accepted. For me it means the story is told with the voices included.

Gadamer's work can help educators open up these fuller discussions about the nature of truth. While debate can encompass the value of a more circumspect approach to 'objective truth', it can also robustly scrutinise the Gadamerian truth sought through fused horizons. How suitable is the objectivity ideal if we concede one uniquely correct interpretation cannot exist? Equally, if Gadamer's plurality of interpretations is accepted, what kind of reasoning, validity or fidelity can justify why "some interpretations are better than others"? (Caputo 2018, p. 13). Indeed, how do we steer clear of the 'anything goes' relativism that Gadamer wished to avoid? (Weberman 2000). There is rich material here for classroom deliberation; Gadamer can provoke different thinking regarding how we may better understand our world.

Horizons of prejudice: Students' views on situatedness in storytelling

Most students conceded that remaining objective and detached in journalism had human limitations:

> You can never be truly objective, we are not robots; our stories will always have some element of subjectivity … "what's the story?" is [itself] a subjective phrase used by editors.
>
> There is always unconscious bias due to the values you hold as a person.
>
> Our words, choices, sentences and structure style are all from ourselves and our values [in regard to] how a story should be represented. Cold hard facts are objective [but] weaving them into a sentence is not. It [objectivity] can be striven towards but not fully achieved.
>
> Our bias and attachment are an integral part of human psychology and how we perceive the world. In practice, full objectivity and detachment is impossible.

Acknowledgement of Gadamerian prejudices swirl amid these comments. Yet some students appeared confident in their ability to bracket their pre-understandings. They aimed to "remove conscious bias as much as possible", to try to "put their opinion aside" and "not let their own thoughts and experiences influence [stories]". For some, any hint of subjective encroachment jeopardised impartiality and professionalism; resulting journalism "could not be considered news". One was "obsessed with the truth" and required "objective viewpoints".

Students commonly discussed a detachment quandary which also served to highlight the hermeneutic challenge. On the one hand, the attempt to objectively distance could feel easier if one had no personal experience of the subject. However, these subjects could then remain remote, elusive and difficult to adequately understand. As one put it, "Most of the time I have not lived the experience to be able to relate to my interviewees. Instead we can imagine through empathy." Another revealed:

> [I have a] lack of experience in other ways of life. For example, I wrote about a fire in a slum in Sierra Leone but my life experience is so far removed from those affected that it seemed hard to have a level conversation where I could understand the issue in a deeper way than the facts I had at hand.

Conversely, the relatable rather than the alien poses its own challenges to personal situatedness. For this student, feelings of "sympathy" required negotiation:

> Often I can relate to and understand the stories I write. The difficulty is listening to stories and reflecting back on my own experience. For example, I've done mental health and eating disorder stories and it opens up a range of personal emotions in myself. Trying to manage myself after interviews or

writing stories without biasness is truly a challenge … My background has allowed me to be open, to interact with a multitude of characters and walks of life … it makes me listen more. It hasn't changed my view but it expands my thinking to be able to see two sides of a story and make a judgement on where I stand.

From a Gadamerian perspective, these students were 'brought up short' by feelings of difference or familiarity – the crucial hermeneutic prerequisite to understanding. Fellow students gave further insight into their "openness to the other" (Gadamer 2004, p. 361), an approach often conveyed as being "open minded". In so doing, they offered glimpses into the experience of pursuing understandings that are grounded in one's own and another's standpoint:

> I am a Christian. I have these views that influence my lenses on the world. When I focus on how that affects my reporting, then it allows me to be conscious of my own bias and being self-critical in how I can improve … It has allowed me to see the world through the lenses of a storyteller and ignited a passion for the role of journalism in society. [It's] allowed me to see my own bias and views and how that characterises me as an individual.
>
> I understand myself more as a person and as a potential journalist during these [University] studies due to time to critically reflect … I have transferrable views that are open to being changed.
>
> You may project your point of view on theirs and ignore points they make. For example, when you are talking about the legalisation of marihuana and you are [personally] against it. You then talk to someone who is a great defender of legalisation because it effectively helps those with health issues. You might not dive deeper into why they defend it, what health issues they themselves may have etc and just stay in your "thinking bubble". That's why it could be a good idea to inform yourself well about the topic before an interview and also challenge your own views prior to the interview. I have learnt that you must be open to anything that you encounter on the way and also accept that there will be other viewpoints out there. Apart from that, by informing yourself about the topic, your view might change or intensify, depending on the situation. I believe that so far, my views have not particularly changed. I rather feel that I have become more open-minded.

Nonetheless, strongly held standpoints – often of a political nature – appeared to require particular hermeneutic attentiveness in order to create shared meaning, a 'fusion of horizons':

> Political opinions are really challenging … it's difficult to not go into a debate when you disagree with others' views … I have learnt it's important not to suppress your views but to share them in a non-argumentative and correct way at appropriate times.

> I want to give people a voice. Sometimes you may not completely agree with someone but you have to hold their views ... I don't think my views and standpoints have changed but they have definitely been challenged.
>
> I am very opinionated and [a] stubborn person at times, especially in controversial subjects which could be seen as both a blessing and curse in journalism ... I find I only pay attention to the stories that interest my interests. I've learnt to expand my horizons and educate myself in different affairs and problems.
>
> Always questioning things is a good thing to do ... while my opinions may not have changed much, my eyes and ears are more open. I'm learning facts rather than changing opinions.

Again, *Truth and Method* proved helpful in teasing out important student self-reflections and prompting debate. For example, those workshop storytellers who believed they should banish their prejudices – typically expressed in the desire to "remove my personal opinions" – were invited to consider an alternative to self-extinction. They could instead get in touch with their pre-understandings and use them to mediate and create shared understanding. Perhaps they might then view their standpoints with perspective and as the means with which to remain open to others and their horizons.

Horizon journalism: A new direction for future storytellers

Truth and Method's workshop cameo indicated that Gadamerian thinking can inform journalism education and practice. Despite the dense complexity of his opus, accessible and evocative takeaways like 'horizon' can initiate rich deliberation upon personal standpoints, objectivity, prejudice, interpretation and truth. While the workshop and questionnaire achieved this goal, the pedagogic experience additionally informed the following final reflections.

The questionnaire was designed to first glimpse what students thought about their world and journalism. I wanted to be challenged and "pulled up short" by their textual responses (Gadamer 2004, p. 270). I was subsequently struck by the depth of concern some students had about society and the future; there was a disturbing sense of despair over global developments, trust in government and social media's perceived inwardness and insularity. Their journalistic horizons were meanwhile shrouded by anxiety over establishing trust in a social media age. Again, I was hermeneutically challenged to unpack my responses. Educators open to engagement with the unexpected and unscripted strive to keep ignorance and complacency at bay. Students can help by questioning what teachers say to them – and to do so more often (Harcup 2021). *Teachers require these questions to help them question themselves.* The adoption of a hermeneutic mindset can help teachers continue to evaluate their own horizons in relation to those of their students. These educators become alert to the harmful and socialising transmission of old practices, old traditions and old ways of thinking and doing. They are also mindful that closed horizons serve only to deny teachers important insights and concerns; teachers with defiantly fixed horizons remain forever blindsided to potential solutions. Exploration of student horizons through questioning and ongoing reflection effectively contemporises teaching; educators' horizons formed in the past can pulse with renewed energy and relevance in the present. Gadamer, in short, reminds us of the narrowness of our own perspectives and the enrichment derived from knowing "what other possibilities there are in our world" (Taylor 2002, p. 141). True student emancipation and freedom becomes dependent on the broadening of their teachers' horizons.

The questionnaire next encouraged students to reflect upon their situatedness in storytelling. I sought their opinions on objectivity, truth and how they 'handled' their own views and prejudices. A full spectrum of responses resulted, ranging from determination to remain objectively detached to the pursuit of truth via dialogue. The importance of openness, the Gadamerian key to understanding, was often mentioned by students. Openness and understanding are inextricably linked and their encouragement should be the goal of a hermeneutically inspired journalism education. Hermeneutics ordains that understanding comes from self-openness; this allows us to bring our own prejudices into question in the process of understanding others and coming to the best interpretations possible. *Students, like staff, need to question their feelings and ask: What does my reaction tell me about myself, my prejudices and my viewpoints?* Teachers must, however, be mindful that "real understanding always has an identity cost" (Taylor 2002, p. 141). While we have "a deep identity investment in the distorted images we cherish of others", coming to see others inescapably entails altering our understanding of ourselves (Taylor 2002, p. 141). Such self-exfoliation can be revelatory yet demanding. One workshop attendee advised journalism education to help students protect themselves in the stories they tell, adding:

> You are human before you are a journalist. To tell stories, to find stories and to research stories is to understand who you are and why you are doing it.

Teachers must be supportively aware of the courage involved. Another workshop student issued a rallying cry of encouragement by urging journalism education to:

> Create more open and understanding storytellers who are less reactionary and more critical and understanding of the part they play in public opinion.

I call the pedagogic approach explored in this chapter *Horizon Journalism*. It aspires to offer a missing hermeneutic dimension to educational delivery by focussing on the better understanding and interpretation of others. Horizon Journalism clearly moves beyond the dominant 'standard model' of a skills-focused journalism education where practitioners are prepared "to operate as objective observers" with a "primary mission" to support and hold democratic institutions to account (Solkin 2022, p. 451). Horizon Journalism rather adopts the features of a more 'radical' educational model; it seeks to enable journalists to "understand their relationship to the communities they serve" and wants to listen to learners as well as practitioners (Solkin 2022, p. 451). It is essentially humanist. While Horizon Journalism concurs that horizon acquisition *is* education, it stresses, like Gadamer, that education is always self-education (Grondin 2011). Education is not something that is handed down to students from parents or teachers. Education starts and remains with "the pupil we never cease to be"; it concerns "our quest to become at home in this world" (Grondin 2011, p. 18).

Turning to practice, Horizon Journalism necessarily challenges the hegemonic epistemology that has long driven objective journalism. Instead, it joins calls for journalists "to reorient themselves from detached, data-driven social scientists toward caring, storytelling humanists" (Parks 2020, p. 1242). Converts will accept there is no point seeking the marginalised if one approaches from entrenched, marginalised standpoints. Rather, Gadamer would want journalists to reflect upon their own pre-judgements (Matheson 2009). However, Horizon Journalism does not recklessly abandon objectivity or casually discard its importance. Horizon Journalism highlights objectivity's insufficiency while drawing attention to the understanding, truth and quality journalism residing within inter-subjective conversational encounters. Yet while Horizon Journalism serves to scrutinise journalism's historically transmitted and unquestioned traditions, it also offers synergy. Where 'engaged' journalism has been seen by practitioners as a "mechanism to build or restore trust" (Wenzel and Nelson 2020, p. 515), Horizon Journalism can contribute reflexive interrogation of one's own horizons as a means to do so. Similarly, Horizon Journalism may afford another way to undertake and enrich 'immersive storytelling' where the aim is to transform perspectives (Fowler-Watt 2021).

Journalism's fundamental challenge remains the challenge that has always confronted and confounded society: How can we better understand each other? Horizon Journalism can play its part through addition of a humanist and hermeneutic dimension to education and practice. Gadamer's hermeneutics – so richly infused with the virtues of understanding, dialogue and tolerance – is ultimately a philosophy of faith and hope. While faith is placed in our sincerity to respect and understand the unique individuality of others, we must also hope that we are up to the interpretive challenge. We are tasked to question more and listen better. Above all, we must not stop looking for "the real meaning of an utterance" (Gadamer 1984, p. 63). There can surely be no better guidance for future storytellers.

References

Barthold, L.S., n.d. *Hans Georg-Gadamer (1900–2002).* Internet Encyclopedia of Philosophy (online). ISSN 2161-0002. Available from: https://iep.utm.edu/gadamer/ (Accessed: 7 April 2022).

Cairncross, F., 2019. The Cairncross review: A sustainable future for journalism. Department for Digital, Culture, Media and Sport. Available from: https://assets.publishing.service.gov.uk/government/uploads/system/uploads/attachment_data/file/779882/021919_DCMS_Cairncross_Review_.pdf (Accessed: 24 May 2022).

Caputo, J.D., 2018. *Hermeneutics. Facts and Interpretation in the Age of Information*. London: Penguin Books.
Edelman Trust Barometer, 2021. Raging infodemic feeds mistrust (online). Available from: www.edelman.com/trust/2021-trust-barometer (Accessed 11 March 2022).
Fiske, J., 2011. *Reading the Popular*. London: Routledge.
Fowler-Watt, K., 2021. Immersive storytelling. *In*: Mihailidis, P., Shresthova, S. and Fromm, M., eds. *Transformative Media Pedagogies*. New York: Routledge, 100–108.
Freire, P., 2005. *Pedagogy of the Oppressed*. 30th Anniversary Edition. Translated by Myra Bergman Ramos. London: Continuum.
Gadamer, H-G., 1984. The hermeneutics of suspicion. *In*: Shapiro, G. and Sica, A., eds. *Hermeneutics. Questions and Prospects*. Amherst, MA: University of Massachusetts Press, 54–65.
Gadamer, H-G., 2004. *Truth and Method*. London: Continuum.
Grondin, J., 2003. *Hans-Georg Gadamer: A Biography*. New Haven and London: Yale University Press.
Grondin, J., 2011. Gadamer's experience and theory of education: Learning that the other may be right. In: Fairfield, P., ed. *Education, Dialogue and Hermeneutics*. London: Bloomsbury Academic, 5–20.
Harcup, T., 2021. Making one or two more calls: teaching journalism students the value of news. *Journalism Education*, 10 (1), 83–89.
House of Lords, 2020. *Breaking News? The Future of UK Journalism*. Authority of the House of Lords (online). Available from: https://committees.parliament.uk/publications/3707/documents/36111/default/ (Accessed: 14 February 2022).
Knight, M. and Cook, C., 2013. *Social Media for Journalists: Principles and Practice*. London: SAGE.
Matheson, D., 2009. Hans-Georg Gadamer's philosophical hermeneutics and journalism research. *Journalism Studies*, 10 (5), 709–718.
Parks, P., 2020. Toward a humanistic turn for a more ethical journalism. *Journalism*, 21(9), 1229–1245.
Scott, D. and Usher, R., 2011. *Researching Education. Data Methods and Theory in Educational Enquiry*. London: Continuum.
Solkin, L., 2022. Journalism education in the 21st century: A thematic analysis of the research literature. *Journalism*, 23(2), 444–460.
Taylor, C., 2002. Gadamer on the human sciences. *In*: Dostal, D., ed. *The Cambridge Companion to Gadamer*. Cambridge: Cambridge University Press, 126–142.
Toff, B., Badrinathan, S., Mont'Alverne, C., Arguedas, A.R., Fletcher, R. and Nielsen, R., 2020. *What We Think We Know and What We Want to Know: Perspectives on Trust in News in a Changing World*. Reuters Institute for the Study of Journalism. Available at: https://ssrn.com/abstract=3750935 (Accessed: 14 February 2022).
Ward, S., 2010. Inventing objectivity: New philosophical foundations. *In*: Meyers, C., ed. *Journalism Ethics: A Philosophical Approach*. New York: Oxford University Press, 137–152.
Weberman, D., 2000. A New Defense of Gadamer's Hermeneutics. *Philosophy and Phenomenological Research*, 60 (1), 45–65.
Wenzel, A. and Nelson, J.L., 2020. Introduction "Engaged" Journalism: Studying the News Industry's Changing Relationship with the Public. *Journalism Practice*, 14 (5), 515–517.
Winston, B. and Winston, M., 2021. *The Roots of Fake News: Objecting to Objective Journalism*. London: Routledge.

3

A "HOTCHPOTCH OF CONFLICTING SCHOOLS"

The problems plaguing journalism education in the 2020s

Graham Majin

Once upon a time in journalism

Hugh Cudlipp was a giant of British journalism. He left school at the age of 14 and worked as a "pupil reporter" for the *Penarth News*, a local paper covering events on the outskirts of Cardiff. It was neither well paid nor glamorous. On a "pocket money salary" of five shillings a week, his autobiography records, he "graduated from the Boy Scout Notes and Church Notes to covering the wheeler-dealing of the less exciting sub-committees of the Town Council." At the local magistrates' court, he reported cases of "wayward revellers, retired and frustrated colonels suspected of the ancient art of indecent exposure and motorists who had jumped the crossings or parked on the wrong side of the promenade." Cudlipp's job was to record the facts accurately and turn them into stories for the next edition. As he recalls, "Their minor follies were recounted in excruciating detail for the titillation or deterrence of their neighbours" (1976, 36). In 1937, at the age of 24, he became editor of the best-selling *Sunday Pictorial* (now the *Sunday Mirror*). He played a major role in developing tabloid journalism in the UK, became Chairman of the powerful Mirror Group and was ennobled, becoming Baron Cudlipp in 1974.

Cudlipp's story provides a useful point of comparison for teachers of journalism in the 2020s. It helps us see how both education and journalism have changed and how they continue to evolve. It helps us see that journalism is not a static, unchanging thing. It is plastic and malleable. It stretches to meet the needs of society and the dominant ideology of the age. This in turn prompts a series of questions: What exactly do we teach and why do we teach it? Are there things we don't teach that we should? Is what we do relevant? Two things from Cudlipp's story strike us as incongruous today. First, there is his lack of education, especially his lack of a university degree, and the corollary that the absence of any formal journalistic qualification was not a barrier to him getting a job as a journalist. On the contrary, it was

DOI: 10.4324/9781003301028-5

considered perfectly normal. The other thing that jars modern readers is Cudlipp's description of the purpose of journalism. It is hard to imagine teachers of journalism today telling their students that the function of news is to titillate readers and deter them from breaking the law. In the 21st century, Thomas Hanitzsch's (2017) description of journalism is far more likely to resonate,

> there is a remarkable consensus about the essential tasks of journalism in society: observation and information; participation in public life through commentary, advice, and advocacy; as well as the provision of access for a diversity of voices.

Many would go further and agree with Hanitzsch that contemporary journalists should aspire to be "involved, socially committed, assertive and motivated." Trying to unpack the differences between Cudlipp and Hanitzsch's descriptions of journalism leads us into a complex labyrinth of philosophy, politics and sociology. It can briefly be summarised, however, by saying that for Cudlipp, the truth-telling role of journalism comes first, while its ethical-political role comes second. For Hannitzsch, the positions are reversed; contemporary journalists are expected to be aware of their ethical-political responsibilities at all times. When, then, did things change and who changed them?

Generational Cohort Theory is based on the idea that certain age groups are shaped by powerful forces during their coming-of-age years, as a result of which they share similar values that remain largely unchanged for the rest of their lives (Huan 2010). Although widely used in historical and social science research, it is understudied in relation to journalism. According to Generational Cohort Theory, the baby Boomer generation changed almost everything with which they came into contact: fashion, music, art, moral values and social attitudes. Their impact on education and journalism was also huge. The Boomer generation ridiculed the old, Victorian Liberal style of journalism practised by their parents and grandparents. Writing in 1975 in the London *Times*, John Birt, who would later become Director General of the BBC, called for a "new journalism" and mocked the old breed of fact-finding hacks, like Cudlipp, who had cut their teeth working on provincial newspapers. Instead, Birt demanded a new generation of elite, university-educated journocrats. Birt explained that the problem was caused by a

> cultural lag in the qualifications and background of the broad mass of reporters, news editors and the like. If the archetype is the cub reporter who, having left school at 16, wins his spurs covering crime in Gateshead, it is not to be expected that the profession will be well adapted to explaining a world of continuing economic malaise and increasing social stress.

Birt's new journalism would be a journalism with far greater power to explain *why* things happen and *how* they could be changed to make the world a better place. What was needed, he said, were knowledgeable and educated journalists, sometimes working in teams and continuously blending inquiry and analysis, so that the needs of understanding direct the inquiry and the fruits of inquiry inform the analysis.

(Birt 1975, 12)

To the Boomers it seemed natural and desirable to spend several years with likeminded people in the finishing schools of higher education. Writing in 1970, the American social psychologist Kenneth Keniston saw the existence of a huge cohort of college students as both the cause and effect of the generation gap – the gulf of understanding between the Boomers and their parents. The expansion of higher education was, he said, an entirely novel social phenomenon that kept the Boomers out of productive employment and placed them in a unique environment where they could indulge their fantasies in ways not available to their parents and grandparents. The Boomers were, he said, "a new generation, the first born in this new era of postwar affluence, television and the Bomb, raised in the cities and suburbs of America, socially and economically secure." Keniston pointed out that only an affluent society could afford to insulate their children from the world of work by sending them *en masse* to college, thus the expansion of higher education was a luxury: "In 1900, there were only 238,000 college students: in 1970, there are more than seven million, with ten million projected for 1980." However, the "prolongation of education," he said, was also a prolongation of immaturity. It was a form of infantilisation that was creating a new type of person, a human being halfway between child and adult:

> We are witnessing today the emergence on a mass scale of a previously unrecognized stage of life, a stage that intervenes between adolescence and adulthood. I propose to call this stage of life the stage of youth.
>
> *(Keniston 1970, 650)*

It was this, Keniston concluded, that explained the Utopian radicalism and rebelliousness of the Boomer generation.

> Many a contemporary adolescent, whether of college or high school age, finds it convenient to displace and express his battles with his parents in a pseudo-youthful railing at the injustices, oppression and hypocrisy of the Establishment.
>
> *(651)*

Credentialism, signaling or human capital? Why it matters

One consequence of the expansion of higher education during the last third of the 20th century is the phenomenon known as "credentialism." The American sociologist David Brown observes: "the expansion of access to higher education and the proliferation of formal degree requirements for entry to employment have been enduring trends over the past century" (2001, 19). This, says Brown, has led to the expectation that an ever-growing proportion of the population ought to have a degree, and to the assumption that those who lack degrees are suited only to non-elite jobs. Brown argues that over-educating people is not a good thing. He argues, it "dilutes learning by 'McDonaldizing' education and by encouraging students to plod mindlessly through degree sequences in pursuit of guaranteed vocational rewards." Even worse, he says it is a process that serves the interests of universities, not students. He therefore questions the need for "mass, state-supported credentialing systems that hold people out of labor markets in ever lengthening educational credentialing sequences."

The American complexity scientist Peter Turchin is another academician who asks, "are we headed in the wrong direction?" Turchin uses the phrase "elite overproduction" to describe the creation of unsustainable surpluses of highly credentialed graduates all chasing a limited number of jobs, "elite overproduction results when elite numbers and appetites exceed the ability of the society to sustain them, leading to spiraling intraelite competition and conflict" (2012, 17).

Turchin argues this is not a process that can go on forever. Like the Tower of Babel, it cannot climb infinitely high. At a time when affluence is rapidly unwinding, Turchin believes the model introduced to serve the needs of the Boomer generation is increasingly anachronistic and may even lead to serious social discontent:

> Since the number of power positions is limited, a growing segment of elites/elite aspirants must be denied access to them. These "surplus" elites must challenge the established elites for access to elite positions, or acquiesce in downward mobility.

The American academic Bryan Caplan draws on Educational Signaling Theory to argue that the contemporary higher education model suffers from a confusion of aims. The real purpose of a university education, he says, is not to provide students with useful skills, instead a degree signals to employers that a student is intelligent, hard-working and willing to conform. Higher grades send stronger signals than lower ones, Masters degrees are more prestigious than Bachelor ones and so on. According to Caplan it is an arms race in which students compete against each other: "You want a better view at a concert. What can you do? Stand up. Individually, standing works. What happens, though, if everyone copies you? Can everyone see better by standing? No way" (2019, 5).

In the 21st century, Educational Signaling Theory poses a challenge to the Human Capital Theory which was favoured by the Boomer generation. As Caplan explains,

> The human capital story says that when you go to school they actually teach you a bunch of useful job skills. You then finish and the labor market rewards you because you are now able to do more stuff. The signaling model says, no, no, no, no; that's not what's going on. What's going on is that people go

to school; they don't actually learn a lot of useful stuff; however, the whole educational process filters out the people who wouldn't have been very good workers. So people who are lower intelligence, lower in work ethic, lower in conformity.

(Caplan, 2014)

The British academician Stephen Davies sees cause for concern in the fact that one-third of all jobs now require a degree, even though the skills required can often easily be obtained without going to university. He concludes the system has "reached a dead end":

> Only wealthy countries can afford to have so many productive young people out of the world of work for three or four years. This seems to make university degrees a pure consumption good, of a luxury kind. For some people this is the case and it was the nature of university education for the majority of those who underwent it until about the 1970s.

(Davies 2020, 13)

One implication of these criticisms is that today we may be operating an outdated educational system designed by the Boomer generation during an age of affluence to suit their needs and aspirations. One way to answer them is to point out that journalism education is, unlike many subjects in the humanities and social sciences, strongly vocational. There is certainly merit in this argument. However, it threatens to saw off the branch on which we are sitting. If university journalism departments are simply providing vocational training, then would on-the-job training not be a superior and cheaper solution? If, on the contrary, we are providing something more, then what exactly is it, and how can we justify it?

A tale of two journalisms

The Boomer generation transformed journalism. Objectivity and impartiality, the fortress guarding Victorian Liberal Journalism, came under a sustained attack. What fired the Boomer imagination was committed, ethical-political journalism with the potential to transform the world. What the Boomers despised was the old-fashioned journalism of detachment – what Cudlipp referred to as a willed neutrality, a "bland professional aplomb" (401).[1] As early as 1962, the American historian of journalism Frank Mott could detect that the winds of change had started to blow. Although the castle was still secure, Mott recognised a growing hunger for opinion and a move away from strict impartiality.

> Despite increased emphasis upon interpretation, the news itself – the objective news facts as nearly as an honest and skilful reporter can ascertain and record them – continued to be the fundamental business of American journalism.

(Mott 1962, 788)

It was during the 1970s that the walls of Victorian Liberal Journalism began to crumble, although the older generation of journalists put up a spirited resistance. A few weeks after Birt's provocative calls for a new type of journalism, the BBC's Editor of News and Current Affairs Desmond Taylor launched a counterattack restating the values of Victorian Liberal Journalism. A journalist, he said, must be "disinterested" and his work must imply neither approval nor disapproval.

> He must have the same attitude to his raw material that an employee of a bank has to its money – it isn't his. He is handling it on behalf of other people, he must preserve it scrupulously, never convert it to his own use. He must not try to change people's minds, or confirm their beliefs; he must give them the untainted information they need to make up their own minds. He cannot aim to move events, from however worthy a motive and for however worthy an end.

But Taylor's views were out of date, the incoming tide could not be stopped. Cudlipp sensed it and announced his retirement from journalism in 1972. "There was a new scene in Fleet Street," he said, and it jarred with the "standards and philosophy I had favoured in the past." University-educated Boomer journalists had strange, new values and wanted to do things their own way. Cudlipp felt the time had come to stand aside; "the bolshie undergraduates," he wrote, "would have to carry on in future without my advice or admonition. The younger generation would have to fend for itself" (414). And fend for itself it did. By the late 1980s, Boomers were in positions of power and influence in American and British newsrooms and Boomer Journalism was everywhere replacing journalism on the Victorian Liberal model. The differences between them were complex and involved, not just a different understanding of the role of journalism, but also a different understanding of the nature of truth and knowledge. As I have written elsewhere,

> Boomer Journalism saw itself as having ethical-political responsibilities, and truth came to be understood as the consensus of people with shared ethical-political values and goals. Journalism's methodology shifted to the creation and management of narratives intended to help create a better, more socially-just world.
>
> *(Majin, 2022)*

By the end of the 20th century, senior, mainstream journalists were openly calling, not for a journalism of *detachment*, but for a journalism of *attachment*. As the veteran BBC foreign affairs correspondent Martin Bell famously wrote (1997, 8),

> In place of the dispassionate practices of the past I now believe in what I call the journalism of attachment. By this I mean a journalism that cares as well as knows; that is aware of its responsibilities; and will not stand neutrally between good and evil, right and wrong, the victim and the oppressor.

However, the triumph of Boomer Journalism brought unexpected consequences. The tendency of journalism to rely on shared ethical-political narratives, its willingness to self-censor and its intolerance of uncomfortable "unethical" opinions triggered a reaction. Taking advantage of the internet and social media platforms, an entirely different type of journalism began to emerge. This Unofficial Journalism rejected the assumptions of Boomer Journalism and sought inspiration in pre-Boomer approaches. It saw its mission as putting back into public discourse the other side of the argument that Official Journalism had stripped out. The reaction of Official Journalism to this insolence was harsh. It accused Unofficial Journalism of peddling misinformation, disinformation, conspiracy theories and hate speech. The clash between the two journalisms, and their different epistemological approaches, can be illustrated by looking at how they cover the climate change story. For example, in the summer of 2021 a heatwave struck the Pacific Northwest of the United States . Official Journalism was careful to stress ethical-political elements of the story and recognise its responsibility to environmental justice. CNN's Rachel Ramirez reported:

> Researchers say it's important to understand that climate change is already affecting our lives today – that unless climate resiliency or heat action plans are put in place, particularly in historically marginalized communities, multiple people will suffer and die from extreme heat as climate change accelerates.
>
> (Ramirez, 2021)

The BBC's approach to the story was similar and referred to climate experts who were confident:

> the heatwave that scorched western Canada and US was "virtually impossible" without climate change. The team, which is part of the World Weather Attribution network, described it as a one-in-a-1,000-year event which would have been 150 times less likely without human influence on the climate.

The article, by the BBC's Environment Analyst Roger Harrabin, continued, "temperatures will push onwards to 2C and above unless policies radically change," adding that, "some scientists are warning that areas of the world will become uninhabitable if current trends continue. So what are our leaders doing to keep us safe?" Underlying the CNN and BBC coverage is the philosophy of Boomer Journalism and its desire, not merely to describe the world, but to change and improve it. For example, in September 2018, the BBC's Director of News and Current Affairs Fran Unsworth emailed guidance to her journalists advising them:

> climate change is accepted as happening, you do not need a "denier" to balance the debate ... To achieve impartiality, you do not need to include

outright deniers of climate change in BBC coverage, in the same way you would not have someone denying that Manchester United won 2-0 last Saturday. The referee has spoken.

(Hickman, 2018)

The contrast between Unsworth's approach and that of Taylor, who occupied the same job 40 years earlier, is instructive. Unsworth's document referred to the BBC's "Greener Broadcasting" strategy and stressed the importance of the BBC "doing its part to tackle environmental factors that could impact our futures." Whereas Taylor made it clear that tackling problems was something journalists were neither qualified nor entitled to do: "it would be arrogant and insupportable if we tried to take a hand in solving them ourselves and strayed outside the strictly journalistic role" (op. cit.). The same underlying approach can be seen in contemporary journalism in the US. For example, a manifesto entitled *A New Beginning for Climate Reporting*, published by the *Columbia Journalism Review*, urged journalists to be more committed to environmental activism, not less. The role of journalism, it said, was to shape public opinion, help engineer consent for ethical-political policies and make the world a better, fairer place. Its authors explained, "Journalism has always been about righting wrongs … It is in our best traditions to shine a light on our most vexing problems, in order to help fix them." The essay concluded, "transforming the news media is fundamental to achieving that goal" (Hertsgaard, 2019).

In this example, what is missing from Official Journalism's reporting is the other side of the argument. To find it, one must climb over the fence into the world of Unofficial Journalism. For example, the American blogger Cliff Mass accuses Official Journalism of selectively cherry-picking information to support its chosen narrative. According to Mass, at the same time the heatwave struck the Pacific Northwest, a cold wave struck the central Pacific Ocean. These, he said, were two parts of the same atmospheric phenomenon. The heatwave was visible and made headlines because it occurred over inhabited land. The cold wave could be conveniently ignored because it took place far out into the sea. Thus, although the heatwave was real, it was only one half of the story.

> Other large temperature anomalies scattered around the world, both warm and cold … Extreme temperatures happen all the time in a somewhat random fashion. They just don't happen where YOU are located very frequently.
>
> *(Mass, 2021)*

Mass concluded that "human-caused global warming played a very small role in the extreme heat event that we just experienced here in the Pacific Northwest." In his opinion, Official Journalism was putting "political agendas ahead of truth." To Official Journalism, however, the "other side of the argument" presented by Unofficial Journalism is not legitimate opinion at all. It is "misinformation" and "climate denial." The same epistemic controversy can be seen in the debate concerning "false balance." The science journalist David Robert Grimes explains:

> False balance arises when journalists present opposing view-points as being more equal than the evidence allows. But when the evidence for a position is virtually incontrovertible, it is profoundly mistaken to treat a conflicting view as equal and opposite.
>
> (Grimes, 2016)

In the early 21st century, Official Journalism often justifies a one-sided approach by citing the dangers of "false balance." According to Grimes, when we know what is true, it is ethically and politically wrong to allow advocates of what is false to spread their dangerous misinformation. Hence the views of climate deniers, he says, should be suppressed because publishing them "risks giving debunked or dangerous fringe views an air of legitimacy and the oxygen of publicity – and ultimately, such sophism leaves us all more divided." However, Victorian Liberal journalists, working with a different understanding of Journalistic Truth, would have found Grimes' case for censorship baffling or absurd. They would have argued that people can only form an opinion about what's true after listening to *both* sides. If one side is denied the "oxygen of publicity," knowledge becomes impossible. As the philosopher of Victorian Liberalism John Stuart Mill put it,

> There is the greatest difference between presuming an opinion to be true, because, with every opportunity for contesting it, it has not been refuted, and assuming its truth for the purpose of not permitting its refutation.
>
> (Mill, 2011)

The journalistic landscape of the 2020s is characterised, therefore, by intolerance and hostility between two mutually incompatible journalisms with different sets of facts, different opinions and different understandings of Journalistic Truth. As Majin summarises,

> Official Journalism, drawing on the Boomer Epistemology, understands legitimate knowledge as official truth – the consensus of benevolent experts in positions of authority. Unofficial Journalism, seeking inspiration in the tradition of Victorian Liberalism, sees legitimate knowledge as the responsibility of each individual. The wider epistemic problem is that it is impossible to agree what is true, until there is agreement about the nature of truth.
>
> (op. cit.)

Back in 1975, Desmond Taylor warned the incoming Boomer generation of journalists that, if they suppressed information, it would inevitably produce a reaction. The BBC, he said, "does not exist in a vacuum and the audience would soon turn to other sources of news." His words were, arguably, very prophetic.

Discussion

The Boomer generation created our journalism, our approach to education and even the epistemic assumptions about how we understand the concept of Journalistic Truth. It is the right of every generation to rearrange the philosophical and ideological furniture to suit its tastes and serve its needs. Indeed, not doing so is a recipe for social stagnation. However, is the Boomer's matrix of assumptions, ideas and values still valid in the rapidly changing world of the 2020s when the taken-for-granted, endlessly increasing affluence that underpinned their ideology is no more? In the 2020s we dance to different tunes. In the US, the former House Speaker Newt Gingrich warns of dramatically rising food prices, shortages, stagflation and rising levels of "misery": "I think people have no idea how bad the food situation is going to get ... we have a grave danger of being worse off in another year or a year-and-a-half than we were under Jimmy Carter" (Gingrich, 2022). Similarly, the Guardian reports,

> Britain's cost of living crisis has another potent symbol: Elsie, a 77-year-old woman who found the cheapest way to keep warm was to switch the heating off, leave home and ride the buses all day.
>
> *(Butler, 2022)*

We are living at a time of stress and change. As a consequence, the dominant ideology of the last 60 years is beginning to fracture. But ideology abhors a vacuum. Thus, we see fragments of competing ideologies around us; incomplete and incoherent, like protoplanets trying to form themselves out of swirling dust. And, as a result, we have competing, incoherent journalisms, uncertain of their purpose, rudderless journalisms tossed by the storm, trying to anchor themselves to passing pieces of ideological wreckage. For educators, the urgent task is to recognise where we are so we can understand more clearly where we're going, and whether or not we want to go there. What type of education and what type of journalism will be needed to meet the challenges of the present and the future? What sort of journalists are we trying to produce? Official Journalists who understand their ethical-political responsibilities, who have been taught not to challenge the consensus narratives and who have learnt the delicate art of self-censorship? Or curious, impartial journalists capable of critical thinking with the courage to challenge accepted orthodoxy? Is it possible for us to produce both? If so, how? What, one wonders, would Hugh Cudlipp think about the state of journalism and journalism education in the 2020s? His description of joining the Daily Mirror in 1935 might provide a fitting verdict. It was, he said sadly (op. cit. 55), "a hotchpotch of conflicting schools of thought and no thought at all."

Note

1 Cudlipp preferred writing op-eds to factual news reporting. He understood the two roles were very different and felt that opinion writing was his special talent, "I was always in the propaganda business myself so far as a newspaper's opinions were concerned" (ibid.).

References

Bell, M. (1997) TV news: How far should we go? British Journalism Review, 8 (1), 7–16. doi: 10.1177/095647489700800102. (Accessed 13 December 2021).

Birt, J. (1975) Television journalism: The child of an unhappy marriage between newspapers and film. *The Times*. 30 September 1975.

Brown, D. (2001) The social sources of educational credentialism: Status cultures, labor markets, and organization. *Sociology of Education*, 74, 19–34 [29].

Butler, P. (2022) *Woman who rides bus to stay warm is tip of pensioner poverty iceberg. The Guardian*. 3 May 2022. www.theguardian.com/business/2022/may/03/stories-like-elsies-highlight-pensioners-plight-and-the-inadequate-help

Caplan, B. (2014) *Bryan Caplan on college, signaling and human capital*. Econtalk. 7 April 2014. www.econtalk.org/bryan-caplan-on-college-signaling-and-human-capital/

Caplan, B. (2019) *The Case against Education; Why the Education System Is a Waste of Time and Money*. Princeton: Princeton University Press.

Cudlipp, H. (1976) *Walking on the Water*. London: Bodley Head.

Davies, S. (2020) To a radical degree: Reshaping the UK's higher education for the post-pandemic world. Institute of Economic Affairs. Briefing. 12 August 2020.

Gingrich, N. (2022) Newt Gingrich: People have 'no idea' how badly food prices will rise over the year. MSN. 6 May 2022. www.msn.com/en-us/news/world/newt-gingrich-people-have-no-idea-how-badly-food-prices-will-rise-over-the-year/ar-AAWYtGr

Grimes, D. (2016) Impartial journalism is laudable. But false balance is dangerous. *The Guardian*. 8 November 2016. www.theguardian.com/science/blog/2016/nov/08/impartial-journalism-is-laudable-but-false-balance-is-dangerous Accessed 20 May 2022.

Hanitzsch, T. (2017) Professional identity and roles of journalists. Oxford Research Encyclopedia of Communication. https://oxfordre.com/communication/view/10.1093/acrefore/9780190228613.001.0001/acrefore-9780190228613-e-95

Harrabin, R. (2021) Why North America's killer heat scares me. BBC News. 9 July 2021. www.bbc.co.uk/news/world-us-canada-57729502

Hertsgaard, M. and Pope, K. (2019) A new beginning for climate reporting. *Columbia Journalism Review*. 16 September 2019. https://www.cjr.org/covering_climate_now/climate-crisis-new-beginning.php

Hickman, L. (2018) *Exclusive: BBC issues internal guidance on how to report climate change*. Carbon Brief. 7 September 2018. www.carbonbrief.org/exclusive-bbc-issues-internal-guidance-on-how-to-report-climate-change

Huan, C. (2010) Advertising and generational identity: a theoretical model. American Academy of Advertising. Conference. Proceedings. Lubbock: American Academy of Advertising, 132–140.

Keniston, K. (1970) Youth: A "new" stage of life. *The American Scholar*, 39(4), 631–654. www.jstor.org/stable/41209802

Majin, G. (2022) The unhealed wound; official and unofficial journalisms, misinformation and tribal truth. In: Fowler-Watt, K., and McDougall, J. eds. *Palgrave Handbook of Media Misinformation*. Palgrave Macmillan, pp. 233–247.

Mass, Cliff. (2021) Was global warming the cause of the great northwest heatwave? Science says no. Cliff Mass Weather Blog. 5 July 2021. https://cliffmass.blogspot.com/2021/07/was-global-warming-cause-of-great.html

Mill, J.S. (2011) *On Liberty*. London: Walter Scott Publishing, 35. https://gutenberg.org/files/34901/34901-h/34901-h.htm

Mott, F.L. (1962) *American Journalism*. New York: Macmillan.

Ramirez, R. (2021) Climate change is fueling mass-casualty heat waves. Here's why experts say we don't view them as crises. CNN. 13 July 2021. https://edition.cnn.com/2021/07/12/weather/climate-change-mass-casualty-psychology/index.html

Taylor, D. (1975) Editorial responsibilities. BBC Lunch-Time Lectures. 10th Series, (2), 13 November 1975.

Turchin, P. (2012) Dynamics of political instability in the United States, 1780–2010. *Journal of Peace Research*, 49 (4), 577–591.

4

SPORTS JOURNALISM'S DILEMMA

All about celebrating the spectacle?

Max Mauro

Introduction

On 30 March 2022, the *Independent's* chief football writer Miguel Delaney tweeted on his way to Doha, Qatar, to cover the FIFA Men's World Cup draw.

> Of course, journalists are going. The job is to report, and the fundamental of reporting is going, looking and talking to people. Journalists, as a rule, shouldn't boycott events.

A few minutes later, he tweeted again.

> The job isn't to promote, or celebrate. It's to report, every aspect. Human rights groups are also encouraging journalists to go, albeit with a critical eye. This is more pronounced with this World Cup than most. Otherwise, PR-friendly perspectives are spread.

The 2022 FIFA World Cup is one of the most controversial sport events ever organised. According to the *Guardian*, 6,500 migrant workers have lost their lives in Qatar since the World Cup was awarded to this country in 2011, many of them employed in the construction of the venues and associated infrastructure.[1] Unsurprisingly, Delaney's tweets elicited a good number of replies and retweets (by 2 April it had received 576 comments and been retweeted 270 times). However, while some social media users appreciated the critical stance taken by the journalist, the majority of the comments to his tweets were from Newcastle United FC fans accusing him of "hypocrisy" for having previously criticised the takeover of their club by a company controlled by the Saudi Arabia kingdom. According to these fans, someone criticising "sportswashing" in one case should not engage with

DOI: 10.4324/9781003301028-6

the same practice in a different context. As contradictory as this form of criticism may appear, it arguably epitomises an underlying tension in contemporary sports writing and reporting and the type of challenges posed to the moral authority of sports journalists by sport fans and the wider public. It further underlines a question which is at the heart of the relationship between mass media and professional sports at the present time: How can we separate the narration and interpretation of sport events, including lucrative national leagues and international tournaments and competitions, from the multiple ethical, political, social and cultural issues in which they are embroiled? From *sportswashing* to racism, from corruption within the sporting bodies to doping, from human trafficking of young talents to growing mental health issues among professional athletes, the list of "non-sporting" issues affecting contemporary sports is long and constantly growing.

This question and these issues matter particularly to journalism educators. A critical challenge in forming future sports journalists and sports media professionals is, in fact, that of equipping them with multiple practical skills, needed to navigate in a competitive multimedia industry, alongside an appropriate critical lens that would allow them to read through the complexity of the contemporary sporting spectacle. The present chapter will explore the state of sports journalism in Higher Education with the aim of unpacking established trends and emerging fissures. It will start with an overview of the role of sport in the contemporary media industry, with particular attention to the "sports/media complex" (Rowe, 2013) and to the transformation of journalistic practices over the past three decades. It will then explore the evolution of the teaching of sports journalism at university level and the creation of dedicated degrees in sports media. Finally, it will pay attention to the main challenges faced by prospective sports journalists, offering some suggestions based on the review of the literature and conversations with professional journalists and educators.

The sports media landscape

From the end of the 19th century, mass media have been instrumental to the growth of sport as popular culture and a form of entertainment among different social classes. At the same time, professional sport leagues and competitions have contributed to the commercial appeal of newspapers in different countries. This is the case, for example, of the diffusion of the popular press among the working class in Britain parallel to the professionalisation of football, the first baseball leagues and then the Major League Baseball in the USA and cycling events such as the Tour de France and the Giro d'Italia, both created at the beginning of the 20th century by sports dailies (Holt, 1989; Laucella, 2014; Wille, 2003). The same role was played by sport in the early popularisation of cinema newsreels, radio and television broadcasting (Whannel, 2009). International sport competitions such as the Olympics and the FIFA World Cup have, since the 1930s, further intensified the relationship between sport and media (Tomlinson, 2017). All this testifies to a long history of sport as a key subject for mass media and journalism. However, this relationship changed in nature with the technological advancement of broadcasting and the mass availability of television sets in Western societies.

From the 1950s, and more prominently through the 1960s and 1970s, television acquired a different role in the definition of the sporting spectacle. Up to that point, sport and media had been related through distinctive functions such as advertising, promoting, and reporting, but they remained separate entities: sport was just a subject, although of growing importance for the media industry. According to Rowe (2013, p. 64),

> the key change occurred when (sport) became scheduled media content in the form of events rendered as audiovisual texts, especially when presented "live" through broadcasting at the same moment as in-stadium spectators were experiencing the temporally and spatially fixed event.

The USA, with their professional leagues of baseball, American football and basketball, and a few private broadcasters competing for lucrative deals with the leagues, pioneered these changes, which decades later became the norm in other parts of the world.

Such a critical development led, in the 1980s, to the conceptualisation of the "sports/media complex" (Jhally, 1984), which has been influential for a growing body of research in the fields of sports media and the sociology of sport. The sports/media complex highlights the implications of the intimate association of live images and sport events, made available to millions of people at national level and globally, which provides a powerful transnational marketing language for sponsors. As it happened, it is through the combination of sport as media content, television and sports marketing that the Olympic Games and the FIFA World Cup were transformed, in the 1980s, from popular and expensive sports festivals into profitable commercial enterprises (Roche, 2019).

From the point of view of the journalistic profession, it is interesting to observe that, while television has been the driving force of the growth of sport events in the second half of the 20th century, it has also determined an increase of attention toward sport among other media, such as newspapers. This has been particularly the case in the UK. From the 1990s, and notably following the 1990 World Cup in Italy and the birth of the Premier League in 1992, the so-called quality press increased their sport sections, especially the coverage of football. For example, the *Daily Telegraph* devoted 18% of its space to sport in 1974, but by 2004 sport occupied about 30% of the newspaper (Boyle, 2006, p. 50). A similar trend was followed by the *Times* from the moment it was acquired by Rupert Murdoch, in 1981. These changes brought the quality press closer to the level of attention historically paid to sport by the popular press.

Understandably, the creation of the Premier League produced a seismic change in the television coverage of sport in the UK. In just over three years, between 1996 and 1999, coverage of sport on terrestrial TV stations (BBC1 and BBC2, ITV, Channel 4 and Channel 5) increased by 56.9% to 4.302 hours (Horne, 2006,

p. 43). On satellite (which in the UK at that time meant essentially SkyTV) and cable TV the percentage increase over the same period was 46.6 (but amounted to 26.435 hours). Football was the most widely covered sport on TV followed by golf, motor sports, cricket, tennis, horse racing, boxing and rugby union. In 1999 football accounted for over one-quarter of BBC1's sports coverage and tennis for over one-fifth of BBC2's output, closely followed by snooker (ibid., p. 44).

These figures show the importance of sport for the media industry in the UK in the first decade of the internet. Since then, the commercialisation and commodification of professional sports has continued to increase, progressively extended to more sports and a variety of competitions. It is therefore not surprising that media mogul Rupert Murdoch emphasised the role of sport in the media industry, advocating its use as the "battery ram" in the penetration of new markets (Andrews and Ritzer, 2007). These developments arguably implied a growing demand for content, and therefore more job opportunities for journalists and sport communication professionals. However, further deep transformations were heralded by "the digital revolution", first with the wider availability of internet among the population at the turn of the century, and then with the technological advancements exemplified by the smartphones and other portable digital devices. Although interest in sport has never been so prominent, boosted by the multiplication of channels and ventures enabled by the digital environment, and by the use of social media by fans, protagonists and media outlets, the profession has entered a critical stage. On the one hand, traditional media such as newspapers have been affected by a constant decline in both circulation and advertising revenue. This has led to a number of print media outlets to focus primarily or essentially on the digital, and to significant staff reductions across the sector (House of Lords, 2020). Television has also witnessed an erosion of audiences, particularly among the younger generations, which has also affected sport events, particularly in the USA. However, the value of television sport programming has increased with growing focus placed on the (online) social dimension of spectatorship. An example of this trend is the Super Bowl, the most important media sport event in the USA and one of the most lucrative globally. According to viewing figures, the Super Bowl is watched by fewer people on television compared to previous decades, but its commercial value for television advertising has continued to increase, boosted by social media traffic: in 2019 the cost of a 30-second spot on the Super Bowl was up 60% from 2008.[2]

New pressures and opportunities have emerged within the "networked media sport", which Rowe and Hutchins (2014, p. 44) define as

> a dense, rich media environment in which sport can be viewed, discussed and, in some cases, organized among online sport constituencies in ways that challenge the traditional distinction between audience and participant.

It is precisely the blurring of the distinction between producers and audiences that characterises the contemporary media landscape, and which makes the work of sports journalists particularly challenging, more so than that of news journalists (sports fans are the first experts in their favourite sports or about the teams/athletes they support). According to Laucella (2014, p. 259),

> sports journalism is at a crossroads as new media producers and bloggers have challenged traditional journalistic norms and news values. Pressures come from within the organization, as well as outside the organization, and social media have accelerated the process.

Hutchins and Boyle (2017, p. 497) contend that sport journalists have reacted to this pressure by establishing a "community of practice", described as a situation in which

> professional journalists distinguish themselves from so-called semi-professionals, amateurs, enthusiasts and purveyors of sponsored content (e.g. bloggers, citizen journalists, social media commentators, marketers and public relations practitioners), privileging the actions and logics they use to produce knowledge about events in the social world.

What is at play is the status and the interpretative authority of sport journalists in the face of a fragmented institutional and organisational scenario. Having said that, we should not overlook the fact that this analysis, as much of the literature in this field, is primarily focused on the Global North; the digital divide is still a tangible factor in determining developments in the media industry across the globe (ITU, 2021).

Finally, a possibly even more disruptive challenge for the job of sports journalists comes from the fact that sport organisations (leagues, national associations and international federations) and athletes no longer need to rely on journalists to communicate with fans and the public. Digital media and social media have provided an effective instrument for the protagonists of sport to reach out to their audiences. The growth of in-house media and communication departments within sport organisations displaces the authority and the operational independence of the journalist (McEnnis, 2018). Bradshaw and Minogue (2020, p. 112) believe that

> now that clubs have their own websites and social media platforms – platforms that enable them to bypass journalists and produce content that goes directly to supporters – the journalist is marginalised.

At the same time, however, media departments of sports clubs and sports organisations increasingly provide professional opportunities for young people who may have completed a journalism or sports journalism degree but find restricted options with traditional media outlets (Hutchins and Rowe, 2017; Lloyd and Toogood, 2015). Taking stock of this trend it is timely to pay attention to its implications for the evolving professional and ethical boundaries of (sports) journalism, something that also pertains to the work of university educators. What happens to journalistic standards if the news is produced and disseminated in growing measure directly by the protagonists? Drawing on a study conducted in the USA, Mirer (2019, pp. 75–76) argues that

> in-house sports reporters are seeking recognition as part of the profession, but in producing work that looks like traditional journalism they raise important questions about the professional claims sports journalists make about their work.

Sports journalism education

Historically, sports journalism has often been considered something of a sub-genre of the journalistic profession, referred to as the "toy-department" of a media outlet (Miller, 2020). This is due to the perception that sport events are simply games, entertainment, and those writing, reporting and commenting about them, should consider themselves lucky enough not having to deal with more serious issues (Rowe, 2005; Steen, 2014). However, the evolution of sport as a media spectacle, and its prominent role in the media industry, particularly in the Global North, has arguably changed this perception. According to Farrington et al. (2012, p. 1)

> during recent times, sports journalism has moved from the toy department to the finance department. Where once the profession was seen with amusement or scorn, it is now seen as crucial to the incomes and audiences of many media organizations.

This sort of cultural shift has been reflected in the renewed attention paid by scholars and journalism educators to the field of sports journalism and sports media. Higher Education in the UK is a particularly pertinent setting in which to observe this development. As noticed, the inception of the Premier League in the early 1990s has transformed the British sports media landscape, and its effects have reverberated in other European countries where football is the leading sport, such as Spain, Italy, Germany and France. It is therefore not surprising that British universities have, over the past two decades, directed attention and resources to develop sports journalism degrees and degrees that explore the complex relationship between sport and the media and communications fields. Sports journalism courses were introduced in British Higher Education in the first decade of the 21st century, at a time when the "marketisation" of British universities was a completed process (Vernon, 2018), and universities were multiplying their provision of undergraduate and postgraduate studies, particularly in the field of media (Brienza, 2016).[3] Since then, the number of institutions offering this type of degree has grown constantly. At the time of writing, 26 British universities offer 51 undergraduate degrees in "sports journalism" or sports media related subjects, up to 14 universities in 2015 (Price, 2015).[4] Some universities have further specified the focus of their provision, creating degrees in "Multimedia Sports Journalism", in "Football Journalism" and even in "Esports and Sports Media". Eleven universities offer postgraduate courses, which include degrees in "sports broadcasting", "sports communication" and "international sports journalism". The increasing popularity of sports journalism degrees among young people, particularly males, is proved by the fact that in some universities the number of students enrolling in these degrees has outnumbered traditional journalism courses.[5]

Two professional training bodies, the National Council for the Training of Journalists (NCTJ) and the Broadcast Journalism Training Council (BJTC), offer accreditation to journalism courses in the UK. According to the NCTJ, the accreditation is "a benchmark of best practice" and provides standards against which "potential students can judge prospective courses".[6] The NCTJ accredits more than 80 journalism courses at 40 universities[7]. Among the universities offering undergraduate degrees in sports journalism, nine are currently accredited by the NCTJ, and four are accredited by the BJTC.[8]

In a European context, the variety of offers in the field of sports journalism and sports media by British HE institutions appears quite unique compared to other countries. In fact, where available, "sport" is generally offered only as an option as part of undergraduate journalism or communication degrees. This is the case, for example, in Spain (although some Spanish universities offer postgraduate courses in sports journalism), Italy and Germany. Looking at the case of Turkey, Büyükbaykal reflects on the importance of sport in popular culture and laments the poor quality of sport journalism writing and reporting in the country. He underlines the "importance of sports journalism education", advocating "a close cooperation of Press Institutions, Faculties of Communication, Sport Vocational High Schools and Sport Sciences Faculties" (2016, p. 667).

But how is sports journalism taught at university? Are there common trends and established practices, despite the limited history of this specific educational path? Weedon and Wilson conducted an analysis of the most popular "handbooks, field guides and other educative texts", used in sports journalism courses in the English-speaking world, with the aim to understand "how tomorrow's would-be sports journalists might learn to report on serious matters such as racism, corruption, environmental degradation and other issues identified as besetting sports media" (2020, p. 1377). The eight books surveyed were authored by current or former sports journalists who hold faculty positions in British and North American universities. One of the emerging themes analysed in this study is "objectivity", which seems to play a key role in the definition of the professional identity of sports journalists. In general terms, a recurring argument across textbooks is that "the capacity and responsibility to 'be objective' is what distinguishes sports reporters, and journalism, from sports fans and supporters" (ibid., p. 1385). Objectivity is interpreted as impartiality, not "taking a stance", in reporting on sport events. However, this idea of objectivity seems oblivious to the kind of debate that has animated journalism for much of the 20th century, reflecting concomitant developments in philosophical and scientific thought (Post, 2015). According to

Weedon and Wilson, "objectivity is enlisted in these books as a journalistic *rite of passage*". Differently from objectivity, ethics is a theme that is confined at the margins of the books in their analysis, and in some cases is only addressed in the appendices. The tone of the conclusion of the two authors is defined by a sense of perplexity and, possibly, hope. They ask: "Might sports journalism itself place the social, cultural and political significance of sport at the centre of ongoing attempts to define quality?" (ibid., p. 1397).

Challenges and opportunities

As we have seen, the growing importance of the sporting spectacle, and the role that media play in magnifying its significance across cultures and countries, forces journalists, scholars and educators to reflect on the ethical and practical boundaries of the (sports) journalistic profession. The coverage of sport by media outlets has grown parallel to the commodification of sport, but while the mutual promotional support of sport and media was evident since the early days of professional sports, the digital environment has intensified competition, something that is reflected in the broader commercialisation of the media (McManus, 2009). This affects all media outlets, including broadsheet/quality news organisations. A study of leading "quality" news organisations in Australia, India and the UK revealed the pressure of sports editors to "monetise" sports-related content (English, 2016). For example, a senior editor at *The Times of India* noted how "sports columns were designed around advertisements for alcohol products" (ibid., p. 1010). A sports editor at the *Sydney Morning Herald* said that he "would now meet with advertisers, while his counterpart at the *Guardian* believed in trying to 'monetise' the sports section" (ibid., p. 1012).

This trend arguably contrasts with the moral and ethical dilemma of sports journalism highlighted by Oates and Pauly (2007, p. 336). They argue that "even when sports coverage does not offer citizens crucial information, it may offer them cultural narratives that frame and shape their understandings of the group identities and relations of democratic society". They consequently emphasise "the moral obligations of sports reporting as a form of cultural representation" (ibid., p. 333). However, the pressures coming from the industry appear to push the profession in a different direction. Samindra Kunti is a Belgian freelance journalist who has covered major international sports events for Forbes, World Soccer, BBC and other media. He believes that the demand of sport content is higher than ever, but the quality of the product is going down.

> My view is that you should always try to put sport in a social and economic context, otherwise it does not make sense, but good quality journalism requires funding and time, and most media are not interested. Visual, quick content is more important: this is what drives the industry today. We also need to consider that there are less people working at the desk, also in big media, and articles are often not edited or even sub-edited. On the other hand, social

media headlines drive content towards young people's interests which are increasingly shaped by what circulates on TikTok or YouTube.

So, where does sports journalism education position itself in the face of these opposing pressures? How can young prospective journalists learn to proficiently navigate through competing obligations? Weedon et al. (2018) believe that positive change in this journalistic field could come from a closer dialogue between sociologists of sport, sports media scholars, journalists and journalism educators. They seek shared criteria to define "quality sports journalism" and, taking stock of the heightened significance of sport in the economy of the 21st century news media industries and the continuous interest of sociologists of sport and media scholars in sports journalism practices, they interpret quality as "public service journalism", which implies "a concern with civic issues and inequality" (Weedon et al., 2018, p. 645). They further refer to Rowe's definition of "excellent" sports journalism, one that is "capable of reaching beyond sport into the more universal and profound sphere of individual motivation, the 'human condition', the state of society and so on" (1999, p. 59). They conclude:

> positive change is more likely to come from the education of tomorrow's sports journalists, and collaborations with current ones, than from critiquing the institutionalized practices of reporters and broadcasters who already have hundreds if not thousands of critics below the line.
>
> (Weedon et al., 2018, pp. 662–663)

As aspirational and laudable these goals may be, they arguably clash with the practicalities of the job carried out by many sports journalists in the digital environment: a 24/7 news cycle which demands shorter and quicker forms of information. As noted by Domeneghetti, "it is hard for even the most succinct journalist to articulate their thoughts clearly in 280 characters (the maximum length of a tweet on Twitter) or 10 seconds (the maximum length of a snap on Snapchat)" (2021, p. 175). This appears particularly problematic when journalists deal with sensitive issues, such as racism in sport, homophobia and transgender rights. A Tweet or social media post can be easily misunderstood and the journalist or the protagonists of the story, or both, can find themselves at the receiving end of abuse. This is a risk highlighted by Bradshaw (2021, p. 29), who contends that "social media has introduced – or intensified – a host of ethical issues for sports journalists, not least self-censorship and the connected phenomenon of how to deal with the online abuse that is directed at them". As a consequence, in order to avoid controversies journalists may be tempted to censor themselves.

Social media can be a powerful tool in the hands of the journalist, but they can also undermine their authority. Steve Menary has worked in the industry since the 1990s, for print media, BBC World and others, and authored seven books. He links social media with click bait.

> You may write something that's just a fact but because it touches a certain club, you will get people (fans) on social media piling on, just saying you're wrong, you're wrong. 100 people shouting you're wrong doesn't mean you are wrong. It just means there's 100 people shouting that you're wrong. These may be the same people that rate your articles, which is what digital media often encourage readers to do. Journalists end up getting measured on that, which I think is bad.

No one should be surprised by the fact that, in the contemporary media landscape, the use of social media is considered by editors and media managers as part of the set of skills expected to be possessed by young recruits. Ketter et al. (2014) argue that sports editors and television sports directors rank "writing ability" as the top skill desired for news reporters. However, the definition of writing appears to be changing in a multimedia scenario, as "many sports editors and sports directors stressed writing includes the 'ability to blog – aggressively, several times a day'". Another editor said: "we're now asking for writers to develop, maintain, and interact using blogs, Twitter, and other web tools" (ibid., p. 293).

The professional boundaries of sports journalism have expanded, and the way journalists report and comment on sport is going through a novel transition. However, change and evolution have characterised different moments in the history of professional sports. One can think, for example, of the innovation in sports writing stimulated by the Tour de France in the early decades of the 20th century; the influence that the film *Olympia*, about the 1936 Olympic Games, had on the evolution of sports broadcasting, or the impact that televised football had on the British press from 1960s and through the 1980s, with more attention being paid to personal stories, and a more prominent use of quotes. Thus, the apparent "complications" brought about by the digital scenario should be read within a historical framework, which demands that journalists adapt. In fact, "adaptability" is one of the key traits that sports editors believe journalism schools should instil in students (Ketterer et al., 2014).

What is remarkably different today compared with previous eras are the heightened social and political ramifications of media sport events (Wenner and Billings, 2017). Miller (2020) ponders on the challenges faced by sports journalism and invites to pay attention to three aspects: one is technology, exemplified by the role of automation and clickbait in the production chain and particularly on labour; the second is (the lack of) diversity within the industry, in terms of gender and race; and the third is partisanship and nationalism. Jonathan Liew, sportswriter for *The Guardian,* believes that automation represents the main challenge, but only in the long term:

> Once the machine can simulate the artistry of writing, which it's nowhere near being able to do yet, then we're all in trouble. I think the other problems are far more imminent. Gender and ethnic diversity have historically been

a huge problem in sports journalism, but I think there is a broad recognition across the board of the issue. A lot of new media, whether it's fan media or startups are a lot more cognizant of the need to have a broader range of opinions, voices, and life experiences. It is slowly improving also in the traditional media. It's important because it shapes public opinion and shapes the way we see the world.

A growing body of literature highlights the need for the sports media industry to address the historical hegemony of (white) men. To this day, women are still a tiny minority in sports journalism. Price (2015) appropriately directs the attention to sports journalism courses in the UK. At the time of his study, female students were just 7% of the total 55% in journalism courses. He therefore makes two suggestions to sports journalism educators to become more inclusive of female students: "First, it is important that courses cover a wide range of sports and clearly advertise this to prospective students. Second, institutions with a variety of journalism courses could organise individual modules and classes with gender balance in mind" (ibid., p. 18).

Even more striking is the lack of representation of racial and ethnic minorities among sports journalists in the face of a consistent presence of ethnic minority players in top competitions such as the Premier League, the NBA, the NFL and others. Bradshaw and Minogue (2020, p. 127) cite a study of the National Council for the Training of Journalists which found that only 8% of black candidates were able to secure newsroom jobs six months after graduation, in comparison to 26% of their white peers. Although some media institutions and professional bodies are addressing issues of inclusion in the sports media, a less discussed issue is the way partisanship and nationalism are normalised in contemporary sports reporting and writing (Mauro and Martinez-Corcuera, 2020). In light of the global dimension of sport, and of the increasing ethnic and racial diversity within professional leagues and national teams, sports journalism educators should encourage students to look beyond their national boundaries and their own personal passions to embrace the universal power of sport to connect and bring people together.

Conclusion

This chapter has looked into the intersection of sports and media, and into the growing interest paid to it by scholars and journalism educators. It is undeniable that, over the recent decades, sport news and the coverage of sport have acquired unprecedented prominence in the media industry. The heightened economic and political value of sports events and competitions highlights the role "naturally" played by sport as malleable popular culture, but, more importantly, it stresses its force as a transnational marketing language for global capitalism, a dynamic asset of the entertainment industry and as a strategic tool for the national(istic) ambitions of both democratic and authoritarian governments. Sport has increased its importance parallel to the hegemonic positioning of the neoliberal ideology in the post—Cold War world, and Miller argues that sport is actually the "most spectacular embodiment of neoliberalism, through the dual fetish of competition and control, individualism and government" (2013, p. 24).

Journalism educators and media scholars should be cognisant of this, and of the fact that the growth of sports journalism courses is a reflection of, and a reaction to, these developments. Mass media are not only key to the functioning of the sporting spectacle, but they are also responsible for its credibility in the eyes of the public amid multiple challenges. Therefore, the coverage of sport events cannot be reduced to their "celebration". The education of young prospective journalists and media professionals in the field of sport is a complex task, which demands novel perspectives for engaging with the moral, political and social dimensions of the sporting spectacle. Norman Denzin believes that "a new sports media culture is required" (2013, p. 298) and contends that schools of journalism should be "committed in training sports journalists … who want to do more than report on history. They want to interrupt and interpret sport cultural history as it is being written". Are we ready to embrace this challenge?

Notes

1 www.theguardian.com/global-development/2021/feb/23/revealed-migrant-worker-dea ths-qatar-fifa-world-cup-2022
2 www.cnbc.com/2019/01/30/how-much-it-costs-to-air-a-commercial-during-super-bowl-liii.html (Accessed 20 April 2022).
3 Brienza (2016, pp. 99–100) observes that "UK universities have tripled their provision of undergraduate and postgraduate media studies at virtually the same time as undergraduate tuition fees for UK/EU students also tripled from £3000 to £9000 p.a."
4 AA.VV. The complete university guide 2022. Available from thecompleteuniversityguide. co.uk (Accessed on 15 April 2022).
5 This is the case, for example, of Solent University and Bournemouth University.
6 www.nctj.com/ (Accessed 15 April 2022).
7 The accreditation is granted on the basis of a number of "performance standards", such as "Quality journalism education and training and results", "Close industry links and practical up-to-date journalism experience" and "Innovation, ambition and continuous improvement".
8 www.sportsjournalists.co.uk/training/other-training-courses/ (Accessed 15 April 2022).

References

Andrews, D.L. and Ritzer, G. (2007). 'The grobal in the sporting glocal'. *Global Networks*, 7(2), pp. 135–153.
Boyle, R. (2006). *Sports journalism: context and issues*. London: Sage.
Boyle, R. and Haynes, R. (2009). 'The sports pages: Journalism and sport'. In R. Boyle and R. Haynes (eds.), *Power play: Sport, the media and popular culture*. Edinburgh: Edinburgh University Press, pp. 19–42.
Bradshaw, T. (2021). 'Benefit or burden? Social media and moral complexities confronting sports journalists'. In R. Domeneghetti (ed.), *Insights on reporting sports in the digital age: Ethical and practical considerations in a changing media landscape*. Abingdon: Routledge, pp. 17–30.

Bradshaw, T. and Minogue, D. (2020). *Sports journalism: The state of play*. Abingdon: Routledge.
Brienza, C. (2016). 'Degrees of (self-) exploitation: Learning to labour in the neoliberal university'. *Journal of Historical Sociology*, 29(1), pp. 92–111.
Büyükbaykal, G. (2016). 'Importance of sports journalism education'. *Journalism and Mass Communication*, 6(11), pp. 661–668.
Denzin, N. (2012). 'Afterword: Sport and neoliberalism'. In M.L. Silk and D.L. Andrews (eds.), *Sport and neoliberalism: Politics, consumption, and culture*. Philadelphia: Temple University Press, pp. 294–302.
Domeneghetti, R. (2021). 'Conclusion'. In Domeneghetti, R. (ed.), *Insights on reporting sports in the digital age: Ethical and practical considerations in a changing media landscape*. Abingdon: Routledge, pp. 172–183.
English, P. (2016). 'Mapping the sports journalism field: Bourdieu and broadsheet newsrooms'. *Journalism*, 17(8), pp. 1001–1017.
Farrington, N., Kilvington, D., Price, J. and Saeed, A. (2012). *Race, racism and sports journalism*. Abingdon: Routledge.
Holt, R. (1989). *Sport and the British*. Oxford: Clarendon Press.
Horne, J. (2006). *Sport in consumer culture*. Basingstoke: Palgrave Macmillan.
House of Lords/Communications and Digital Committee (2020). *Breaking news? The future of UK journalism*. 1st Report. London: House of Lords.
Hutchins, B. and Boyle, R. (2017). 'A community of practice'. *Digital Journalism*, 5(5), pp. 496–512.
ITU-International Telecommunication Union (2021). *Measuring digital development: Facts and figures*. 2021 Report. Geneva: ITU.
Jhally, S. (1984). 'The spectacle of accumulation: Material and cultural factors in the evolution of the sports/media complex'. *Insurgent Sociologist*, 12(3), pp. 41–57.
Ketterer, S., McGuire, J., and Murray, R. (2014). 'Contrasting desired sports journalism skills in a convergent media environment.' *Communication & Sport*, 2(3), pp. 282–298.
Laucella, P. (2014). 'The evolution from print to online platforms for sports journalism'. In A.C. Billings and M. Hardin (eds.), *Routledge handbook of sport and new media*. Abingdon: Routledge, pp. 244–274.
Lloyd, J. and Toogood, L. (2015). *Journalism and PR: News media and public relations in the digital age*. Oxford: IB Tauris/Reuters Institute for the Study of Journalism.
Mauro, M. and Martínez-Corcuera, R. (2020). 'Hypermasculinity and racist discourses in the Spanish media'. In J. O'Brien, R. Holden, and X. Ginesta (eds.), *Sport, globalisation and identity: New perspectives on regions and nations*. Abingdon: Routledge, pp. 90–106.
McEnnis, S. (2018). 'Sports journalism and cultural authority in the digital age'. In T.F. Carter, D. Burdsey, and M. Doidge (eds.), *Transforming sport: Knowledges, practices, structures*. Abingdon: Routledge, pp. 207–219.
McManus, J. (2009). 'The commercialisation of news.' In K. Wahl-Jorgensen and T. Hanitzsch (eds.), *The handbook of journalism studies*. New York: Routledge, pp. 218–234.
Miller, T. (2012). 'A distorted playing field: Neoliberalism and sport through the lens of economic citizenship'. In M.L. Silk and D.L. Andrews (eds.), *Sport and neoliberalism: Politics, consumption, and culture*. Philadelphia: Temple University Press, pp. 23–37.
Miller, T. (2020). 'Reporting'. In H. Richards, J. Novick and R. Steen (eds.), *Routledge handbook of sports journalism*. Abingdon: Routledge, pp. 367–376.
Mirer, M. (2019). 'Playing the right way: In-house sports reporters and media ethics as boundary work'. *Journal of Media Ethics*, 34(2), pp. 73–86.
Oates, T.P. and Pauly, J. (2007). 'Sports journalism as moral and ethical discourse'. *Journal of Mass Media Ethics*, 22(4), pp. 332–347.

Post, S. (2015). 'Scientific objectivity in journalism? How journalists and academics define objectivity, assess its attainability, and rate its desirability'. *Journalism,* 16(6), pp. 730–749.

Price, J. (2015). 'Where are all the women? Diversity, the sports media, and sports journalism education'. *International Journal of Organizational Diversity,* 14(1), pp. 9–19.

Roche, M. (2019). *Mega-events and social change: Spectacle, legacy and public culture.* Manchester: Manchester University Press.

Rowe, D. (1999). *Sport, culture and the media: The unruly trinity* (2nd ed.). Maidenhead: Open University Press.

Rowe, D. (2005). 'Fourth estate or fan club? Sports journalism engages the popular'. In S. Allan (ed.), *Journalism: critical issues.* Maidenhead: Open University/McGraw-Hill, pp. 125–136.

Rowe, D. (2013). 'The sport/media complex'. In D.L. Andrews and V.B. Carrington (eds.), *A companion to sport.* Hoboken: John Wiley & Sons, pp. 61–77.

Rowe, D. (2017). 'Sports journalism and the FIFA scandal: Personalization, co-optation, and investigation'. *Communication and Sport,* 5(5), pp. 515–533.

Steen, R. (2014). *Sports journalism: A multimedia primer.* Abingdon: Routledge.

Tomlinson, A. (2017). 'Twenty-eight Olympic summers. Historical and methodological reflections on understanding the Olympic mega-event'. In L.A. Wenner and A.C. Billings (eds.), *Sport, media and mega-events.* Abingdon: Routledge, pp. 51–68.

Vernon, J. (2018). 'The making of the neoliberal university in Britain'. *Critical Historical Studies,* 5(2), pp. 267–280.

Weedon, G. and Wilson, B. (2020). 'Textbook journalism? Objectivity, education and the professionalization of sports reporting'. *Journalism,* 21(10), pp. 1375–1400.

Weedon, G., Wilson, B., Yoon, L., and Lawson, S. (2018). 'Where's all the "good" sports journalism? Sports media research, the sociology of sport, and the question of quality sports reporting'. *International Review for the Sociology of Sport,* 53(6), pp. 639–667.

Wenner, L.A. and Billings, A.C. (2017). *Sport, media and mega-events.* Abingdon: Routledge.

Whannel, G. (2009). 'Television and the transformation of sport'. *The ANNALS of the American Academy of Political and Social Science,* 625(1), pp. 205–218.

Wille, F. (2003). 'The tour de France as an agent of change in media production'. *The International Journal of the History of Sport,* 20(2), pp. 128–146.

5
WHY POLITICS AND PUBLIC AFFAIRS STILL MATTER

David Brine

This chapter is presented as an essay written from the perspective of a journalism educator immersed in teaching public affairs to undergraduate students and those studying for their professional journalism diploma in the UK, as apprentices and as trainees working in newsrooms on the Meta Community News Project.

Introduction

The coronavirus disease 2019 (Covid-19) pandemic touched every part of our lives – and therefore every area of what we call the public realm. For journalists it was a health story, a science story and an economic story. However, it also swept through social care, welfare, education, devolution and local government – not to mention the power dynamic between our elected politicians and their appointed special advisors.

To get to the heart of stories about the crisis in our care homes – why there was a shortage of Personal Protective Equipment (PPE) – and to investigate the extraordinary road trip made from London to County Durham by the UK Prime Minister's special advisor, Dominic Cummings,[1] journalists needed a solid grounding in public affairs – that is, how government (both central and local) works.

Within the UK context, reporters who can tell their Clinical Commissioning Groups (CCG) from their Care Quality Commission (CQC) and their civil servants from their special advisors (SPADs), have always been at an advantage, but never more immediately than in the teeth of this all-consuming story. That understanding allowed the best journalists to carry out their prime functions – holding power to account and telling the public what they need to know.

The importance of these roles has never been greater. As many reporters, academics and political observers have warned, we are working in a different era to journalists of the past. Former BBC Newsnight anchor Emily Maitlis argued in her

2022 MacTaggart Lecture at the Edinburgh International Television Festival that politics has massively changed, politicians have massively changed but journalists have not yet caught up. For those charged with training the next generation of journalists, this should be an acute concern – and in no arena more than public affairs. In the past decade we have seen norms trashed as people in power show they are prepared to test the limits of the constitution in countries around the world to achieve their aims.

This new generation will need to get used to politicians using populist rhetoric to discredit and disempower journalists, so they are less likely to be held accountable for their actions. This messaging propounds the idea that the media is somehow getting in the way of the relationship between the people and their government and is framed as the media's grand conspiracy against the populist as the representative of the people.

Journalism educators are now having to show students how industry professionals are practising a sophisticated form of soft censorship – strategic bias – whereby reporters under attack end up employing bias to signal their impartiality, the curse of so-called both-side-ism or false equivalence.

It is against this backdrop of attacks on democracy itself that the importance of public affairs should be seen. As Maitlis said, "We show our impartiality when we report without fear or favour, when we are not scared to hold power to account even when it feels uncomfortable to do so."

She added: "Whatever our journalism does, it must earn the trust of our audience otherwise we are mouthpieces of those in authority, disconnected from the very people we are trying to serve" (Maitlis, 2022).

This essay argues that to fulfil this role, tomorrow's journalists need a strong working knowledge of public affairs as one of the key weapons in their armoury.

Challenges

Even as the Covid-19 pandemic – this once-in-a-generation event – was at its height with daily televised press conferences and unprecedented lockdowns, the engagement of many young people – including those aspiring to a career in the media – with politics and public affairs continued to decline.

It seems extraordinary to me – someone who has had a passion for politics since their early teens, studied the subject as an undergraduate, covered town halls for more than 25 years as a reporter and newsdesk staffer on regional daily newspapers and now a public affairs tutor since 2016. Surely there is never a dull moment in politics, even if it is not every week that throws up a new Prime Minister, fresh cabinet and a new sovereign – as we have witnessed recently in the UK.

Yet the lack of engagement from many students did not come as a surprise – a reaction that was also evident in my conversations with editors and colleagues teaching public affairs nationwide. However, it was disappointing that such a fundamental news event that affected everyone did not create a spike in interest.

Why is this the case? We know many young people are politically active on single issues. Strikes in schools to focus attention on the climate change crisis and campaigns around student mental health are evidence of this but it is not translating into engagement with the country's political institutions. Many times, students have told me that "politics is boring" when asked why they are not enjoying learning about public affairs.

Anonymous feedback from undergraduates on the public affairs module that I teach contained a typical observation. The student wrote: "It's a tedious subject. Unfortunately, it's a boring subject but that's just a personal opinion. I don't know how you can make politics interesting, who knows?"

We also know that the laudable policy of widening access to Higher Education is changing the nature of the students attending journalism degrees. Entry requirements have been eased which has brought undergraduate courses within reach for far more people than previously. Many of them have grasped the opportunity and gone on to great success both academically and in their later journalism careers. However, there is no denying that it has presented challenges to journalism educators as a significant number of students now need more support – both academically and pastorally – than previously.

This is a particular challenge on university courses with large cohorts where under-pressure staff simply do not have the time to give individual attention to students who do not engage with teaching sessions and materials. This is magnified when institutions offer programmes with specialist options or a suite of courses – for example, sports journalism – and students do not see the relevance of this general journalistic knowledge to their individual career. This can create a resistance to learning a subject like public affairs, when their schema for journalism is narrow, and, in the case of sports journalism, this might be limited to match reporting or blogging.

One student I recently encountered who arrived at university with the aim of becoming a football journalist illustrates this mindset. When asked whether an interest in politics had played a part in his ambition to become a journalist, he said:

> In all honesty, politics played no part. I found the world of politics so complex I didn't consider it. My inspiration for journalism was purely football. Football was my passion so I thought I should do a job in my passion, but this has now changed.

Reflecting on his thoughts about studying public affairs on his multimedia journalism course, he said:

> I found it a beneficial and necessary subject. It taught me everything I needed to know about the infrastructure of the UK. Sure, some people may have found it boring but for those that want to go into journalism it is absolutely necessary.

Why politics and public affairs still matter   65

He described the learning of politics as "key knowledge":

> To be a journalist in a certain field you need to be an expert on it. Therefore, if you want to be a UK political journalist then you need to have strong, contextual understanding of the infrastructure in the UK.

However, the student is in a minority as he revealed he rarely has discussions with fellow students about politics or public affairs. He said:

> I feel as though a lot of young people are dis-incentivised to talk about such subjects. I can feel really isolated at times as I don't feel as though people want to have these discussions or at times do not know enough for them to be able to have a conversation.

So, the question remains: "How do you show a predominantly apolitical group of people that public affairs knowledge is vital to journalists, even though it is not seen to be a 'sexy' subject?"

A different kind of journalism student

I am also involved in teaching trainee journalists on a contract basis under schemes such as the Meta-funded Community News Project and the Level 5 Journalism Apprenticeship. These 'students' are working in newsrooms, usually at local and regional newspapers and websites. For four days a week, they are working journalists. On the fifth day, they become remote online learners, studying for the National Council for the Training of Journalists' Diploma in Journalism. This includes public affairs as an elective skills module, still greatly valued by editors.

Even though a tutor's first contact with these trainees may be mere days after they first set foot in the newsroom, what is striking is their appreciation of the importance of public affairs knowledge in the creation of news stories and other editorial content.

The role of a Meta community news reporter is to engage with people in a defined group or geographic area and to curate, collate and create content relevant to them. It is not primarily to report hard news. They are tasked with building and developing community networks in person and online. The identified patch or demographic should be one that has been under-served, and material must be additional to the news provider's normal output.

However, it does not take long for these student reporters to be working on stories that require them to dip their toes into the world of public affairs. For example, why does a particular community – geographical or demographic – find it harder to access certain health services? Why can't parents in that community get their children into the area's 'better' schools?

Where does an inexperienced trainee reporter go to research these stories? Who should they interview? Without a solid grounding in public affairs, the reporter would not know that health services are planned and purchased by local CCGs, part of whose role is to improve the general health of the community and address health inequalities. They may also fail to grasp the different types of schools bundled together under the aegis of state education – community schools, academies, free schools – and their varying admission policies.

One student who has obtained their National Council for the Training of Journalists' Diploma in Journalism through the Community News Partnership said her newsroom experience meant it was clear immediately why the public affairs module was relevant to on-the-ground journalism:

> All stories are rooted in some form of public affairs – health issues (obviously relevant with Covid), political stories, policing issues, education etc. It is key to the journalism role I am pursuing. Without even a basic knowledge of everything taught in public affairs it would be hard to understand the political landscape unless you do all your own research.

The journalist, who has since moved jobs from a regional daily newspaper and website to a national newspaper and website, added that public affairs had helped her enormously in her latest role as a political reporter at the *Scottish Daily Mail*.

> Having grown up in England, I had little knowledge of how the political system worked in Scotland – what issues were devolved for example. Having taken the public affairs module, I felt much more confident putting myself forward for the job and then when working in Parliament I didn't have to ask questions about devolution as I already knew a lot of it.

NCTJ public affairs – is there a better way of teaching?

As every public affairs tutor teaching the NCTJ diploma would acknowledge, the programme of study is content-heavy. Alongside Essential Media Law, it is the most 'academic' of modules in the Diploma of Journalism. Whereas reporting staples such as content creation, story development, digital techniques and broadcasting skills can seem fun and practical, law and public affairs can be viewed as a chore, complete with their own dedicated textbooks (see key texts listed at the end of the chapter).

Reaction from new students is mixed. Many have no idea what is covered in the programme of study. When they find out, some are interested but many immediately write it off as we have already established, as 'boring politics'. Back with the new entrants for sports journalism, I have won some of them round with an explanation of the subject's importance with reference to the key role of organisations such as the Department of Culture, Media and Sport and UK Sport in the administration of sport in the UK. However, there was a core of students who remained unconvinced. It did not seem to occur to them that major news stories can break out at any moment and as the reporter on the spot their editors would want them to step in seamlessly. In that case a little public affairs knowledge could be useful. Anyone remember Hillsborough, where a perfectly normal football match turned into a disaster, with 97 people killed in a horrific human crush at the stadium? Sports journalists suddenly found themselves reporting on a major news story, which led to a series of inquiries into the policing on the day.

So, the challenge remains how to make public affairs more engaging and interesting and also more relevant. What might inspire students other than practical examples of the kind of news stories that relate to public affairs? Is it useful to take a more practical approach such as field trips enabling students to cover a council meeting, or visit the Houses of Parliament or listen to guest speakers from education or the National Health Service?

One of my former students, who arrived as an undergraduate with a passion for journalism and politics, said:

> Although predominantly theory, it was useful to see how real-life journalism in public affairs made use of the key knowledge. On reflection, it would have been great to visit the civic establishments at the heart of the module to better gain an understanding of how they worked in real life. Theory can be re-learnt but an engaging guest speaker or a trip to the Houses of Parliament will never be forgotten.

What can militate against this approach is a lack of time and number of students. Trying to schedule outside speakers when you need to cover the entire NCTJ programme of study in 12 weeks or organise visits with large cohorts of students is often a challenge too far.

Ironically, the pandemic and its migration to online meetings has been beneficial in getting access to council meetings, for example, and a wider range of guest speakers have been available, albeit from a remote location.

Putting the theory into practice

It would appear that practicality is the watchword here. Expanding the use of real-life examples of public affairs journalism is the way forward. This is a tried and tested formula that works, and results in some of the most effective teaching sessions that stick in students' memories.

No workshop on the Freedom of Information Act would be complete without reflection on the MPs' expenses scandal – duck houses, moat cleaning and flipped second homes – uncovered thanks to the outstanding work of City University professor Heather Brooke and reported by the national press. Or the infamous request from a student on work experience at the regional newspaper, the *Yorkshire Post*, who asked Wakefield Prison what items had been confiscated from inmates. The *Sunday Times'* investigation of the extraordinary saga of civil servants' search for the Loch Ness Monster is a reminder that Freedom of Information requests can also be used to reveal lighter stories.

Similarly, this can be fertile ground for engaging sports journalism students. While many seem interested only in what happens on the pitch, track or court, can we inspire others to look beyond the action and dig out those public affairs stories that impact the lives of our audience? For example, how much does it cost to police that flashpoint local derby football match? How much has the council cut back on its spending on sports pitches and other facilities?

One of the most memorable public affairs sessions from the past year was watching live with my students as former Yorkshire cricketer Azeem Rafiq gave tearful evidence to the Department of Culture, Media and Sport select committee about the racism scandal at the county club. Much better for the students to understand the scrutiny role of backbench MPs by immersing themselves in this significant developing story than by their tutor talking over slides, although that type of teaching still has its place.

This was surpassed only in September 2019, when I was teaching Community News Project trainees about the flexibility of the UK's unwritten constitution in our newsroom while the President of the Supreme Court, Baroness Brenda Hale, was literally adding another layer to that constitution on the television screen above my head as she gave her reasons for ruling then Prime Minister Boris Johnson's proroguing of Parliament unlawful.

The other weapon at our disposal is communication. More than ever it is important that we engage with our students and attempt to meet them where they are. What are their concerns about the world? Is it the environment, the availability of health services or simply whether they will be able to enjoy a fulfilling career in journalism and be able to afford a home? The chances are that whatever the answer, we can show them how the subjects covered in the public affairs syllabus impact on their hopes and fears. Listening to these interests and concerns could, I believe, provide a fruitful route to engaging more of tomorrow's journalists with politics and public affairs.

What is more, post-pandemic, public affairs tutors now have fresh, shining examples of relevant reporting to inspire young trainees and students who bring less and less political knowledge – and often interest – to the table.

One example is journalist Jack Shenker's 'Death at the Ministry', a long read for 'slow news' outlet *Tortoise*. This tells the heart-breaking story of Emanuel Gomes, who died after contracting Covid-19 as he continued his cleaning job in the heart of London. It led to questions about why the people he worked for seemed so casual about the risks he faced during the pandemic. This matters, as Shenker argued, because Gomes worked for the British government, the very body responsible for setting the rules around lockdown.

Another is *The Sunday Times'* 'Failures of State' series, a damning account of errors made by the British government starting from then Prime Minister Boris Johnson's failure to attend five emergency Cobra crisis meetings in the early days of the pandemic. Produced by the newspaper renowned Insight investigative reporting team, the stories were critical of Johnson's leadership but also explore the terrible effect the pandemic had on Britain's health care system.

The lesson? Knowledge and understanding of politics and public affairs are vital for those covering the biggest stories of the 21st century and defending the very essence of journalism when it is under attack like never before. It can also lead to more active civic engagement from young people, balancing out the democratic deficit. It is incumbent upon us as journalism educators to use these shining examples as models to get students thinking about how they can create public interest journalism in the public affairs sphere, translating theory into practice.

Key texts for the teaching of public affairs and media law in the UK

>   Baker J., 2021. *Essential Journalism: The NCTJ Guide for Trainee Journalists*. Abingdon, Routledge.
>   Harrison S., and Hanna M., 2020. *McNae's Essential Law for Journalists*, 26th ed. Oxford, Oxford University Press.
>   Morrison J., 2021. *Essential Public Affairs for Journalists*, 7th ed. Oxford, Oxford University Press.

Note

1 Dominic Cummings was chief advisor to the British Prime Minister Boris Johnson in the Covid-19 pandemic. In May 2020, following investigations by a number of national newspapers, it emerged that Cummings had broken lockdown rules and public health protocols by travelling out of London, at least once. This included a trip to County Durham when he had coronavirus symptoms. He initially denied the allegations, and eventually was cleared by a police inquiry, but the incident affected public trust in the government at a time of national crisis. Cummings was sacked by the PM in November 2020.

6
MEDIA LITERACY AND/IN JOURNALISM EDUCATION

Learning from (media) action

Julian McDougall

Introduction

This chapter discusses the design and implementation of a media literacy theory of change for Media Action, the BBC's international development charity. Media Action were seeking to integrate a more strategic media literacy approach into their existing work in 20 of the world's poorest, most diverse and most fragile countries. To build on their approaches and partnerships, the objective was to continue supporting independent media, combined with new training and outreach work on media literacy for journalists and publics in audience and community contexts. The theory of change informed a field review and approach paper, practitioner toolkit, training guide and 'train the trainers' programme for the organisation. These elements combined in a strategy for BBC Media Action's in-country practitioners to work with audiences, local media partners and publics to strengthen media ecosystems and promote resilience to information disorder through media literacy.

BBC Media Action is the UK public service broadcaster's international charity, using media and communication in developing countries and fragile societies to "save lives, protect livelihoods, counter misinformation, challenge prejudice and build democracy" (www.bbc.co.uk/mediaaction/). The approach is to "tackle information disorder by providing audiences with accurate, trusted and engaging information, and improving media and digital literacy" (BBC Media Action, 2021: 2). The organisation's multi-stakeholder, collaborative ecosystem approach, whilst being agile and nuanced to local contexts, is also typical of media literacy approaches that assume positive consequences:

> People have knowledge and skills (including the critical appraisal of information and emotional scepticism) that help them navigate their information ecosystem with care, identify false and misleading information and consume,

DOI: 10.4324/9781003301028-8

produce and share information in a more considered, safe and responsible way. (2021: 9)

Methods at work include interventions for discerning and mindful engagement with news and social media, innovative media forms such as gamification and 'pre-bunking' (the practice of educating people about misinformation as a preventative measure, so they can recognise it, an inoculation strategy, similar to a vaccine for public health), with the strategic intention to further develop work in these areas at scale for mass-reach application, from within mainstream media, to extend and bolster the organisation's response to information disorder through 'ecosystem hygiene' as well as with the added value of contributing new knowledge to the field of media literacy, where work has most typically been educational, produced through non-formal media, youth-led NGO partnerships and/or 'counter-script' media work, as opposed to being generated by 'the mainstream media'.

Integrating media literacy into journalism practice is essential to restore trust in the era of 'information disorder', as stated by UNESCO: "Media and Information Literacy can enable quality and ethical journalism, build trust in media through citizens, government, and media partnerships, as well as stimulate civic engagement" (2019). This means that increases in publics' media literacy, ideally progressing into their dynamic uses of media literacy for positive change, need to be combined with interventions in media ecosystems *by* 'the media'. When combined with critical engagement with journalism by media literate audiences, public interest media and trustworthy journalism can play a vital role in making fragmented, polarised and overloaded information environments healthier.

But media literacy is contested and complex. When solutions, or at least responses, are sought to misinformation, discursive polarisation, the lack of trust in professional media or the negative effects of our engagements with social media more broadly, media literacy is often cited, as David Buckingham observed:

> Media literacy is often invoked in a spirit of "solutionism". When media regulation seems impossible, media literacy is often seen as the acceptable answer – and indeed a magical panacea – for all media-related social and psychological ills … This argument clearly frames media literacy as a protectionist enterprise, a kind of prophylactic. It oversimplifies the problem it purports to address, overstates the influence of media on young people and underestimates the complexity of media education.
>
> *(Buckingham, 2017)*

This contested and complex nature of media literacy is manifested in the oxymoronic neutrality endemic to such solutionism. Such a way of thinking about literacy, of all kinds, but in this case media literacy, ignores the paradox that unhealthy media ecosystems are not caused *by* a lack of media literacy but rather by the toxic use *of* it.

Media literacy: Complex and contested

Positing media literacy as complex and contested in this way is to understand it as dynamic, living and unsettling (Potter and McDougall, 2017 Pahl and Rowsell, 2020; Lee et al, 2022).

Voices from the diverse field of media literacy shift the focus to indigenous media literacies and Global South perspectives, combining literacies with activism for social justice through g/local application, intersecting with movements for 'mining back' in algorithmic cultures, and mobilising counter-representations of nature, ethnicity, indigeneity and various forms of difference towards media literacy edu-cologies; the field is exploring diverse cartographies. These include considerations of how media literacy relates to feminism, critical race theory, postcolonial and intersectional practices, and embracing how these perspectives, politics and geographies can decentre the field. This is very far from the binary, deficit logic of solutionism and the situating of media literacy in either regulatory or instrumentally educational spaces.

Given all of these more fluid, agentive, shifting and negotiated sets of ways of thinking about media literacy, it is also necessary to learn from the longer history of social literacies research, in which positive change through, with and for literacy is generated by third space partnerships involving education, training, subcultural and community activity, activism and media 'artivism' (Medrado and Rega, 2022).

The third space (Gutiérrez, 2008; Bhaba, 1994) is where lived experience meets educational or developmental practices in or by institutions

> This third space involves a simultaneous coming and going in a borderland zone between different modes of action. The third space is thus a place of invention and transformational encounters, a dynamic in-between space that is imbued with the traces, relays, ambivalences, ambiguities and contradictions, with the feelings and practices of both sites, to fashion something different, unexpected.
>
> *(Bhabha, 1994: 406)*

Recent research into media literacy work in third spaces developed a way of thinking about literacy of all kinds as dynamic rather than static (Potter and McDougall, 2017)and generated a set of transferable design thinking and working principles for this kind of activity (Rega and McDougall, 2021), which were adapted for Media Action to include negotiating media literacy objectives, nuanced for local contexts; working with values for capacity and resilience – sharing across cultures, refining, agreeing and reviewing – as this constant re-negotiation of media literacy is at the core of the 'uses of media literacy', for positive change.

Resilient communities require conducive media environments which we can, subject to certain conditions, understand *as* third spaces. In these spaces, we can generate new knowledge about the potential connections between media literacy, communities and civic engagement. Media literacy is understood in this way as a *conduit* for the capacity of civic action. Locating this process within third space, through 'design thinking' for projects and programmes, is also a useful way of thinking about the meeting point between international (usually Western) frameworks for media literacy, the needs of local communities and the specific problems with media ecosystems in diverse regions, so as to support decolonising approaches to intercultural media literacy work.

This is very different from the kinds of vertical, 'voice-giving' work we might see, albeit unintentionally, in the media for development paradigm and most certainly in the 'universal', Global North epistemology at work in media literacy solutionism. It is therefore of great importance, not only with regard to politics but also to understand better and more deeply how media literacy works, or even, what it is, to think about it as deeply situated in cultural, geopolitical and media ecosystem contexts.

All of this means that Media Action's decision to so directly foreground media literacy strategy is at once interesting and loaded with challenges. Hitherto, it can be argued that the 'version' of media literacy favoured by media development actors, involving fact-checking and source-checking, not only reproduces binary thinking but may unintentionally enact epistemic violence, further alienate subaltern audiences (see Spivak, 1988) and thus strengthen the appeal of conspiracy theories and increase the polarisation of discourse. In these ways, media development organisations seem to struggle to adapt their intervention logics to contemporary information environments, tending to invest in reforming traditional media, notably by generating incentives to be more inclusive, rather than supporting activist counter-media:

> It is unclear whether such approaches are symptomatic of media development actors' inability to step out of their comfort zone – after all, they are often rooted in traditional media themselves – or if these are desperate but deliberate attempts at status quo maintenance. Fixing media institutions which are often resistant to change and may soon slip into obsolescence is, arguably, less of a worthwhile endeavour than supporting the emergence of alternative media which are in tune with contemporary information paradigms.
>
> (Sayah, 2022)

Theory of change

BBC Media Action's conceptual framework sees media literacy as an enabler for reducing information disorder, increasing trust in public interest media and thus improving the health of media ecosystems in the countries where they work. Speaking from Nepal, on the organisation's work in South Asia, Bhattarai states:

> BBC Media Action believe that supplying accurate, trusted and trustworthy Information on media platforms that reach people at scale is one of the most effective antidotes to information disorder. At the heart of BBC Media

Action work is training and mentoring journalists, editors and other media professionals working in local and national media organizations, supporting them to deliver trusted information in the public interest.

(Bhattarai, 2022)

Media Action's relationships with journalists, audiences and media partners, informed by research into deeper understanding of peoples' attitudes, values and motivations, are potential third spaces for reciprocal exchange and the production of content and development of programmes which can 'cut through' and impact on diverse publics and, at the same time, move out of the development paradigm 'comfort zone', with its unintended hegemony, as described by Sayah above, in the context of the Tunisian media ecosystem.

In the theory of change produced for BBC Media Action, media literacy develops in people in four interrelated areas of social practice, from access to awareness to capability to consequences, potentially disrupting media ecosystems in positive ways as these elements accumulate among and between publics as a collective media literacy.

To move beyond skills and competences alone to focus on the *uses* of media literacy (Bennett, McDougall and Potter, 2020), using Sen's capability approach (2008) can enable a greater focus on how media literacy work can develop capability from resources to functioning. Capability, in Sen's terms, emphasises human diversity, the significance of choice-making and the possibilities of flourishing. This view of the positive *uses* of literacy offers more sensitivity to variations and local contexts. This more *dynamic* understanding (Potter and McDougall, 2017) of media literacy as an agentive capability can offer a conduit for social praxis and the *potential* to give voice, reduce marginality and develop communicative resilience (Buzzanell, 2010) and the capacity for citizens to act to make positive change in media ecosystems (see Figure 6.1).

Access means that people have or acquire the ability to engage with the full media ecosystem that is available to them in their sociocultural and geopolitical

CEMP's theory of change for media literacy

People with media literacy can demonstrate

Full and safe **ACCESS** to digital technology and media	Critical **AWARENESS** of media representations and what content and information can be trusted
ToC for media literacy	
The **CAPABILITY** to use our media literacy actively, rather than as passive consumers	The critical understanding of the **CONSEQUENCES** of our actions in the media ecosystem and how to use our capabilities for positive consequences

FIGURE 6.1 Theory of change

situation. This is, of course, also complex, since the media ecosystem is in some regards global, so the theory of change takes this into account in g/local framing of what we mean by 'full access'. But access is also sometimes a matter of personal choice, so this framework recognises that people can, as their media literacy develops, increase and / or change their access through changing media behaviours.

Awareness develops as media literate people understand more and think more critically about media representations of people, issues, places and events and, as this accumulates to a 'macro-level', the relative health of their media ecosystem, in terms of trust, public interest, diversity and pluralism.

Capability is where people can use their media literacy for particular functionings in their lives (as stated above, informed by Sen). Such capabilities can include self-representation through media, interacting with media organisations differently, making more sustainable media behaviour choices, using media for civic engagement, employability or community actions. However, and this is central to the theory of change and what distinguishes it from solutionism, there is absolutely no reason why such capability *will* necessarily lead to what would be considered positive uses of media literacy (from a social justice, liberal democracy lens) without a tangible and productive combination of capability with consequences.

Consequences are measurable examples of the conversion of media literacy capability into *positive* change, requiring an active desire for media to promote equality and social justice and democracy. Again (to emphasise the fundamental status of this assertion within the theory of change), any notion that positive consequences of more media literacy in the world are inevitable are not only naïve, but beyond neutral; such thinking is to be complicit in the problem that media literacy is assumed to resolve. The protagonists of misinformation and the cynical commodification, for profit, of the mediated living literacies of people with and through technology (e.g., through the algorithmic processing of their data and the intention thereafter to influence their behaviour) *are* the media literate. Information disorder, capitalist realism, strategic ignorance and deceitful media are all the products of a media literacy which is anything but neutral. If a 'solution' is possible, it can be achieved only through a clear focus on alternative consequences, for social good.

BBC Media Action's mixed methods and multi-stakeholder involves

> providing audiences with accurate, trusted and engaging information, and improving media and digital literacy; working with media practitioners and local and national media organisations to strengthen their capacity to provide accurate, trusted information and ... strengthening media ecosystems by supporting the wide availability of relevant, engaging and trusted public-interest content, creating or supporting networks and coalitions of media and civil society organisations working to tackle information disorder and increasing the capacity of media to produce content that tackles information disorder on an ongoing basis.
>
> *(2021: 2)*

However, information disorder needs also to be understood within a meso-level analysis of the social inequalities that impede equal access to mediated civics. These are often more deep-rooted and structural than binary discourses of truth and fake or centres and margins or trust and mistrust can account for. For this reason, those more 'neutral' frameworks for media literacy skills and competences often fail to address not only the implicitly or overtly desired uses of media literacy, but also the way that such competences are related to traditional hierarchies of social capital and intersect with other forms of stratification:

> Women, ethnic minorities, younger people, and those with fewer socio-economic resources historically have less access to formal social capital. It is mostly their lack of this formal social capital, rather than their lack of skills, interests or economic resources, that drives inequalities in digital civic engagement.
>
> *(Helsper, 2021: 113)*

Therefore, the aspects of Media Action's work which *do* focus or *can* focus more on the 'dynamic' uses of digital media literacy for social justice and pluralist, counter-hegemonic media ecosystems than on the 'static' training of participants in media skills alone are those with the greater potential for development within the theory of change.

In Table 6.1, the organisation's stated approaches to media ecosystems and information disorder are mapped to the theory of change.

TABLE 6.1 Mapping organisational strategy to the theory of change

	Strengthening media ecosystems	*Reducing information disorder*
ACCESS	Audiences develop ML through equal and sustained access to public interest media content which integrates ML. Diverse publics can represent themselves, as projects and programmes include them.	The increase in public interest media reaching more people and increasing ML through integrated content channels' attention to trustworthy content. This both reduces exposure to misinformation and increases resilience to it, when exposed, through the integrated ML increase. Increased access to advocacy media and diverse representation increases trust in media as inclusive.

TABLE 6.1 Cont.

	Strengthening media ecosystems	*Reducing information disorder*
AWARENESS	Through critical ML, people can assess and evaluate the health of media ecosystems and how media are representing people, places and issues, who is othered or excluded. This leads to risk calculations with regard to media engagement and information circulation; decision-making, action and capability.	Critical ML enables evaluation and assessment of the accuracy of information (including health information), representation of groups within the society, ideology in media discourse and the persuasive intentions of content. A higher level of critical ML leading to this raised awareness of media re-presenting and self-reflexive awareness of bias increases resilience and mitigates against the media environment in which misinformation can thrive.
CAPABILITY	ML converts into (1) the capability for people to act to strengthen the media ecosystem by making decisions about what to consume, what to trust and how to ensure pluralist media engagement and (2) the capability to put ML into action by making media to contribute to the health of the ecosystem.	As the ecosystem is strengthened through increases in ML, this enables people to assess and deal with resilience to content abundance, act positively in response to and with media and information. Mediated societal engagement increases, with benefits to public health, gender equality and climate literacy and with aligned reductions in polarised discourse.
CONSEQUENCES	Awareness and capability combine to make the ecosystem healthier as a result of people making different decisions about what media to consume and support, what content to share and how to challenge media representations and unverified information. These choices are driven by a desire for positive change and to reduce harmful consequences from media.	Higher level ML moves from awareness of media representation and the persuasive/ideological context of information and the capability to act differently and positively in the media ecosystem to an understanding of the consequences of how people act in their social media lives, share their data and subject ourselves to socio-technical algorithms and surveillance. The ultimate goal of ML is to increase awareness of all conditions in which all media, information and data are produced and circulated to the extent that information disorder is reduced through inoculation.

Cluster analysis

Thematic analysis of activity where media literacy is developed through the projects the organisation facilitates identified four clusters (see McDougall, 2022; McDougall and Rega, 2022).

As the four elements in the theory of change do not happen through linear progression, from one to the next, these are clusters of activity where the elements of the theory of change are evident, but often partially.

Cluster 1: DML is *baked in* to the intervention, rather than explicitly stated as a discrete objective, but it could be easily foregrounded as such and then developed and measured. Strengthening the media ecosystem in Zambia through a mixed methods approach to supporting local radio was informed by a deep diagnosis of potential impacts through this medium and addressing barriers. The combination of community outreach and co-production enabled a partial third space for journalists to work with BBC MA (partial because this was an exchange between two second spaces and did not engage publics' first space media literacies). The self-testimony of audiences reached provided evidence of media engagement moving to the action / capability stage, for civic and political participation – *Regular listeners were 1.5 times as likely to think that they could positively influence politics and governance issues that affected members of their community compared to those who did not listen regularly* (BBC MA Zambia Research Summary: 7). However, the digital and media literacy levels or the uses of media literacy for the civic capacity desired were not addressed. *Access* was a core objective, *Capability* is evident (on the basis of self-reporting), *Consequences* are implicit, *Awareness* is not addressed. The communication interventions made in Cox's Bazar, Bangladesh – focused primarily on solving an *Access* to information problem rather than the media literacy needed for refugees to source such content – discern it from misinformation and engage with mainstream media in the longer term. Similarly, the remote 'pivot' and 'scaling up of partnerships in Nigeria (*Talk Your Own Talk* and *Mu Tattau Nu*) to create inclusive platforms for citizens (*Access*) changed perceptions and actions about the coronavirus disease 2019 (Covid-19) but any impact on media literacy at a broader level (*Awareness, Capability, Consequences*) cannot be gauged from the crisis-response initiative. BBC MA interventions which directly support and bolster media ecosystems through working with public service and independent media organisations (e.g., in Ukraine, Ethiopia and Iraq) have media literacy baked in, indirectly, as in the short term they improve *Access* but the sustainability of publics evaluating (through media literacy) this access for themselves (*Awareness*) and the *Capability* for audiences to be active in the ecosystem are longer term 'by-products'.

Cluster 2: Media related capability intentions *partially* address media literacy: *Klahan 9*, a reality TV and social media intervention addressing youth employability in Cambodia, fused a reception study with the potential for third space media development, but the media content and audience separation was maintained throughout the project, with data generated by interviews (rather than by the social media activity, for example). Engagement with the text provided (through self-testimony) motivation for action and the project as a whole provided new knowledge on the need for diversification. However, like the Zambia project mentioned, the kinds of media literacy at work in engaging with the textual world (*Klazhan 9* and social media extra-texts) and converting engagement into capability for gaining employment were not subject to analysis. *Access* was a core objective, *Capability* is evident. *Weather Wise* in Kenya improved the media ecosystem by providing *Access* to climate information with direct actions by both citizens and journalists, and *Awareness* of the importance of media providing robust advice and of the role of partnerships between journalists and scientists in healthy ecosystems. However, *Awareness* of ecosystem challenges in the future and less immediate contexts and *Capability* to engage and address *Consequences* are, again, indirect possibilities. *Wae Gyal Pikin Tinap* in Sierra Leone uses storytelling and advocacy (#choosetochallenge) for change for women and girls through radio co-presenting. This is a form of 'changing the story with Access and Capability at the core of the intervention. Awareness (of how 'the story' needs to be changed) and Consequences (of accepting 'the story') are more long-term aims. Similarly, *Talo iyo Tacab* in Somalia, enabled a third space for youth media empowerment and *Radio Television Afghanistan* and *Open Jirga* address gender inequality in media work (Access) and visibility (Awareness), with the longer-term objective of increasing Capability (for women to work in media) and Consequences (for the wider society of gender inequality in media representations). *Let's Talk about Us*, in South Sudan, provides the same rich evidence of community mobilisation and gender empowerment through media, bringing lived experience, advocacy for change and medical advice together in radio, with the same focus on Access to developmental media but Awareness of the issue being covered as opposed to normative media representations.

Cluster 3: Media literacy is the *what* but not the *how*: *Increasing Women's Digital Literacy* in India is the most explicit media literacy intervention reviewed. The project does address both what and how, in terms of describing the situation at the level of *Access* and sharing impactful practice to address barriers and inequalities, for example, handset cost, social norms in rural settings and gendered perception barriers to digital investment. Leveraging women's empowerment collectives involved peer and community support, moving towards third space. However, a lack of impact on the external normative environment combined with the lack of criteria with which to define and measure outcomes impeded progression to the *Capability* stage because working to change the conditions required for media literacy to develop at the *Access* stage were not within the scope of the activity. This project speaks compellingly to the complexity of media literacy in specific contexts and the need for the g-local adaptation of the theory of change. A study of Algerian social media use and experiences of misinformation was entirely diagnostic, leading to a recommendation that people "need sensitive support to help them recognise their own vulnerabilities, and they need better media literacy skills and confidence to help them identify false and misleading information" (2021: 3). Rich data from this research reveals the inherent contradiction in the media literacy situation, which may be exacerbated in Algeria due to specifics at the *Access* level but is transferable to many contexts. For example, respondents felt a false sense of security in their resilience to misinformation, whilst half of those confirmed they had shared information which they later realised was not trustworthy. At the same time, the 'power of shares', whereby trust is associated with both the amount of distribution and personal familiarity with distributors (e.g., family and friends sharing material) appeared to be a feature of the social media ecosystem. Importantly, as the research found a desire for action among participants, specifically to use social media to help others (e.g., with reliable Covid-19 information), the most important contribution for media literacy in this case will be to align *Capability* with *Awareness* (of own vulnerabilities) as a reflective understanding of *Consequences* appears to be in the higher range. The *El Kul* project in Libya reported similar findings, with the combination of Covid-19 misinformation and the national election proving another highly specific, situated context. Here, the evidence of proliferating misinformation and overconfidence among citizens was at work with altruistic motivation, a rich resource for media literacy to develop in the future. Both studies and sets of recommendations show the potential for BBC MA to be at the forefront of work in the intersection between media literacy as 'innoculation' against misinformation in general (debunking, but in a broader context) and the urgency of a rapid response to misinformation about Covid-19, specifically. Media literacy in this context takes on a role in public health.

Cluster 4: There is rich *potential* for the work to integrate media literacy: *Balada Yayang Bebeb* in Indonesia is a multi-platform youth-engaging media project combining audio dramas with public service announcements to counter health misinformation related to Covid-19. The key media literacy aspects of this intervention are the focus on partnerships and connecting to lived experiences, both of media use and Covid-19-related concerns. *Access, Awareness* and *Consequences* are evident, *Capability* could be easily developed. *Tea Cup Diaries* in Myanmar shares many characteristics with media literacy projects in educational contexts, raising awareness of source and healthy scepticism about trustworthiness of material, acknowledging young people's emotive engagement with media and information rather than only imposing the 'false binary' of true or false. The potential for this approach to address media literacy 'head on' is capturing the more critical or mindful engagement with information on social media that participants reported – how did the 'playful' questioning translate into sustainable media literacy practices, post-project, and how can this be replicated for peers, to progress from short-term, reactive treatment to more developmental inoculation, among the community? *Action* and *Consequences* are evident; *Awareness* is partially demonstrated. The *Climate Change Asia* report on Cambodia disseminates findings from a mass survey of citizens' experiences and perceptions to inform the creation of communications that motivate people to act. The 'journey' framework for media intervention, integrating media audience segmentation, is agile, developmental and dynamic and offers perhaps the closest 'fit' to the media literacy for capability framework: "When a media intervention begins, people in Cambodia may find themselves at any stage on the communications ladder. The goal is to help them move up the ladder, towards the adapting rung" (Southall, Chandore and Otdam, 2019: 69). This development but segmented 'ladder' approach can be easily applied to media literacy, where audiences and beneficiaries of MA work might be at the *Access* stage, or they might demonstrate high levels of media literacy but have no means for *Action*. Or they might be using their media literacy for negative action, and need to be reached for educational work on *Awareness*. The proposed collaboration with Luminate, to combine digital storytelling methods with inoculation theory, is another rich space for the kind of dynamic media literacy activity proposed in the theory of change. The proposal is clear in the intention to support media literacy within a mixed methods approach working with transmedia narrative creation, to reflect and disrupt, rather than 'correct' misinformation, in Global South contexts. There is the potential to both identify more discreetly and measure the impacts of the media literacy component of this project. This potential to develop media literacy activity as a more measurable component should be fully informed by the challenges presented by the hardest groups to reach with media literacy being at opposite ends of the spectrum. At the one end are those without safe *Access* to media literacy, for either economic, technological, educational or political reasons. At the other are those with *Access* and *Awareness* who are already demonstrating *Capability* and are aware of *Consequences* but for whatever reason are not concerned about them.

Toolkit and training

The toolkit and training guide produced out of the theory of change and review of current practice places emphasis on the third space design principles (for content and activities) that move the strategy away from the 'top-down' media development tradition and solutionist, binary thinking. A series of 'train the trainers' workshops were facilitated with in-country practitioners, and third space media literacy activities were modelled. This phase provided indicative content to be locally adapted for delivery: a set of third space activities within three phases and suggestions for debriefing on each activity and feeding forward from one session to the next. The way the training modelled works is that each element links to the next, so first trainers work with participants to link *Access* to *Awareness* in the first phase, then they develop *Awareness* into *Capability* in the second phase and finally they work together to progress *Capability* into *Consequences* in the third and final phase.

In the phase that links *Access* to *Awareness*, participants are supported to understand the role of media in society and the impact of media access on their lives and their communities; critically evaluate the health of their media ecosystem and reflect on the choices they make about media access and, where required, commit to making different choices about what to access and what to access less or engage with differently. In debriefing, the activities culminate in trainees being able to work together to summarise the media literacy levels of the whole group and identify the 'known unknowns' – where the media literacy gaps are. For these known unknowns, depending on the context, there can be areas for the trainees to follow up before the next session, or the trainer can fill in the gaps in the debrief. The training had to be designed with the maximum of flexibility in these regards, since the range of participant groups and in-country contexts is so diverse.

Linking *Awareness* to *Capability*, the objectives are for participants to apply textual analysis skills to media texts and digital information sources; relate access to awareness by critically assessing how media representations impact on their lives; identify disinformation and use strategies for media mindfulness to pause and think about media representation and trust before sharing. Depending on the in-country context and the training design after adaption, the ideal debrief will feed forward to participants bringing with them their own examples of media texts and digital information where a mindful approach helps them to 'think again'. This is what we mean by the third space between training and participants' lived experiences of digital and media literacy. This way, the next time trainers run the exercise, they can replace their chosen texts with the examples their participants bring to the training. That said, the important learning outcome here is to realise that the texts may be quite different, but the process of mindful media literate awareness is the same, whether people are watching a documentary, moving image fiction, listening to a podcast, playing a videogame or reading information shared with us on social media. If the 'receiver' can stop to think about the techniques used by the 'sender' of the messages, then they are more aware of persuasion and resilient to misinformation. In turn, they are less likely to share manipulative or harmful media and information.

In the final phase, where *Capability* is linked to *Consequences*, the intended outcomes are for participants to audit their own digital literacy skills and gaps, understand the benefits of using media literacy for active engagement in communities and society and to assess the value of public interest media and the importance of trust.

The final evaluation of the training programme is not designed to formally assess or accredit individual participants, but each session concludes with discursive feedback designed for self-evaluation and reflection. On the evidence provided by these debriefing sessions, trainers will be able to informally evaluate the learning against the stated outcomes, as follows.

Understand the importance of media literacy in their own lives: Participants have reflected on ten key aspects of media literacy and identified gaps in their own media literacies. They have evaluated their media ecosystem for diversity and trustworthy information and learned lateral reading skills to help them evaluate information and be more generally mindful and critical in their engagements with all media. The importance of media literacy was applied to a range of media formats and types of text – film and television, internet, news and social media, focussed on the most influential platforms in the participants' lives.

Critically evaluate media and information: By focusing on the importance of understanding all media and information as representing reality, people, ideas and events and trying to persuade us of a particular version of reality, participants were encouraged to see all media as a kind of propaganda. Throughout the training, they continually asked critical questions – who is representing the world, how and for what purpose? This critical evaluation mindset will enable them to stop and think and be mindful about all media and information and this provides a greater, sustainable resilience to misinformation and media manipulation over time than only using fact checking and verification tools. If we see misinformation as being like a virus, an 'infodemic', then the latter is more like a medicine after infection; the former – the approach our training took – is more like a vaccine providing resistant antibodies to fight infection from within.

Apply media literacy skills actively in their lives: Participants evaluated their own media literacy capabilities – the potential they have to use their media literacies actively rather than as passive consumers or audiences – and were encouraged to support one another as peers where they had capabilities that others lacked or had partially.

Act as positive peers in the media ecosystem: The concluding session required participants to think about why we need to trust the media and how they can be media activists for positive change.

Feedback on the implementation of the toolkit and training was provided in July 2022 from activities in Tunisia, Algeria and Libya, collated by Maurice Aaek, Senior Training Manager for BBC Media Action in the Middle East and North Africa region, based in Tunisia. The approach had been embedded into two projects. In the first, a media development project relating to agriculture in Tunisia, journalists, media practitioners and actors from civil society and non-government organisations (CSOs and NGOs) were working together to provide information about soil protection. In the second, media practitioners and CSOs working in health contexts were collaborating on health information literacy work, fact-checking and debunking health information with publics. These two interventions combined provide a significant pilot context for the toolkit and training, since they integrate the work directly with three of Media Action's strategic pillars, information disorder, climate change and health information.

The key findings from the application in the MENA region were as follows:

1. The media texts used as examples and/or exercise prompts need to be locally adapted for cultural and contextual relevance (this was already stated in the training guide, to at best avoid but at least acknowledge Global North, Western and potentially colonial dynamics in the use of English language materials as 'train the trainer' exemplars, but there was also the need for more direct guidance for trainers with regard to how to source locally situated alternatives and for what purposes).
2. Media practitioners at the level of initial content creation can be trained together with CSO and NGO workers, but media producers and journalists need to be given discrete training, or at least strands/breakouts need to be facilitated to tailor to the different needs.
3. For some groups, the four elements of the theory of change need to be differentiated, so that people bringing different experiences from first and

second spaces can spend more time on awareness, with less need to cover digital media activism, whereas other groups can progress more quickly to thinking about using digital media literacy for positive consequences. Whilst this might be the subject of a diagnostic needs analysis by trainers, in the MENA experience, this was more related to participant cohorts and less differentiated within them.

4. For some participants, there was a desire for 'right answers', so the reflexive, critical questioning of ecosystems and people's own media consumption behaviours needs to be combined with more factual learning – for example, about ownership of media companies or how algorithms work – when activities in the toolkit are designed to 'self-audit' group awareness, but stop at the point of unearthing the 'known unknowns' for the participant cohort, it was felt that simply knowing what people don't know and being left to find out for themselves was inadequate. This is a challenge for third space learning design and the need to tailor training to the immediate needs of participants in-country as well as mobilising more constructivist objectives.

5. Terminology within aspects of the theory of change needs also to be adapted with cultural sensitivities in mind – for example, 'media for change' is loaded, and in some contexts the word 'development' is preferable. This was an interesting finding, since in Tunisia, for another media literacy project, the 'media development paradigm' had been rejected by the in-country partners as being top-down and, again, potentially colonial in its framing of objectives. This feedback presents starkly the problematic tension inherent to the design of a 'toolkit' in the UK being 'implemented' across the diverse and sensitive contexts in which Media Action work, and also the risks of assuming the partnership dynamics will be the same from one media literacy intervention to another (see McDougall and Rega, 2022, for a detailed analysis of how space, partnership and the framing of change across intercultural media literacy projects, including this Media Action work and the other Tunisian project cited here as informing this work).

Conclusions and implications for journalism education

The existing work of Media Action clearly enables, improves and in some cases builds on high levels of first space media **access**, consisting of digital skills; technological resources; informed media engagement and a diverse media environment. There is also evidence of access improvements for second space media organisations.

Awareness, of media representation at the micro level and media ecosystem health at the macro level, was developed for participants working with Media Action to take back to their first spaces, but there was less evidence of the Media Action changing as a second space. This is the direction of travel in which the toolkit and training guide seek to take the organisation.

The conversion of media literacy into **capability** was evident for all of the second space organisations working in partnership with Media Action, as they all developed new ways of working and new ways of using media literacies to further their objectives. There is also potential, as yet partly realised, for capability to be fostered in third spaces between mainstream media, community and audiences.

At the level of observable positive c**onsequences**, Media Action's in-country communities are at earlier stages of ecosystem change, but on a 'dotted line' trajectory to this. Media Action has tangible, positive impacts on second spaces, the local media it supports through the media literacy development it provides for journalists. Currently, third spaces generated by Media Action are catalysts for impacts in the first spaces of participants; the challenge is to make this more reciprocal.

Therefore, the combination of a new, discrete and targeted media literacy strategy for Media Action, to be delivered in partnership with in-country journalists, practitioners and audience in third spaces will, it is hoped, and over time, improve the health of media ecosystems in poor, fragile and diverse societies. The shift in thinking is away from a 'quick-fix' approach to fact-checking and verification, or a debunking methodology which deals only with misinformation, away from a 'top-down' media development paradigm towards third space partnerships and knowledge exchange. However, as the feedback from the training in MENA shows, there are cultural and geopolitical tensions in assuming these objectives are always already shared between projects and contexts.

The longer-term success of these interventions is unknown, but in any case, BBC Media Action are making a brave change of direction with the work described in this chapter. We can justifiably claim this project to be pioneering, as we reflect on a 'mainstream media' organisation embracing a theory of change that situates media literacy as holistic, dynamic and far-reaching, decoupling the development of media literacy from its uses in context. This is a complex and reciprocal challenge for the training of their teams in media literacy in this vital field of journalism education.

Acknowledgements

From BBC Media Action, the work shared in this chapter was supported by Maha Taki, Alisdair Stuart, Anca Toader, Dipak Bhattarai and Maurice Aaek.

References

Bennett, P., McDougall, J., and Potter, J. (2020) *The Uses of Media Literacy*. New York: Routledge Research in Media Literacy and Education.

Bhabha, H. (1994) *The Location of Culture*. London: Routledge.

Bhattarai, D. (2022) 'Combatting Information Disorder: A South Asian Perspective'. Fowler-Watt, K. and McDougall, J. (Eds.), *The Palgrave Handbook of Media Misinformation*. London: Palgrave Macmillan.

Buckingham, D. (2017) *Fake News: Is Media Literacy the Answer?* https://davidbuckingham.net/2017/01/12/fake-news-is-media-literacy-the-answer/

Buzzanell, P.M. (2010) 'Resilience: Talking, Resisting, and Imagining New Normalcies Into Being'. *Journal of Communication*, 60(1), 1–14.

Gutiérrez, K. (2008) 'Developing a Sociocultural Literacy in the Third Space'. *Reading Research Quarterly*, 43, 148–164.

Helsper, E. (2021) *The Digital Disconnect: The Social Causes and Consequences of Digital Inequalities*. London: Sage.

Lee, C., Bailey, C., Burnett, C., and Rowsell, J. (Eds.) (2022) *Unsettling Literacies: Directions for Literacy Research in Precarious Times*. Singapore: Springer.

Marino, S. (2021) *Mediating the Refugee Crisis: Digital Solidarity, Humanitarian Technologies and Border Regimes*. London: Palgrave Macmillan.

McDougall, J. (2022) *Digital and Media Literacy: Toolkit and Training Guide*. London: BBC Media Action.

McDougall, J. and Rega, I. (2022) 'Beyond Solutionism: "Differently Motivating Media Literacy"'. *Media and Communication*, 10(4), https://doi.org/10.17645/mac.v10i4.5715

Medrado, A. and Rega, I. (2022) *Media Activism, Artivism and the Fight Against Marginalisation*. London: Routledge.

Pahl, K. and Rowsell, J. (2020) *Living Literacies: Literacy for Social Change*. Cambridge, MA: MIT Press.

Potter, J. and McDougall, J. (2017) *Digital Media, Culture and Education: Theorising Third Space Literacies*. London: Palgrave Macmillan/Springer.

Rega, I. and Medrado, A. (2021) 'The Stepping into Visibility Model: Reflecting on Consequences of Social Media Visibility – A Global South Perspective'. *Information, Communication & Society*, https://doi.org/10.1080/1369118X.2021.1954228

Sayah, H. (2022) 'Civic Intentionality First: A Tunisian Attempt at Creating Social Infrastructure for Youth Representation'. Fowler-Watt, K. and McDougall, J. (Eds.), *The Palgrave Handbook of Media Misinformation*. London: Palgrave Macmillan.

Sen, A.K. (2008) 'Capability and Well-Being'. Hausman, D.M. (Ed.), *The Philosophy of Economics* (3rd Edition). Cambridge: Cambridge University Press.

Southall, E., Chandore, K., and Otdam, H. (2019) *How the People of Cambodia Live with Climate Change and What Media and Communication Can Do*. London: BBC Media Action.

Spivak, G. (1988) 'Can the Subaltern Speak?' In *Marxism and the Interpretation of Culture*. Cary Nelson and Lawrence Grossberg (Eds.). Urbana: University of Illinois Press, 271–313.

PART II
New directions in journalism education

7
INCLUSIVE APPROACHES TO NEWS

Daniel Henry and De-Graft Mensah

Introduction

Inclusivity continues to present major challenges within journalism practice and education. Despite a move away from "top-down" reporting evident in citizen journalism and different modes of storytelling that encourage interaction with audiences, journalism is still seen as largely the preserve of middle-class elites. Although there have been some advances, with more presenters from minority backgrounds now seen on our screens, newsrooms and boardrooms still lack diversity. Within journalism education, industry councils have intensified protocols to encourage diversity and to widen opportunity, but progress is slow, and an attainment gap persists. These problems are compounded by the pernicious presence of systemic racism and stereotype – in news reporting and in news organisations.

This chapter brings together in conversation two young black journalists working in the UK to discuss these issues, from the standpoint of their own lived experiences and their own practice, and to reflect on calls to action that could help journalism education lead the way in invoking change. Daniel Henry is a journalist and documentary maker, who has taken his own experiences out into journalism schools, to share with students the potential mental health impacts of systemic racism, urging them to consider ways in which they might integrate their own personal reactions to the problem into their professional practice. De-Graft Mensah presents BBC Newsround and the "If You Don't Know" podcast: his focus is young people and news, and how we engage young people in the key issues around class and race, making complex stories, such as Black Lives Matter accessible and inclusive.

Introductions and beginnings

De-Graft Mensah: I'm a young British guy born in London of Ghanaian background raised in Milton Keynes.[1] Anytime I talk about my life and the sort of things that I have navigated through, I always say that a lot of what I've learned about things that I have been through, which weren't necessarily pleasant, I've learned as an adult because, as a kid you think your life is so amazing. Then, as you grow older you start to realise that certain things that you experienced, especially as a young black boy at the time in certain parts of the country weren't necessarily great. One example is, quite recently, we did a (VT) report for Newsround where it was me, Shanequa Paris, another *Newsround* presenter, Rhys Stephenson, a CBBC presenter and Mwaksy, who is a *Blue Peter* presenter sharing experiences about things that we've all had as a kid and you know it was things such as racist name calling and kids asking questions that were racially loaded. I shared one experience of being a little kid and hearing my cousins' neighbours making monkey noises by the window and all this stuff that as a kid you don't really take in until you're an adult. Then you look back and you realise: "Oh, my goodness that was wild racist".

From a very young age, I knew that I wanted to get into the media industry, but I wasn't sure what careers could exist out there for me. I like telling stories and I like talking! It was a Sixth Form careers advisor who suggested journalism and so I did a journalism course. I remember a lecturer telling us "the hard work doesn't stop here it's not like you automatically finished uni then will continue into a journalism job". I definitely found that out: very soon after uni, having to go back to retail work – I worked in a shoe shop – and I was almost begging people to just give me a chance. Luckily, for me, I had so many people who really believed in me and really fought my corner, and so I got into shadowing at BBC Radio 5 Live, which turned into freelancing work elsewhere at the BBC, then eventually at *Newsround* and the podcast. The whole journey has highlighted so many flaws in the journalism world when it comes to being more inclusive. But before we get into that, Daniel should share his lived experiences!

Daniel Henry: We are going to go back and forth in time here! I remember being at *The Independent* newspaper; I had worked my way in there and I was sat opposite this guy, who I asked: "how did you get in here?" and he said, "my uncle works here!". That experience was quite common in the sense that most people that I met who would have that kind of connection with the publication were white people. I didn't meet many – or any – people from minority backgrounds who had that kind of connection. I remember at first feeling that was quite hard – thinking that "I've busted and scraped to get in and the route that this person is talking about seems much easier!"

I am from Walthamstow, a small town in East London. My mum was a single parent for the first seven or eight years of my life, until my stepdad came along; then my real dad came back … so, I think living, where I did, how I did, that definitely shapes a lot of the stories that I like to tell and the understanding and empathy I have for the experiences of people from similar areas where there's not necessarily much available. It is really about the home that you are in and the little community that you have got, because the state isn't really doing much to support you. As you were saying, De-Graft, that is something that you learn when you look back.

I have always been interested in writing; I remember publishing a poem when I was young, then journalism opening the door to me shortly after my beloved football team, Manchester United, won the treble, I realised that people were being paid to watch Manchester United in Barcelona – and then tell the world about it! That switched it on for me, so I started writing for the school newspaper and took it from there. Around that time, I remember telling my mum that's what I wanted to do, and she said, "well, nobody's going to come and knock on this door to say 'I heard you're interested in journalism, don't worry, Uncle John is the chairman of the company'" – so that told me that I had to go out there and basically knock on doors. And that's what I did. The point here is that this is not an exclusive experience to me – that is what we all do. But, in my experience, what I think is shared between people who often come from backgrounds where there's not a lot of money or from a marginalised group is the lack of those connections and networks to just pick up the phone.

Lots of people I *have* met who have done that seem to have a more comfortable route in and I think that balanced with the, often precarious, nature of entering journalism and being part of the creative industries can push people away.

When you were talking earlier, De-Graft, about how you were finishing uni and going back to working in retail, that was me! I finished my undergrad, I was freelancing for *The Independent* and then they started to make their cuts and as those cuts hit, I didn't really have anywhere to go, so then you start working other jobs … I worked in a pub, I worked in retail, I worked as a recruitment consultant – I did all of those things in between trying to keep the journalism ambitions alive. As I say, I realised that there were people from other backgrounds that were not having those experiences – they would have that gap, but they weren't necessarily filling it with having to do this kind of work; they might be taking two or three months out and travelling a bit or just to take time to think about what to do next. That wasn't an option for me. Once a job had finished, regardless of whether it was a journalism job or outside of that, it was a space that had to be filled with more paying work. Whatever came first was what I had to do. I think that is where the realities of race and class intersect with journalism and those two things impact the kind of people who not only come through the door but also those who can stay – the people who have that leg up stay in it, people who don't, have to find something else to keep them going.

De-Graft: It's also that pressure – especially when you're starting out in journalism – of "can I afford to do this?" and I remember at the start of my career doing internships, and all this kind of stuff and even freelancing and shadowing. I had to pay money for trains and then you've got to figure out, "where am I going to stay?", and I agree that this means that only a certain type of person makes it into these spaces, because if you do come from a background where you might not have the money at home, then you're naturally not going to end up in that space. There are so many people who are in just better socio-economic situations whereby doing an unpaid internship in London for a month isn't that big a deal because you can finance that. The only way I was able to afford it was using all the money I had saved doing retail work.

Daniel: I think that is another big thing because I had the slight advantage of being in London at the time – your family was in Milton Keynes, which is not far, but it is a train, it is a cost! The further you go from London and the big cities, the more difficult it is to be part of it all. It's funny bouncing it with you, because it is that kind of shared experience like I remember deciding that I wanted to do a placement in New York and in order to do that I had to work three jobs through that summer to put the money together and my mum had to give me some money too for that to be possible. So that was a massive undertaking, whereas for people from other communities, other groups, socio-economic backgrounds, it's not a thing! It's like, "going to New York? Get your flights! Go!"

De-Graft: Yeah! I think also we've spoken a lot about money being a barrier – and let me not speak for every single black person in the UK, let me speak for myself – but, sometimes you do look at these spaces and if just visually, you're not seeing black people in those spaces, you might start to think: "Is this a space, that I should enter? Am I going to feel welcome there?" Obviously we do have many different schemes to help and people do find amazing diversity apprenticeships or different ways to get in, so I do think it is getting better, getting people from marginalised communities to get into this space. When we speak to kids at *Newsround*, I always say that

> We live in a world right now where luckily, you can open your laptop or turn on the TV and see so many different faces, whereas as a kid I remember watching TV and maybe seeing like four black presenters maximum.

Daniel: Exactly and I guess, that could be about it …

De-Graft: It's weird because, Daniel, it feels, especially if you're black, depending on your age group also depends on the types of people that you saw on your TV.

Daniel: Yes.

Newsroom environments and inclusivity

De-Graft: When I was growing up, I don't remember seeing black journalists, I mean just black presenters like Angelica Bell.[2] So, it can be difficult, sometimes looking at a world where you see that virtually everyone in this space is white. Luckily, I have had the privilege of working in newsrooms which have felt inclusive, especially where I am now and, and I feel like for me anytime I work in a newsroom that is mainly dominated by younger people, those newsrooms for me have felt the most inclusive. But saying that it could obviously be a lot better – I am not by any stretch of the imagination saying it's perfect.

Daniel: Yes. I think it comes back to the general routes that people get access to these kinds of spaces and jobs. Obviously, the big change is social media, YouTube and so on, because you know that in those spaces the cost to entry is completely gone, so what's happening there is pushing the more established legacy media. They see that they will be left behind if they don't put a bit more effort into reflecting a wider group of society and so that's a good thing for people coming through, because then it means it's all about two ways that you get in: either do your own things and set up your own pages and ride the wave of the impact of those pages or work your way through the more established companies, which are now more open to those kinds of stories and perspectives. It is still difficult, though – if you find that you're the only person [of colour] in the room or one of the only people in the room and a story about racism hits the headlines it's a lot, it's a lot.

De-Graft: I've been in that situation.

Daniel: It really is a lot, maybe I am overthinking it, but there are so many things going through your mind when something like that hits the headlines and you're the only person in the newsroom from a minority background. The reason why it's difficult is because editorial meetings, by definition, are effectively persuasive arguments: you try and persuade the editor of the day, to pick up your story and whatever you think is interesting that day. So, when you're trying to persuade somebody that this racist thing is important and important enough to take up space in the bulletin, that is an emotional weight to bear, because – as with any story – the possibility is that there isn't space in the bulletin. The possibility is that you haven't persuaded the editor enough that this is a story worth doing and when that happens, you then have to walk away with that feeling of … next time that you're in the barbershop and people ask "why didn't that story get on? They never listen, and they're never interested", in your head, you are saying, "I tried. I tried to push it. I told them about it and they didn't listen." I think that weight, also, is changing, I think people like Nadine White [Race Correspondent for *The Independent* newspaper] in particular are changing the dialogue on this: the idea that race is an equivalent specialism to science, or economics, or any other beat and that is important, and her work and the work of many others, such as Afua Hirsch[3] – but the weight of having to do that is heavy and I don't think that all newsrooms appreciate that. So, I really did want to say that.

De-Graft: I think, as well as not appreciating the sort of emotional toil, there's also I guess the stance on the opposite end of that spectrum, where some people can overappreciate and what I mean by that is that when you are the only black person in the newsroom the minute a racism story comes up it's, "So what do you think?" or "What are black people thinking?" – but I am only one black person! My experiences are not those of every living black person in this country. I have had many experiences in my career whereby I've had people from other teams, or people that I know have messaged me to say, "we acknowledge that we're a very white team, what should we be doing about this right now?" I can give them my opinion, but when I hear questions like that, the problem is right there – you are a majority white team and you should start to make your team look a bit more inclusive, so, then you wouldn't have to ring up the only black journalist you know to ask them, "how should we be doing x, y or z?" As you suggested, Daniel, some newsrooms obviously don't get it, but some newsrooms absolutely do – or at least they are getting better at getting it.

I can remember back around the time of the death of George Floyd – I know you did lots of amazing stuff on that, Daniel – but on *Newsround*, we were covering it constantly. But it wasn't until I had a meeting with my editors and I suggested that we should do something a lot bigger – it felt like a very big moment in history – and I thought we needed to tackle it in a slightly different way, so we put together a special programme on CBBC[4] about racism and heard from so many amazing kids. But I bring this up as an example of a situation where I thought the team, even though they acknowledge that there aren't many black people in the team, they really gave me and other team members an opportunity to be listened to. That is not to say that just because I'm black my treatment ideas are going to be great. I might have the information, but sometimes when it comes to thinking about how we tell this story the best person in the room might not be a black person; there might be somebody who's got years and years of producing experience who can say "alright cool, I've heard your experiences, let's turn this into something consumable that people want to listen to".

I just wanted to highlight that, because that was definitely an example of when the team really listened and were really kind as well, reaching out to say, "I can understand that this is emotionally taxing on you, if you need to talk to anyone, I am here" and I did appreciate that because I've never had something like that in journalism before or in any career – I've never had somebody say, "the work you're doing is impacting you or could impact you emotionally". I didn't feel I needed to talk to anyone, but maybe I did need to, actually.

Daniel: That kind of example, there is, really what you want to get to, is that this is normal. The reason you are highlighting that is because it is the right thing, but unusual. That should be how newsrooms are run anyway.

De-Graft: Yes! It shouldn't be unusual!

Daniel: If we want newsrooms to be inclusive, we want them to be reflective, if we want them to really be able to make space for the full range of human experiences – that's what we're here to try and reflect – then that has got to be the minimum that's got to be the starting point, not the high bar. That is what we're supposed to do.

De-Graft: A lot of times when we talk about especially telling stories from all different types of communities, I feel that some journalists and some newsrooms get a bit confused. What I mean by that is they tend to home in on one community and by doing so, they think they are diverse – so they might mention a couple of black stories and think they are diverse. There is one thing I would like to push for in particular, as a black person because I know what it's like to come from a community where your stories aren't always told, so I use that same sort of passion and drive to make sure other community stories are told, and sometimes the same things I ask of my journalists who aren't black, I try to ask the same from me, so

I always tell them to look outside of the streams of news that you normally consume, go to different platforms that are not catered for or tailored to you, find the stories from different parts of the community outside of your norm and I try to do the same. Diversity isn't just having black people on, diversity is looking at different communities and – as we have already mentioned – socio-economic diversity is also important. Once you start to tackle class diversity, you will, in turn, also tackle a lot of racial diversity as well-- in journalism and in society – and that's not to say that all black people in the UK are working class because that's absolutely not true! I know many middle-class black people who have had a lot more opportunities than I have. That is why I mention the socio-economic issue. So, let's just focus on being black for a second: yes, it's great to have black journalists and black presenters, but for me personally I've got a strong interest in black journalists and the presenters who do come from that working class financially, because you could argue that, a middle-class black person will face some of the same disadvantages that I face, but they will also have certain benefits that I don't have because they belong to that middle class of society: they might have access to the funds or the family links and that's why I think that diversity should obviously be more than just a tick box exercise. It is not "we've got one black journalist, that's cool" and "cool we've got one black story", but it should be actually how do we *really* tackle this? Some newsrooms get it, but I don't think all do.

Daniel: I know what you mean. It's that intersectionality, isn't it? The fact that people with one particular characteristic crossover with others – that really goes back to how newsrooms can connect with these spaces and how credible they are seen to be in those spaces. For some people in some areas, there's a complete distrust, a complete disconnect. They have seen the way that their communities have been covered, they've seen the way that their friends have been covered and they don't buy it. It's down to us to find ways to get past that because if not, then, you have people who are completely excluded and that's a wider problem: if poor communities are not part of the national conversation that we are facilitating as journalists, then it means that when decisions need to be made by governments and companies – is this company going to move to this neighbourhood and start hiring? Is the government going to invest in this particular area? – when those discussions are taking place, if certain communities are not part of that then nothing ever changes in those areas. It's so important to ensure that everyone's had a chance to speak and using the platform to do that. When we are covering a story, we need to ask – have we got the right people contributing to this? Are we reaching out to the same old [sources]? In my experience, I know why it happens – the pressures of time etc. – so you go back to the people that you've used before and you trust them, but you do that at what cost? You have to bear that in mind, I think people who are from those areas where they've been marginalised before have a sense of what that cost is.

De-Graft: You said something there, about checking we have got the right people and I think that extends to a lot of sectors of journalism. Often when I look at bosses and senior bosses, ideally, we would have the right people there. When you look at certain newsrooms across the journalism spectrum, you might have a diverse newsroom but then you might find that a lot of the bosses aren't that diverse. You could look outside the world of journalism and into the world of journalism education within universities to ask: "are there many black lecturers here?" I think that might be why some people are deterred from going to university or exploring certain options to study. If you already see an industry where people don't look like you, and then you see people who are trying to open the gates for you to go in, who also don't look like you, you might just get to a point where you think "why even bother?" There were obviously black people on my [university] course, but not many and I do think that is a problem.

Daniel: When I did my master's, there were only three other people from a minority background and me – and what bound us together was that we were all on some kind of bursary. I think this demonstrates that bursaries and scholarships do have an impact. The four of us are all working in media jobs now, so they do work – but it is about whether or not there is the will in the industry at large to extend those types of things, because the type of bursary that I am talking about doesn't exist anymore. As you said, De-Graft, not every black person, is from an impoverished background, but you know the statistics are pretty clear in terms of people from minority backgrounds and white people and where the over-representation is. To change that, you have to pay for it. It's that simple. That investment saves you money later down the line, because the more diversity you have in the newsroom, you will make fewer mistakes in coverage. Take Ukraine as an example; this morning, there was a pull-together of a selection of coverage that we've seen so far, including reporters saying things like, "this is such a shock when it's happening in a European country; I'm seeing people with blue eyes and blond hair and I can't believe it's happening to them". At the same time, by definition people from other wars and conflicts who are not blue-eyed and blond-haired are not suffering pain that is any less than we are seeing now, in Ukraine. So that kind of mistake in reporting excludes communities and puts people off from joining, and they undermine the quality of the product and the reputation of the news outlet. So, longer term, if newsrooms want to avoid that kind of thing and want to avoid being pulled up on that and avoid being embarrassed when their reporters make those kinds of mistakes, then they need to invest in ensuring (1) that there are more people from minority backgrounds in the newsroom in the first place and (2) encouraging everybody in the newsroom to take better care with their language.

De-Graft: This is all very important and when it comes to getting younger people involved in journalism, I do think there is another big struggle, a wider issue than getting black people into journalism. The world of journalism has changed a lot over the past couple years: Tik Tok has grown and the whole online sphere has changed massively so there is an ongoing challenge – how do we entice people to join this industry when a lot of people might be at home thinking, "I'll just make a Tik Tok account and do my own thing". I guess it's somewhat great that we do live in a world now where people don't have to go down the traditional routes, but then that's also not great when we end up in situations whereby we have accounts which are just spreading misinformation because they lack the necessary journalism training. So, they are doing their own thing, but their own thing is very harmful! I think that's a big challenge that journalism has to face – how do we keep this world alive and fresh and exciting for somebody who is a lot younger and who sees so many different platforms in front of them and who might have massive distrust in mainstream media? Unfortunately, a lot of mainstream media have made mistakes that have really torn relationships up between news outlets and communities, so how do we change and how do we adapt and how do we look attractive to – not just young black people – but young people in general? I do find my job exciting, but how do we convey that?!

Do you feel you are role models?

Daniel: By definition, journalism is a public-facing job, what I do is seen by people, so influence and role modelling comes from that. It is not an intentional thing, but it is a consequence of the job. You can make things happen, because you're public facing and there's an impact, it's a responsibility. You are trying to represent yourself well, to represent the outlet well and the people that you are speaking to, their stories. With all of that in mind, that is where the role modelling comes into it, because you have all of those considerations and people see that. When it has that connection, it can be really rewarding.

De-Graft: I agree that I don't like to use the word "role model", personally it just feels weird because I'm talking about myself, but one thing that I'm very conscious of is speaking in a way that feels relatable so that when people do come across me they don't just think you've got to talk in a particular way to become a journalist. You can talk in the way that you talk with your friends and still be a journalist. I am very conscious of things like that. At times it feels like a lot but it's just a life that I guess I've been born into. But being a black person who is on screen and who is on air, sometimes it feels that I do have that responsibility not to mess it up, because people are looking at you and thinking "I want to do that and if he can do that, so can I". Sometimes, I feel that mainstream news can be like your dad has come to talk to your mum. How do we sound more relatable, like these are your friends coming to talk to you? Let's just talk in a way that all of us really understand. I have also really tried to focus on – especially on the podcast – the fact that black stories are not all about racism. I feel there is too much on the black trauma side of things – there are many happy things going on within the black community. We absolutely need to talk about racism, but sometimes it gets taxing as a consumer of the news to just constantly turn on the TV and see another black person died, this black person has been murdered. Sometimes you want to turn on the TV and say – Dave's had an incredible moment at the Brit Awards, or check out this incredible black astrophysicist! Sometimes, you want to see light because it can get a bit too heavy sometimes.

Daniel: Of course! Again, it is about reflecting the full range of the human experience and I think for a lot of the reasons we spoke about earlier, there are definitely platforms, individuals that do that, *Newsround* being one of them – but it is not something that is the norm yet in our industry, the sooner we get to that, the better it will be for everyone.

Looking into the future

De-Graft: My vision for the future would be to be able to walk into a newsroom and see more than one black boss or non-white boss, and not having to be so amazed by it I would like it to be as mainstream and as normal as walking into a newsroom and seeing a white boss. I think that could definitely help journalism in the future as well. But then, I would also like to see and hear voices from across the UK – especially non-white voices across the UK.

This is a key issue for me about journalism. I feel that when we do hear black voices they are from London, or southern voices, and there are massive black communities in other cities like Liverpool, Manchester, Birmingham. We are not hearing from those voices as much.

Daniel: I definitely empathise with that. I noticed it a lot doing my undergraduate studies in the north of England, having lived in east London my whole life. In the north, I met black people whose accent was not like mine, but who shared similar experiences. Then you look at what is being broadcast and realise that you are not hearing these voices, they are not getting on air. Why is that?

In terms of a vision for the future, I would like to see more of the bursaries that I had that got me through. I couldn't have done my master's, without the bursary. I didn't have £10,000 that I needed – and it costs more now – and it will be even more in ten years. I don't know how the next generation will find that money. It might be by that point that it isn't the definitive route that you have to take [to get into journalism], but it was for me and my sense is that, despite the fact that, as we have discussed, social media is changing things, it will still be important, because there's a difference between being a journalist and a content creator. They are both of value, but the journalist needs to know media law to put stuff out and the other one doesn't and to do that you need to complete a course. So, if we want the kind of industry that we've been talking about that needs to be invested in, there needs to be some sort of collaboration: Channel 4, Sky, ITV, BBC – you would think that the money that goes through all of those companies, it is not some sort of utopia to think they could create a fund to finance people between them. The whole industry says it wants more minority voices so could they do that? It's not some sort of pipe dream! They all agree and they are all going to benefit because people move around all the time! Nobody stays at any news organisation forever! It would be amazing!

Journalism education can play its part too: I have shared lectures with journalism schools about the coverage of race – comparing the progress made in covering mental health to the way some outlets approach stories about race. I think that is certainly an area where universities could take a lead, because at that stage young people are really developing. If you can establish the ground rules for covering race – and as more than a one-off lecture – but integrated into teaching or as a module that everyone has to take and pass, then you are setting up a generation of journalists on the right foot so that they come into the industry knowing how to cover race; that these are the kinds of areas we should really be considering. This is an area where education can have more impact, because by the time you are in the industry, the kind of training that is given is the practical stuff – how to use a camera, how to edit, those are short courses that you are put on to do your job – but the soft skills, but important skills, are generally learnt through telling a story, or telling it wrong and getting pulled up on it, whereas at uni if you have that time to learn and then you start your job, I think you are in a better position.

De-Graft: If I look at what I would have benefited from whilst studying at university, I think one thing that could really change would be to learn how we make content that actually has impact, by giving students the tools and the means to amplify a story. Young people know how to use platforms, like Instagram, Twitter and Tik Tok casually, in their everyday lives, but how can we teach students to use these platforms to spread their content so they can show it to editors and say, "this got 30,000 views on Tik Tok – it was more than just an assignment, for me it was real life journalism". I was asked that a lot, I was asked for my show-reel, but editors would say that they were assignments, not "real stories". I had covered some new stories, but they lacked impact. Sometimes it can be hard to teach people to look bigger than what they are studying at the time – for me, at university, impact would have been ending up in the local paper, or getting onto the local radio station. But how can we teach people to use the Internet to get their stories out nationally and internationally? I think that would mean that some more diverse stories would get out and students would come out of university with a bit more weight behind them, operating as a full-fledged journalist. Student journalists need to stop calling themselves that, because they are journalists and they should believe in themselves and believe in what they are doing.

Daniel: I agree.

Notes

1 Milton Keynes is a town situated 80 km north-west of London in the UK.
2 Angelica Bell is a British television presenter, best known for presenting children's programmes on CBBC in the UK (2000–2006).
3 Afua Hirsch is a writer, broadcaster and former barrister who writes for *The Guardian* newspaper in the UK.
4 CBBC is a free-to-air channel owned by the BBC and the brand used for all content it produces for children and young people aged 6–17.

8
INTEGRATING JOURNALISM EDUCATION AND THE SUSTAINABILITY AGENDA

Fiona Cownie and Michael Sunderland

Introduction

Sustainability is edging towards the centre of journalism educators' practice. The United Nations Sustainable Development Goals (SDGs), with their 2030 target, provide a lens through which to articulate the world's key challenges. We argue that meaningful journalism education should capture these goals as part of Education for Sustainable Development (ESD) now expected by the Quality Assurance Agency (QAA) across all Higher Education curricular (AdvanceHE 2021). ESD provides pedagogical guidance which can steer the embedding of social, economic and environmental issues within journalism's curricular and extra-curricular activities. The ultimate aim of ESD is to equip students and graduates with the knowledge, skills and experience to contribute to ethically responsible societies (AdvanceHE 2021). But do journalism educators prioritise such growth in their students and how might they seek to further integrate sustainability to enhance the educational opportunities they design and lead?

This chapter examines the place of sustainability within journalism education in the context of Higher Education (HE). It introduces ESD, the SDGs and UNESCO learning outcomes, sharing good practice within two case studies from undergraduate and postgraduate journalism education. A conceptual framework emerges from these case studies to synthesise the integration of sustainability within journalism education. We use the framework to propose ways that journalism educators can embrace the sustainability agenda, in so doing, enhancing students' learning experiences, generating meaningful actions and inspiring students' career aspirations. In short, this chapter is interested in exploring how journalism educators can augment their positive contribution to our shared future.

DOI: 10.4324/9781003301028-11

Sustainable development goals

At the heart of our integration of sustainability within journalism education are the SDGs. At the turn of the century, the United Nations Millennium Development Goals (MDGs) were created to encapsulate some of the key challenges faced by countries in the developing world. By 2015, the United Nations had rearticulated the world's challenges as the SDGs. No longer were these targets designed to be achieved solely by countries in the so-called Global South; they were set for governments and organisations across the breadth of the planet. The 17 SDGs have increasingly been adopted by governments, non-commercial and commercial organisations as a framework for sustainability. The simplicity of the goals is reflected in titles including *'Goal 1: No Poverty'*, *'Goal 13: Climate Action'*, *'Goal 5: Gender Equality'*, *'Goal 4: Good Education'*, providing a clear vision of external priorities upon which to focus energy and effort. These targets articulate the shared values of sustainability, which can reinforce the meaning and purpose of journalism education.

Although the goals are not always a perfect match for the world's challenges, they are ambitious and provide a focus for change. The goals' reductionism and infographic presentation bring clarity and focus to areas sustainability conversations can occupy. Arguably, such clarity gives stories about sustainability a backstop and a reference point for readers to increasingly understand the challenges we face. Could journalism educators play a role in furthering affective connections to the goals through their integration within journalism training? Despite widespread adoption, critique of the goals is evident. If sustainability is concerned with having enough for everyone forever (Association of Sustainability Practitioners, 2020) how does this square with economic growth (*Goal 8: Decent Work and Economic Growth*)? Do efforts to address one goal potentially diminish the success of another? If organisations are purposefully focusing their activities upon the goals, where does that leave the challenges neglected within the targets? Such challenges may be considered to be real and important, but absent within the 17 SDGs. Nuclear disarmament, animal cruelty, global security, eradication of genocide – where do these issues sit? If not clearly evident within the goals, do they lose potency? Will excluded topics be relegated in importance by organisations and by journalist educators?

Education for sustainable development

The HE sector is being encouraged to embrace ESD and 'ensure that every graduate has not only the knowledge and skills but the attributes that will enable them at least to cope and ideally thrive in the face of the multiple challenges they will face' (A 2021:1). Kemp (2017) argues that integrating ESD can result in a range of benefits to students including intellectual development and fostering a diverse range of skills to offer employers.

Sustainable development is defined as an 'aspirational ongoing process of addressing social, environmental and economic concerns to create a better world' (AdvanceHE 2021:3). We are interested in how journalism educators can create structures and content to enable journalism students to enact sustainable development. Students want to see sustainability being covered in their study. Drayson et al. (2014) claim that over 80% of undergraduates believe that courses should incorporate sustainability and should actively promote their coverage of the sustainability agenda. Nine out of ten students expect to be learning about sustainability within their degree (SOS 2021). Whilst this research population embraces students from all HE subject areas, journalism educators must take these expectations seriously as they design programmes, units, delivery and assessment.

It is clear that the inclusion of ESD within HE faces challenges (Cotton et al. 2009; Shephard and Horsley 2015) including concerns about overcrowded curricular; perceptions of irrelevance by academic staff; limited staff awareness and expertise; and sparse institutional drive and commitment (Dawe, Jucker and Martin 2005). We would argue that since Dawe et al.'s (2005) study, these challenges have reduced. Times Higher Impact rankings now inform many institutions' thinking and priorities. Many academics appear to see the relevance of sustainability. However, expertise around sustainability and awareness of structures such as SDGs may still constrain journalism educators' progress. Indeed, for some academics, constructs such as ESD and the SDGs may still be seen as reducing academic self-determination and autonomy (Jickling and Wals 2008).

Building on UNESCO learning outcomes

The SDGs' articulation has a government-level focus which can prove complicated to apply to an educational setting. UNESCO developed guidelines for translating the goals into educational opportunities and practices within ESD. Of particular value to journalism educators are UNESCO's learning outcomes, aligned to each of the SDGs.[1] Originally designed for pre-university education, the outcomes maintain significant value in higher education journalism programmes, partly due to the fact that such objectives can be achieved by students as part of their reporting on related issues and by reflecting on these activities afterwards.

UNESCO learning outcomes serve as a bridge between the SDGs and the design of journalism education. They highlight what students should know and what they should be able to do related to each goal. To illustrate, *Goal 10: Reduce Inequalities – reduce inequality within and among countries –* is translated into the educational context through UNESCO's learning outcomes. The knowledge which journalism educators could integrate within their curricular, teaching and assessment might include 'knows indicators that measure and describe inequalities and understands their relevance for decision making'. Students' understanding could be evaluated when they realise that 'inequality is a major driver for societal problems and individual dissatisfaction' and become aware of 'inequalities in their surroundings as well as in the wider world and is able to recognize the problematic consequences'.

This awareness and understanding are core to journalists' aim to bear witness to the challenges of our time, whether they are evident within UK or European cities, or across continents.

UNESCO learning outcomes also give us clarity regarding the behaviours journalism educators can seek to instil within their students. For example, we can develop learning environments in which 'students can identify an objective indicator to compare different groups, nations, with respect to inequalities'. Such behaviours will ground student output in journalistic rigour. UNESCO outcomes ask that students 'feel empathy for and show solidarity with people who are discriminated against'. Such a demand on students aligns to the discipline's increasing attention towards journalists' own emotional labour in particular in response to trauma, whether that trauma be in conflict zones or reporting within the coronavirus disease 2019 (Covid-19) pandemic (Jukes, Fowler-Watt and Rees 2021).

Behavioural outcomes associated with *Goal 13: Climate Action – Take urgent action to combat climate change and its impacts* include being able to 'encourage others to protect the climate' and 'evaluate whether their private and job activities are climate friendly and – where not – to revise them'. Journalism educators can use these learning outcomes to inform the development of their curricular teaching and assessment to address Climate Action in a meaningful, well-informed manner. Students preparing for placement experiences can reflect upon journalism's practices, researching each in terms of its climate friendliness, highlighting priorities for change and identifying a meaningful action for them to take into the professional environment. Returning journalism students can draw from their experiences of seeking to adopt climate-friendly practices within the workplace, sharing successes and perceived barriers and proposing recommendations to the sector. For journalism educators embarking on embedding sustainability within their curriculum, teaching or assessment, the UNESCO learning outcomes are a valuable resource, demonstrating how the range of SDGs can find a place within our discipline.

Integrating sustainability into journalism education

Climate change and other global sustainability challenges are the defining news stories of our time. Affecting every person and community on the planet, such issues are imbued with news value, requiring educators to equip future journalists to tackle them with foresight and clarity. Journalism students must understand both the scale and urgency of the sustainability agenda as well as how to lessen their own environmental impact through more sustainable production practices.

Global challenges are among the root causes of many problems faced in communities across the planet today such as outcomes of flooding, reliance on foodbanks, polluted rivers and seas. Facilitating an understanding of these underlying challenges arms audiences with the agency to address the problems they encounter in day-to-day life. Journalism graduates must be prepared to enter their industry with the mindset to navigate and provide leadership within this environment (Royle 2021).

Journalism educators can develop these skills within their students, bringing long-term global issues into the hearts and minds of audiences often concerned with the local and immediate.

The sustainability agenda has risen in prominence within our professional and personal lives; it is critical that it is also asserting its position within our lives as educators. Vukić (2019) notes that there have been few scholarly attempts to conjoin journalism with sustainability. This is the moment for journalism educators to take sustainability seriously and give it priority within their design and delivery of journalism courses. Rao (2012) proposes a 'green pen' model of journalism with a focus on sustainability and climate crisis. Indeed Vukić (2019:253) calls for journalists to be 'professionally educated, autonomous and responsible, (self)-conscious humanists' able to cope with and respond appropriately to the world's challenges. We must work hard to create opportunities for students to tell their sustainability-informed stories, in a manner which engages audiences, captures interest and ultimately contributes to meaningful change in behaviours.

We argue that within journalism education we have educators who care and are committed to putting ESD at the heart of their curriculum, delivery and assessment. Whilst some claim that precious space within the curricular might be preserved by integrating ESD into interdisciplinary or co-curricular activities (Shepherd and Horsley 2015), others are making concerted efforts to explicitly integrate sustainability within the journalism curricular. Kolandai-Matchett, Spellerberg and Buchan (2009) found that a bespoke 'sustainability in journalism' module enhanced students' understanding of sustainability, interest in reporting related issues and understanding of the need for enhanced media coverage of sustainability to build public awareness. Alternatively, journalism educators can embed sustainability within units; we share examples of this within two case studies. Whilst the move towards embracing sustainability is carefully planned by these journalism educators, the pandemic of 2019–2022 with its transition to online delivery methods has also been part of the story. The challenges of bringing stories into the online classroom has presented serendipitous opportunities to create teaching experiences which centre around the SDGs.

However, as a community we must challenge ourselves. Is care about sustainability widespread amongst journalism educators or are there pockets of endeavour which other educators rely upon to 'tick the sustainability box' continuing to teach topics which immediately excite and provide short-term visible success? Indeed, as a community, do we overly emphasise small-scale successes implying that these are more representative of the ways in which we engage with sustainability than is reality? Are we sufficiently self-reflective about how much we are doing and how much has to be done; ultimately are journalism educators knowing or unknowing participants in greenwashing their own turf?

ESD for journalism educators embraces supporting students to pursue sustainable visions of the future, appreciating the complexity inherent in the 'wicked problems' which characterise sustainability and envisaging ways in which students can personally and professionally contribute to positive change and a future characterised by hope. Transforming our journalism curriculum towards ESD takes care, commitment and a sense of courage that a focus on creating stories which centre on the world's challenges will inspire students' engagement and learning. We need to take the strategies and techniques which we know work for our students and transform them within the world of sustainability. Through our students' endeavours we can create solutions informed by hope.

Learning from good practice

We now turn to two case studies of the integration of sustainability within practice and theory-focused journalism units delivered within a large media faculty in a UK university. Presenting these two experiences allows us to draw out key themes which inform a conceptual framework of sustainability within journalism education, and in turn our recommendations to journalism educators.

Case study 1: Integrating sustainability within practical journalism projects

Student journalism activities, including news days designed to mirror industry practice, offer opportunities to embed themes of sustainability into a range of learning experiences. During news days, students are required to work in teams to produce original content for TV and radio bulletins and to maintain their own news websites. News days are sometimes assigned broad themes which focus on the creation of news content. In one UK university, these days are now regularly built around sustainability and the SDGs. Indeed, entire news weeks have been constructed around one SDG or the goals as a whole. Embedding SDGs within these popular and important learning experiences take the sustainability agenda to the centre of students' experiences of what journalism is as well as how to practice.

The sustainability news day brief is for students to create news content which speaks to the goals. This can be implemented in a number of ways. A final-year converged journalism unit responding to the challenges of remote learning during lockdown reinvented delivery and, in parallel, successfully embedded themes of sustainability. This unit, with a three-week full-time block of delivery, requires students to work together as a team to create news content. Traditionally students would be set to operate within a local context, interviewing contributors face-to-face and producing TV and radio bulletins as stories unfolded. Lockdown fundamentally changed this. As academics and students worked entirely online and access to production kit and people was curtailed, a new plan for pedagogic delivery had to be speedily developed and implemented. Online content and working assumed a central place, and the staples of studio-based TV and radio bulletins were no longer options. Strengthening online content in terms of production and assessment was key. Each team would manage their own news website, each of which focused on a single SDG. Whereas the teaching team initially were concerned that students' learning experience would be far more restricted than previously, the new approach prompted a widening out of themes and stories. Students' outlook moved from the local to the global. They embraced interviews, carried out via Zoom or Teams, with people all over the world and reported on subjects including inequalities facing the education system in South Africa and Australian wildfires.

A second-year journalism unit required students to produce short documentaries that spoke to one of the SDGs. This demonstrated that the work would have importance both in terms of the process of learning and in the story being told. Importantly, as part of that process, students had to pitch the documentary, explaining which SDG the work was facing and why this issue was both relevant and important. Students were encouraged to investigate targets and indicators aligned to the goals, to justify the proposed content. This encouraged students to research the goals, and in doing so, sparking conversations about them and building students' understanding of the challenges the goals addressed. These conversations brought the SDGs to life and created personal connections between them and the students, encouraging effort and energy to be invested in the project.

These learning experiences seek to demonstrate that the SDGs impact every part of life. If students want to make a documentary about trans-rights, their tutors discuss how *SDG 10 Reduced inequalities* might speak to that. If they want to create content about sewage and its impact on sea swimming or over-fishing, tutors talk about how *SDG 14 Life below water* is relevant. A sense of connection with the broader challenges of life was key to the success of these approaches to learning which students found rewarding.

In reflecting upon sustainability in practice within journalism delivery, it is interesting to consider how students engage with the goals. Do some SDGs appear to be more fruitful for student journalists to tackle? Do some goals assert a dominance within students' interpretations of sustainability? Journalism educators' experience within these production units suggests that *SDG13 Climate Action* and plastic pollution (*SDG12 Responsible Consumption and Production*) are salient in initial discussions with students about the goals. Students tend not to think about how working conditions might be part of the sustainability agenda (*SDG 8 Decent Work and Economic Growth*). However, once the conversations unfold, students become far more receptive to the relevance of a broader range of goals, understanding that they really do underpin so many areas of journalistic interest. Academics working with sustainability on these production units have found that a broad interpretation of the goals is good practice to prompt student engagement, rather than expecting an absolute match of content to the goal, its targets and indicators. So, the goals provide students with a helpful structure to underpin storytelling, but the intent is that they are not limiting or restrictive.

One of the challenges students find daunting is identifying original story ideas and important people to talk to about these stories. This may be the most challenging skill students have to develop. Students regularly get the confidence-sapping experience of repeatedly being knocked back by people. Sustainability can be a help here; the goals give students focus; importantly, they give a sense of purpose. Happily, students find that experts in the areas of SDGs are often more inclined to speak about their area; that sense of purpose is energising. This builds confidence in students that their interview is of real value. The SDGs provide students with genuine issues which need solving. Suddenly students' work feels important and relevant to the challenges we face. Students really do care about these issues; sustainability provides a bridge for students to walk along to a destination which they sense is worthwhile and empowering. Indeed, there has been a noticeable shift in the interest students are showing in campaigning and advocacy work, and in work with humanitarian and environmental NGOs. Students' involvement in tangible projects, working with interns within international NGOs, is a powerful agent for change and future career aspirations.

Journalism educators' integration of sustainability within production projects injects a real sense of purpose and meaning to students' work. Students' confidence about the importance of their work alongside their care about the stories they are telling energises production work and in turn informs career aspirations.

Case study 2: Asserting the place of sustainability within a theoretically aligned journalism unit

Theoretical units alert students to the broader contexts which inform practical journalism work. 'Global Current Affairs' is a second-year unit delivered to undergraduate students. It has been recognised within an institutional Excellence in Education for Sustainable Development Award; celebrating best practice in embedding ESD within curricular, co-curricular and extra-curricular opportunities and encouraging students to develop the skills, knowledge and values to contribute to a sustainable future. At the heart of 'Global Current Affairs' are two core themes: sustainability and global security. The unit aims to enable the journalists of tomorrow to understand why the public need to engage with sustainability and global security and to be able to explain these themes to their future audiences. The unit seeks to equip students with the knowledge and skills to be translators. Translation is not about scientific complexity, but about demonstrating how the themes of sustainability and global security interact and affect our lives. The unit seeks to navigate the complexity of sustainability and interpret this in a systematic way which demonstrates the interrelatedness of the sustainability agenda.

Sustainability is interpreted broadly to include planet and civilisation as an ecosystem, indeed the unit leader sees sustainability as 'existential survival of species and people and civilization'. So, within 'Global Current Affairs' whilst climate has a key place, global security is also central to the sustainability agenda – a nuclear incident, intended or unintended, would have a devastating impact on environment and people.

The unit curriculum covers a range of topics which clearly map onto the SDGs – food and water, poverty, the environment and global institutions such as the United Nations. Indeed, in an SDG mapping exercise the unit aligns to the full range of 17 SDGs. Case studies from across the world provide students with understanding about the topics and importantly the interdependence between these topics. Multimedia teaching artefacts (documentaries, infographics, reports, slideshows) are used to direct learning, evidencing discussions on sustainability and global security and are central to assessment.

The interdependence of the sustainability agenda is at the heart of one of two assignments – the production of a Reflective Sustainability Mind Map. This works well for students who need to be succinct, smart about what they highlight and able to personalise storytelling. Each week students are encouraged to identify key elements of the multimedia content which were important or interesting to them. In parallel students identify key challenges which face our move towards a more sustainable world. The Reflective Sustainability Mind Map combines these reflections into a substantial visual artefact capturing the key linkages and interdependences between global current affairs, world regions and individuals who are driving global change in the world today.

The Reflective Sustainability Mind Map has been a great success, generating positive student feedback and is at the heart of the 'Excellence in ESD Award'. The mind map gave students the space and creative freedom to raise sustainability-related issues that they feel passionate about and to reflect on what they've learned from each week of teaching, and to do that visually. The mind map offers students the opportunity for personalisation and agency within the world of sustainability. It evokes a sense of hope rather than fear, so important in motivating action particularly in relation to climate crisis. This agency enhances student engagement which in turn was reflected in achievement, with marks reaching the 80%s and even 90%s. There is real evidence of the effort students invest into selecting and curating content, reflecting on their learning within sustainability and highlighting global interdependence drawing from examples from teaching delivery. Weaker assignments tend to lack a personal narrative and missed the opportunity to be bold in their visual display. However, the unit generates visually accomplished artefacts, themselves tools for inspiring other students and scholars to engage within the sustainability agenda.

The unique and personalised nature of content enables students to present their narrative about sustainability in creative ways. This has the positive impact of enhancing student engagement and avoids the challenge of plagiarism. The unit allows students to be empowered to engage with issues – such as climate change, nuclear proliferation, poverty, terrorism – that they care about and that embody the sustainability agenda. This gives students an outlet to reflect on why they think these issues matter, not just to identify problems but also to seek solutions and identify change-makers, people who can act as positive role models such as Malala and Greta Thunberg.

The treatment of theory related to sustainability within this unit works well. Conceptual models are coupled with specific real-world examples of sustainability in practice. 'Global Current Affairs' demonstrates how important the local context is in discussions around sustainability; the history, geography, personalities, politics and international relations affecting an issue or region enable discussions about sustainability to be brought alive and connected clearly to the here and now. The unit starts discussions with a specific event, incident, case study or real-world incident, using that as an entry point into deeper conceptual or theoretical analysis. A shortage of celery at Tesco's which may be observed within students' day-to-day life, is tracked back to broader discussions about Brexit, Covid and the Russian Invasion of Ukraine, together resulting in pressures on the availability of CO_2, workforce supply and costs which ultimately may result in the closure of the celery producer's business. 'Feeling it in our fridge' is a real lens for students' understanding of the sustainability agenda and how they can work to ensure their stories resonate within individuals' lives. Pairing these discussions with visual assignments which might include infographics, photo essays, mind and concept maps connect the global to the local. This encourages students to engage with the big issues which journalism educators seek to address within a sustainability-informed curriculum. Journalism educators can take several key principles from this unit into their provision of education for sustainable development: the currency of hope; the role of student agency, personalisation and creativity to interpret and translate sustainability; the emphasis on interdependency within sustainability; the 'feeling it in our fridge' factor; and the ultimate focus on meaningful action.

Developing a framework for sustainability within journalism education

Synthesising these experiences and reflections, we propose a framework which highlights key themes which inform how journalism educators can engage with sustainability within practice and theoretically orientated curricular-based activities. We propose four tiers: journalism educators' strategic approaches to sustainability; tools which may be helpful to engage students with the sustainability agenda; aspects of the student learning experience which result from these approaches and tools; and four key outcomes – student achievement, student engagement, sustainability-informed career aspirations and meaningful action.

Journalism educators may draw from this framework to create curricular structures and sustainability-informed content to support and enact sustainable development in a manner which addresses the HEA's (2021) ESD ambitions. Whilst the focus of this analysis is curricular based, these meaningful actions may be evident within curricular, co-curricular and extra-curricular contexts. Ultimately, we hope that this framework will demonstrate an approach to journalism education which will encourage students to develop the skills, knowledge and values to contribute to a sustainable future.

Tier 1: Journalism educators' approaches to sustainability

We suggest that as journalism educators design curricular and delivery approaches which speak to the sustainability agenda, they focus on making content relevant to students' everyday experiences: the food for which students shop, the clothes they buy, the transport they take. The movement between local and global contexts is key and demonstrates both the relevance and scale of sustainability issues. Interdependency, geographically (local-global) and between the different strands of sustainability, is key.

Engagement of students and, ultimately, prompts of meaningful behaviour will be best achieved through delivering learning material and encouraging the production of content with a hopeful orientation which speaks to solutions, not just challenges. Journalism students need to feel that the content they create will make a positive difference to how the world moves forward and addresses the challenges articulated through the SDGs. This will be best received within a context of demonstrable institutional and academic commitment to the sustainability agenda underpinned by shared values speaking to aspects of sustainability which we know are so important in driving this commitment (Morgan and Hunt 1994).

Personalisation is a fruitful part of the strategic approach to journalism education. Designing personalised learning strategies which allow students (and academics) to focus on areas which matter to them and to which there is a prospect of meaningful action is important and should be prioritised within journalism educators' approaches to designing ESD. These strategies can then be couched within educational strategies which embrace creativity, curation and, of course, storytelling.

Tier 2: Tools for sustainability within journalism education

We recommend a range of tools to prompt productive learning in the area of sustainability. We saw within the practical journalism projects that the traditional news day continues to provide a lively and fruitful context for news stories which reflect sustainability. The increasingly central place of online content alongside the use of online tools which has become so fundamental to journalism practice characterises journalism education within the realm of sustainability. Multimedia artefacts, so often thought of as the preserve of practice teaching, can provide real value within theoretically orientated units, especially if they are combined with a reflective mindset. The reflective mind map demonstrated within the 'Global Current Affairs' case study can be used to demonstrate the interdependences of the sustainability agenda.

Sustainability-informed content should explicitly relate to the SDGs, and the UNESCO learning outcomes are highly recommended as a bridge into those SDGs. Units on journalism programmes should be assessed in their coverage of the SDGs to ensure that journalism students are exposed to all aspects of sustainability within their degree, even if areas such as climate crisis are intentionally given priority.

Tier 3: Student learning experience related to sustainability

Sustainability offers benefits to the student learning experience. The sense of purpose the sustainability agenda offers students is rewarding and builds confidence in the value of their production and theoretical work. Students have the opportunity

Integrating journalism education and the sustainability agenda **111**

to invest their time and energies into investigating and telling stories about issues about which they care. We saw how the confidence generated by working with stories that matter, combined with enhancing access to prospective interviewees makes a difference to student journalists in their practical modules.

Both practical and theoretical artefacts place students in the place of translator, drawing from their broad understanding of the sustainability agenda, to communicate important stories to their audiences. Understanding the interdependence between sustainability challenges makes students more receptive to engaging with a wider range of issues through a broadening of the SDGs considered to be relevant and worthy of students' effort and energy. Finally, students, through an ability to make choices about how they engage with the sustainability agenda, are conferred with a sense of agency which in turn drives important outcomes.

Tier 4: Outcomes of sustainability informed journalism education

Journalism educators' investment in the sustainability agenda as encouraged here results in important outcomes. Meaningful action which may be manifest in the assessed content within curricular, or broader extra-curricular contexts, such as an increase in activism or volunteering, is an important outcome. We argue that well-informed sustainability orientated journalism education, as a result of the benefits it offers to the student learning experience, can enhance student achievement and student engagement. Authentic engagement with sustainability can in turn have lasting impacts on students' aspirations, increasing the intention to seek or at least consider jobs related to finding solutions to the challenges we face. These may be within traditional journalism roles, or in broader activism or NGO contexts.

ESD embedded within journalism programmes can have a long-lasting positive impact on the world. The skills journalism educators bring to the learning environment help make this happen.

Recommendations for action

Drawing from our analysis of sustainability within journalism education, our case studies and proposed framework, we conclude the chapter with a series of recommendations to journalism educators.

1. Use the UNESCO learning outcomes to build understanding of how journalism programmes and individual units can effectively engage with each ESD: learning objectives – UNESCO Digital Library; Padlet is a useful tool to facilitate programme-level discussions about how learning outcomes might be appropriately addressed within units.
2. Map units within journalism programmes against each SDG. Adapt this SDG programme mapping tool to help you do this www.bournemouth.ac.uk/about/sustainability/academic-opportunities

112 Fiona Cownie and Michael Sunderland

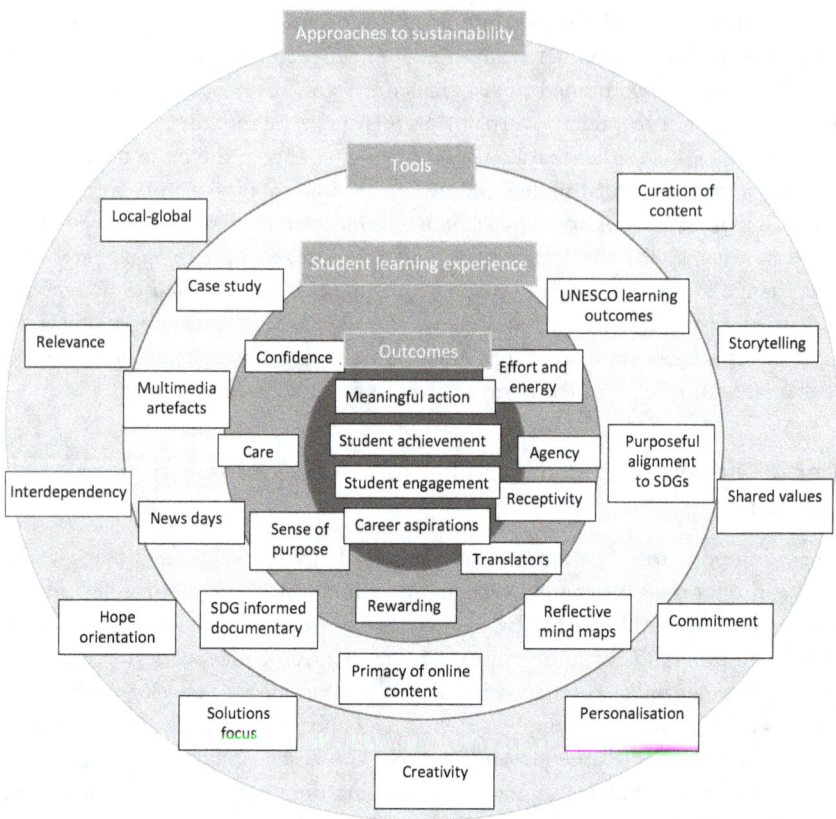

FIGURE 8.1 Framework for sustainability within journalism education

3. Analyse journalism programme coverage against SDGs and check that you are confident that your coverage of sustainability is appropriate in terms of breadth (numbers of SDGs covered) and depth (coverage of UNESCO learning outcomes within each SDG).
4. Utilise the reflective mind map within journalism teaching, either within assessment or as an ongoing group exercise.
5. Design personalised learning and assessment opportunities so that journalism students have choice and thus agency about how they engage with the sustainability agenda.
6. Use local stories and events to build relevance and connect to broader global challenges within journalism content. Encourage students to articulate solutions; encourage a hopeful orientation.
7. Demonstrate your personal commitment to the sustainability agenda, articulating shared values which can cohere the student and academic journalism community; you might add the SDG/s you feel passionate about to your email signature.

8. As a team of journalism educators, ensure that your practice reflects the sustainability agenda and draw examples from this practice. Avoid inessential carbon-generating travel, consider carbon offsetting carefully rather than as an automatic contingency for business as normal. Show that you are prepared to make compromises in your practice as an academic in order to support the sustainability agenda. Ensure that inequities within your journalism educators' community, in terms of access to resource and opportunity to present at conferences, are identified and addressed.
9. Embrace the sustainability agenda and act as advocates, share your successes and failures within communities of ESD practice, internal to your institution or externally through events such as Advance HE's sustainability symposium. Learn from your colleagues; aim to inspire others.

Note

1 https://en.unesco.org/themes/education/sdgs/material.

References

AdvanceHE. 2021. Education for Sustainable Development Guidance, Executive Summary, March 2021. https://s3.eu-west-2.amazonaws.com/assets.creode.advancehe-document-manager/documents/advance-he/education-for-sustainable-development-guidance-executive-summary_1616774751.pdf

Cotton, D., Bailey, I., Warren, M., & Bissell, S. 2009. Revolutions and second-best solutions: Education for sustainable development in higher education. *Studies in Higher Education*, 34(7), 719–733.

Dawe, G., Jucker, R., & Martin, S. 2005. Sustainable development in higher education: Current practice and future developments. www.sustainabilityexchange.ac.uk/files/sustdevinhefinalreport_1.pdf

Drayson, R., Bone, E., Agombar, J., & Kemp, S. 2014. Student attitudes towards, and skills for, sustainable development. *Higher Education Academy*. New York. https://s3.eu-west-2.amazonaws.com/assets.creode.advancehe-document-manager/documents/hea/private/resources/student_attitudes_towards_and_skills_for_sustainable_development_1568037253.pdf

Jickling, B., & Wal, E.J. 2008. Globalisation and environmental education: Looking beyond sustainable development. *Curriculum Studies*, 40(1), 1–21.

Jukes, S., Fowler-Watt, K., & Rees, G. 2021. Reporting the covid-19 pandemic: Trauma on our own doorstep. *Digital Journalism*, 10(6), 997–1014.

Kemp, S. 2017. Education for sustainable development – a vehicle for socially and environmentally responsible interdisciplinary learning, teaching and assessment? [online]. Available at: www.heacademy.ac.uk/blog/education-sustainabledevelopment---vehicle-socially-and-environmentally-responsible

Kolandai-Matchett, K., Spellerberg, I., & Buchan, G.D. 2009. Sustainability in journalism education: Assessment of a trial module in New Zealand. *Applied Environmental Education and Communication*, 8(304), 204–215.

Morgan, R., & Hunt, S. 1994. The commitment-trust theory of relationship marketing. *Journal of Marketing*, 58(3), 20–38.

Rao, S. 2012. The case for 'green pen journalism' in an age of globalization and liberalization. *Ecquid Novi: African Journalism Studies*, 33(1), 3–14.

Royle, J. 2021. From skillset to mindset: The reconceptualization of entrepreneurial journalism in higher education, Thesis, Bournemouth University.

Shephard, K., & Horsely, M. 2015. *Higher education for sustainable development*. London: Palgrave Macmillan.

Students Organising for Sustainability. 2021. www.sos-uk.org/research/sustainability-skills-survey

UNESCO. 2014. Roadmap for Implementing the Global Action Programme on Education for Sustainable Development [online]. Available from https://unesdoc.unesco.org/ark:/48223/pf0000230514 [University of Bedfordshire 2006 Effecting Change in Higher Education. Available at www.jisc.ac.uk/guides/change-management [accessed 12 April 2019].

Vukić, T. 2019. Sustainable journalism education – the only possible way towards the future. *Croatian Journal Educational*, 2(1), 253–279.

9
FROM SKILLSET TO MINDSET

The re-conceptualisation of entrepreneurial journalism in higher education

Jo Royle

Introduction

In their work 'Beyond Journalism', Deuze and Witschge (2017) assert the need to revisit the definition and breadth of focus for journalism studies. They view the field as a 'dynamic object of study' and challenge educators to approach it 'as a moving object and as a dynamic set of practices and expectations – a profession in a permanent process of becoming' (Deuze and Witschge 2017, p13).

The research shared in this chapter is underpinned by the premise of a journalism industry subjected to radical change, and resultant need to act quickly and effectively in order to sustain its future. The incumbent responsibility on journalism educators to respond to the need to look 'beyond journalism' as it is represented by today's industry is recognised as urgent, as is the need to extend the toolkit of the journalist of the future to encompass 'entrepreneurialism'. On the basis of semi-structured, in-depth interviews – with journalism educators – conducted on-site in two UK-based and two US higher education fieldwork institutions, this research focuses on a need to save 'good journalism' and realise fully the value that still exists in it, and also reflects the urgent need for consideration of how this can be done sustainably. Related literature in the field identifies that the long-held perception of journalism as being 'inherently stable' (Deuze and Witschge 2017) needs to be challenged, given the 'culture of job insecurity' that has come to characterise the contemporary newsroom (Ekdale et al. 2015) and the research focuses on preparing graduates for an environment where further self-sufficiency and independence from the newsroom is required in order to protect the resilience of the profession.

Characteristics of the changing nature of the journalism industry and marketplace

It is evident from the literature in the field and the fieldwork data for this study that the journalism industry is changing fundamentally and now has opportunities to reach people who have never before engaged with it, either as contributors or as consumers. That can be seen as an exciting opportunity, although, as Sparre and Faergemann (2016) highlight, this changed relationship between users and producers also has significant impact on related economic models. With a more empowered audience than ever before, as was emphasised by an associate professor of journalism who was interviewed, the profession needs to establish a new model for revenue generation, as well as how content is generated and gathered.

Emergent new models

The pressures facing the journalism profession point towards the need for news organisations to be more creative about how they are generating revenue, as well as how they're creating and gathering content. Kramp and Loosen (2018) reflect on the changing dynamic between journalists and their audiences in an era of disrupted business models and 'continuous mediatization' (Kramp and Loosen 2018). The resultant expansion of the ways in which journalist and audience communication can occur has inevitably led to a more diverse and dynamic means of interaction (Loosen and Schmidt 2012) which provides a space where new 'deliberative democratic potential' can occur (Collins and Nerlich 2015).

The journalism industry is in a 'precarious' position with lots of individual organisations taking different approaches to monetising content. The disruptive influence of technology and changing business models (Downie and Shudson 2009) also link to this sense of 'precariousness' which Barnes and Scheepers (2017) feel epitomises the work of journalism. Ekdale et al. (2015) focus on the 'culture of job insecurity' that they assert has come to characterise the contemporary newsroom and the varied nature of employment contracts in the journalism industry, including part-time, casual, freelance, temporary positions (Ekdale at al. 2015).

The assertion of Sparre and Faergemann (2016) is that journalism graduates of the future will need to be equipped to embrace the realities of a media environment that is reflected in 'economic restructuring, constant technological developments and job losses' (p266). Deuze and Witschge (2017) also reflect on a new environment and news models with 'participants from different disciplines, with different working arrangements ... different professional identities, along with collaborating publics' (p9). This gradual breakdown of the 'wall between the commercial and editorial parts of news organisations' (Deuze and Witschge 2017, p11) has seen the emergence of the value of enterprise skills. It can be asserted that the radical changes that have occurred within the field of news production and the pressures that have been created can be alleviated only by a very different approach. Focus on the idea of bringing entrepreneurship into journalism makes a lot of sense when there's 'still value in journalism', as asserted by one of my interviewees. Barnes and Scheepers (2017) agree that in order for new innovative business models and projects to emerge and 'save' old journalism, the new journalism landscape will have to be shaped by entrepreneurs.

Extension of the role of journalist

The changing identity of the journalist that is predicted on entrepreneurial skills aligns to Castells' argument (2010) that the relationships of capital and labour are increasingly individualised and characterised by a more temporary work environment, as discussed above. Thus the role of the journalist can be seen as being extended and more self-sufficient. The range of skills required in order to achieve this are perceived to lie within the concept of 'an entrepreneurial journalist'.

Oakley (2014) notes that there is a shift towards stressing the significance of 'enterprise' from an individualistic perspective rather than as a value for organisations. In their work 'Beyond Journalism' (2017), Deuze and Witschge challenge the defined role of a journalist at an ontological level, asserting that journalism requires a perspective of 'becoming' rather than 'being'. Journalists need to have a clear sense of distribution channels, platforms, revenue models and design thinking for what their readers need and where there's an opportunity in the market, thus highlighting the role of the journalist as evolving and expanding in line with the impact of new technologies. Anderson (2011) proposes a new approach in the industry where news production is considered as 'a network that transcends organisational boundaries'.

The need to rethink the framework of traditional news is very apparent, in order to ensure that it becomes more 'participative, open and iterative' (Lewis and Usher 2013). The focus on the interface between journalism and computer science and the notion of open-source culture point towards the need for innovation that goes 'beyond merely swapping tools or tinkering with newsroom culture' (Lewis and Usher 2013, p611). It is asserted that a new framework could 'make journalism more relevant to a participatory, digital culture' that will 'push journalists beyond the newsroom, figuratively and literally' (Lewis and Usher 2013, p609).

New skills needs from journalism educators

The spirit of 'experimentation' and innovation and embracing change required of the journalism industry is also necessary in journalism educators in order to encourage a spirit of community-centred collaboration (Mensing 2010). It can be asserted that journalism education, too, has been influenced by the constraints of the newsroom, and Deuze and Witschge (2017) reflect that the traditional structure of the industry has been dominant over both employment and the organisation of the industry, and how we prepare and educate those entering it. They believe that journalism employees now require a 'toolkit that looks at the field as a moving object and as a dynamic set of practices and expectations – a profession in a permanent process of becoming' (Deuze and Witschge 2017, p13).

One interviewee, with an Associate Dean of Innovation role, asserts the rapidly changing environment calls for a broader skills base in graduates in order to be able to shape the direction of the news industry. Certainly, the literature supports the idea that the model of journalism education has remained unchanged for too long (Mensing 2010) and is overly characterised by the traditional 'age of the reporter' (Carey 2000), and a new approach to what are considered the norms, practices and values is required, thus insisting that journalism educators should 'reimagine the profession' (Glasser 2006). Having a sense of adventure and the willingness to take risks will be critical, and journalism course leader who was interviewed also comments on the need for graduates to be able to not only respond to change but also to help to lead it.

A 'Journalists at Work' survey (2018), which was overseen in the UK by the main industry accreditation body the National Council for the Training of Journalists (NCTJ) and sent to both journalists and industry bodies highlighted the turbulent time that has been faced by the journalism profession in the UK during the last two decades and its consequential fundamental change, as it has dealt with the impact of mobile devices and the internet on its business model (Murphy 2019). This point was reiterated at the Society of Editors 'Future of News' conference, where BBC journalist Ros Atkins (2022) highlights the need for newsrooms to 'constantly innovate, re-structure and produce content in a format that audiences want to consume it' (Atkins 2022) in order to ensure they main relevant to the future of news dissemination. The need for self-sufficiency in this changing environment is also reflected by Storey et al. (2005) who expect journalists to be 'workers as more adaptable, flexible and willing to move between activities and assignments and to take responsibility for their own actions and their successes and failures' (p1036).

It is argued that in order for a media system to re-emerge which both makes a significant contribution to the democratic process and is commercially viable, a more flexible and innovative approach is needed within the workforce. It is advocated that journalism educators should move their curriculum from preparing graduates for an 'industry-conceived model' (Mensing 2010) to a 'community-oriented model' (Borden 2007), changing the journalist role to being that of 'reporter, editor and facilitator' within the context of the community.

Pavlik (2013) asserts that in response to this and to safeguard the industry of the future, a disruptively innovative curriculum is required within higher education to prepare graduates for a future which is increasingly individualised and needs to be more 'participative, open and iterative' (Lewis and Usher 2013). The integrating of practice beyond the newsroom reflects that engaging collaborative enterprise skills are vital to sustainable journalism practice.

Defining 'entrepreneurship'

Enterprise skills thus emerge as being significant in their potential contribution to ensure the sustainability of the industry and address the need to make traditional newsgathering a more participative and iterative process. The creation of an enhanced and dynamic toolkit for the contemporary journalist who will be self-sufficient and can operate in a more fluid environment of experimentation both within and outside the traditional newsroom is identified as an urgent matter. An Associate Dean who was interviewed emphasised that the delivery of entrepreneurship was about 'innovation and creativity in unusual spaces', which can be 'inside or outside a company'. The perspective of another interviewee, with a senior lecturer and course leader role, was similar as he defined entrepreneurship broadly and in relation to a 'higher order' approach to creating flexible individuals with a wide variety of career paths.

Indeed, at an ontological level, entrepreneurship education can be seen as 'opening people's minds' or 'extending their knowledge' (Fayolle and Klandt 2006). Fayolle and Gailly (2008) say the word entrepreneurship is 'polysemous' and can describe attitudes such as 'autonomy, creativity, innovation, risk-taking or the act of venture creation' (p572). A senior lecturer and course leader, who was interviewed, also emphasised the significance of 'trial and error' and that feeling comfortable with this mindset would allow for experimentation of 'different routes' to audiences that haven't been sought before, and which might ultimately lead to monetisation of content in new ways.

Another courser leader also challenges the core of the journalistic identity, suggesting the need for a paradigm shift away from finding stories which are shared, and then the journalist moving onto the next piece of news. He alludes to the need for 'a different connection' which encompasses links within communities outside newsrooms, as is noted above, and harnesses a wider range of resources to build a different level of relationship. Thus the concept of new partnership emerges, which draws on the notion of being enterprising as sharing creative activity more widely in order to add value.

Klerk (2015) builds on the work undertaken in relation to 'entrepreneurial bricolage' as using existing resources to create new opportunities (Baker and Nelson 2015), and uses a new sub-term 'collaborative bricolage' which focuses on creative industries practitioners taking advantage of their 'connections and networks for collaborations, creative work, co-innovation' (p836). Essig (2015) also acknowledges the significance of entrepreneurial bricolage as she applies Sarasvathy's Effectuation Theory (2001) where the assumption is that the 'means are as given' and the significance relates to the impact and outcome that can be created with that set of means. She concludes that the 'mediating structure' which links the 'means' to the 'ends' (Essig 2015, p242) is the process of intermediation which is characterised by entrepreneurial action and notes that further research is required to understand better the structure or activities that embody that action (Essig 2015). One of the course leaders interviewed asserts that by building on existing connections in communities and realising the potential for a different, more reciprocal and deeper type of relationship, the journalist can begin to add further value to the links that are already made. These links and community building, and the related networking, enterprising behaviour, could be seen to add significantly to the democratic process of the news industry and the role of the journalist within it.

Embedding entrepreneurial skills and 'mindset' into the journalism curriculum

An 'exchange of thinking' that is also called for by Kearney and Harris (2013) identifies the need for interlinking the creative and entrepreneurial disciplines, through the development and delivery of a curriculum that meets the needs of today's journalism industry. Research in the fieldwork institutions reflects that while it's still important to teach all the 'baseline skills', like writing, interviewing, thinking critically and presenting a story, it's also key to teach students a broader set of skills that will allow the ability to find new opportunities and problem solve. One interviewee, who was an associate dean of innovation, asserted that her students had to learn to 'dance with uncertainty'. Although reflecting that journalism delivery that embeds entrepreneurship is 'still in its infancy', Willemsen et al. (2021) assert the importance of the 'passionate and improvisational nature of doing innovative journalistic work' (p1487).

The significance of 'mindset'

Concerned that the existing focus of higher education is privileging the needs of industry rather than journalism graduates, a senior lecturer and programme director at one of the fieldwork sites points out that in fact 'the way journalism is changing isn't simply a matter of additional skills'. The enterprising problem-solving approach of Barnes and Scheepers (2017) also highlights the significance of a 'non-predictive learning mindset' instead of a 'predictive, getting it right mindset'. This is based on the notion that entrepreneurship is about not relying on assumptions because knowledge required to succeed or to move things on cannot be predicted in advance (Kerr, Nanda and Rhodes-Kropf 2014); thus related learning must occur through an action-focused approach and necessitates a discovery mindset for graduates (Barnes and Scheepers 2017). Carey and Naudin (2006) reflect on the importance of the role of higher education in instilling 'entrepreneurial spirit' in students of creative disciplines and assert that this is achieved by 'embedding attitudes and including entrepreneurial activities in project-based work', which is characterised by independence, flexibility, and adaptability (Pollard and Wilson 2013).

Curriculum design: co-curricular approaches

As is noted by Murphy (2019), today's journalism educators must plan for the 'ever-changing' future of the industry and organise a curriculum that keeps 'relevant with the technological, audience and business model changes' (p248). Whilst highlighting the ongoing debate between a focus on job skills and intellectual education, Frost (2018) also emphasises the need for journalism educators to prepare students to be flexible and adaptable for an unpredictable future. The Journalist at Work 2018 survey (NCTJ) also emphasised the need for graduates to be prepared for careers in freelancing or in roles with short-term contracts and to be able to work as 'multimedia journalists', that is, working on more than one platform (Murphy 2019).

In terms of appropriate curriculum design and with the importance, as highlighted by an associate dean of innovation, of allowing their journalism students 'a pipeline of experiences and exposures', one of the institutions featured in this research focuses on creating entrepreneurial opportunities beyond the formal curriculum to enhance their adaptability, some of which does, however, interface with credit-bearing assessment, with students being engaged in competitions, live projects and interactions with the university's central 'incubator' unit, which provides a separate space for experimentation and creativity. Students therefore interact with each other in the space, as well as having the opportunity to interface with and contribute to real business opportunities. The work of Neilsen and Stovang (2015) in the development of their DesUni model, 'a tool for designing teaching using design methods', highlights the need for '"real-life" problems' to be encountered by students and envisages the related learning as a contextualised process, which does not focus on the student alone, but is socially constructed. This flexibility between formal and informal modes of study is seen to incentivise student engagement.

In relation to this, it can be noted that Neilsen and Stovang (2015) focus on how knowledge can be defined and used in order to facilitate students to 'act and think in a designerly way'. In addition to asserting that prior knowledge should not be viewed as 'something that there is, or has been' and that 'new knowledge emerges from discovery and exploration', a focus on tacit knowledge is also key to the DesUni model, and Neilsen and Stovang (2015) view it as 'the students' ideas, values and needs', pointing out that 'his or her imagination represents an almost boundless source of knowledge that students are not aware that they have' (p985). The notion that it is possible to develop 'tacit knowledge' by the means of 'facilitation, shared learning, social interaction and brainstorming' (Neilsen and Stovang 2015) is also echoed in the work of Rae (2005). He asserts that through actively engaging and participating in 'social and industry networks' and experiences and the relationships that come from them, it's possible to 'develop intuition' (Rae 2005, p328).

Curriculum design: blended, less constrained approach to subject delivery

The breaking of barriers, in relation to curricular and co-curricular delivery of journalism, plays an interesting role at another of the fieldwork institutions. In order to enhance and build on a flexible skills base, one journalism educator facilitates the ability of his students to be able to move seamlessly between different work streams, including video, audio, text, data, live reporting, and thus encouraging their ability to adapt to change. This links to the work of Barnes and Scheepers (2017) and their assertion that an 'entrepreneurial problem-solving' approach involves experimentation and a 'non-predictive mindset, as opposed to a predictive, *getting it right* mindset' (p98) and a 'discovery mindset'. In order to navigate their way in an industry which is impacted by significant technological change and to 're-imagine' its future, journalism graduates need to question and challenge 'traditional normative value judgments' (Mensing and Ryfe 2013).

In their exploration of the creation of 'new knowledge', Neilsen and Stovang (2015) discuss how, through its being moved into other contexts and combined in new opportunities, 'prior knowledge' can be transformed. They emphasise that interdisciplinary approaches are critical to this happening, in alignment with the 'interdisciplinary reality facing entrepreneurs' (p985). The resultant new knowledge, which relates to the DesUni model and design thinking, emerges from this process of experimentation and discovery (Neilsen and Stovang 2015).

The pragmatism that underpins the creation of the DesUni model (Neilsen and Stovang 2015) allows the understanding of the shift from discovering the present to envisaging the future, building on a design thinking approach, which reflects that

> The transition from one learning area to a new area must be considered as a gradual one and take place with awareness of the existence of other areas. (p984)

This links strongly to Sarasvathy's similarly pragmatic 'Effectuation Theory' (2001). She argues that through using 'means', including the use of contingency planning, and making the most of alliances and partnerships, it's possible to control an unpredictable future, rather than actually try to predict it. Sarasvathy argues that by building bridges and finding links between the range of means, it's easier to deal with challenges and uncertainty (2001).

One fieldwork site builds strongly on their interdisciplinary approaches with an embedded entrepreneurship module being delivered across their creative sector curriculum to courses including journalism, fine art, heritage studies, museum studies and music. They emphasise the significance of these 'creative clusters' in encouraging truly creative ideas to emerge from 'different perspectives and different ideas and different skills, knowledge and understanding' and thus prioritise trying to avoid being 'siloed'. Sarasvathy (2001) highlights the value of engaging with partners in order to capture different and surprising perspectives. She stresses the significance of allowing a project to evolve and change due to the influence of new relationships, in an iterative manner, and calls this kind of partnership 'the crazy quilt principle' (2003) due to it being characterised by brightly coloured and quirky patterns.

Curriculum design: risk-taking

Duening (2010), in creating five minds for an entrepreneurial future, builds on the work of Gardner's five minds for the future (2008) and includes 'risk-managing mind' as linking to 'creation' and 'innovation'. Wilson (2009) asserts that graduates are able to display such attributes only by ensuring more 'experimental' approaches to learning and by instilling a 'risk-taking' attitude in students, as is encouraged as being significant in the delivery of entrepreneurial education (Gibb 2005).

Creating a 'safe environment' in which students can actually benefit from things going wrong can enable innovation (Shank and Neaman 2001). Sarasvathy (2001) claims that progressing projects using the 'means' available, reduces their failure rate, and so it's important that students make iterative steps forward and reflect as part of the process on how they can adapt and change their work as they progress, rather than work towards an unachievable goal.

Barnes and Scheepers (2017) note that this focus on failing as contributing significantly to the learning process is contrary to approaches which could be considered as being traditional in educational pedagogy and, as such, 'provides a unique environment for exploring media work and reimagining journalism' (p99). This approach and experience can also be seen to build resilience in students and enhance their 'entrepreneurial self-efficacy' (Barnes and Scheepers 2017) as they see that they can progress their ideas and projects, in spite of small setbacks.

Embedding an entrepreneurial constructivist approach in journalism education pedagogy

Given that 'entrepreneurial learning is essentially experiential' (Rae 2007), it is significant to investigate how curriculum design and delivery can achieve this. There appears to be no universal pedagogy for teaching entrepreneurship, particularly in relation to the media industries and journalism (Kearney and Harris 2013; Fayolle and Gailly 2008).

External engagement and community networking

Deuze and Witschge (2017) highlight the significant work of journalism higher education, on an international basis, and the contribution of courses focusing on entrepreneurialism in preparing students for the future of the industry, where they will be expected to 'monetize content in innovative ways, connect to publics in interactive new formats, grasp opportunities, and respond to (and shape) its environment' (p11) Wahl-Jorgensen (2009) emphasises the significance of journalism academics paying more 'attention to places, spaces, practices and people at the margins of [a] spatially delimited news production universe' (p23) and criticises the 'newsroom-centricity' of journalism education. It is suggested that educators concentrate on a 'dynamic' vision for journalism and are less focused on the limited and routinised nature of the newsroom (Deuze and Witschge 2017). Anderson (2011) proposes 'blowing up the newsroom' and looking instead at news production as a 'network' that breaks free of the traditional boundaries; and Caplan et al. (2020) emphasise the need to create 'media projects and products that serve communities on and off campus'.

The assertion that entrepreneurial learning helps to prepare students for imagining a journalism industry for the future, not the past, is shared by the fieldwork institutions and their attempts to engage the community reflects the significance and value of embedding 'social networking capacity' (Bridgstock et al. 2011, p126). One journalism course leader makes engaging a 'wider community of practice' central to his delivery, describing it as 'networking and partly about life-long learning'. This links to the assertions of the need to find new structures beyond the newsroom, and also to Sarasvathy's principle of using the 'means' that exist and are essentially at the disposal of the students (Sarasvathy 2001). One of her categories emerges from the question 'Whom do I know?' (2001), which links clearly to 'social networks' and a pragmatic perspective of using connections to move forward.

Duening (2010) emphasises the entrepreneurial mind for the future as linking to 'resiliency' and 'effectuation', and as noted by Essig (2013) these can be built by the interface of the student to the larger community. In contrast, trying to address such areas in the traditional classroom would teach students about resilience and spotting an opportunity, but not how to '*be* resilient' (Essig 2013).

Love and Wenger (1998) make the case that engagement in 'communities of practice' allows student learning to emerge iteratively. They reject the concept of it being essential for learning to be 'decontexualised from practice' to become 'academic'. This links strongly to Gibb's assertion that 'entrepreneurial learning involves emphasis upon "how to" and "who with" and that some knowledge should be offered on a "need to know" basis' (p253). One senior lecturer interviewed advocates the importance of embedding student-led networking and community interaction in the curriculum, noting that 'the only demand made on projects is that they have to have some kind of public engagement' and also that they are entirely devised by the students, saying 'I don't devise projects for them', which is a bold step.

Nielsen and Stovang (2015) also assert the significance of independent, active learning, noting that the role of the 'DesUni teacher is to "facilitate the students" wicked problem-solving process, by exploring and co-creating problem and solution spaces with the students' (p985). They see the solution of wicked problems as involving learning-by-doing, engaging 'internal and external stakeholders' and the whole process being continually iterative. The resultant skills development includes those of 'autonomy, creativity, innovation and risk-taking' which relate to the 'polysemous' nature of entrepreneurship (Fayolle and Gailly 2008). Barnes and Scheepers (2017) note that it's important for 'entrepreneurs to be prepared to adapt, co-create with interested stakeholders' (p99) for the result of an improved solution to a problem. And, Deuze and Witschge (2017) argue incredibly persuasively for 'an ontology of journalism beyond individuals and institutions', which responds to the fact that journalism takes place in increasingly networked settings, and there is an urgent need for education 'to broaden the focus of journalism studies' (Deuze and Witschge 2017, p12).

Student-led delivery

Given the 'experiential' nature of entrepreneurial learning (Rae 2007), it was evident that the fieldwork institutions were making efforts to focus on the learning process, rather than the teaching process, with the delivery of theory being linked to and led by its practical application. Bridgstock (2012) asserts that a significant part of the 'entrepreneurial artist identity development involves experiential project-based work' (p132), thus allowing further co-creation, negotiation and idea generation under the facilitation and guidance of the 'teacher'.

Barnes and Scheepers (2017) also note the significance of viewing entrepreneurship as using unexpected surprises to 'create new opportunities iteratively moving the venture forward' (p100). Davies, Fidler and Gorbis (2011) have highlighted 'novel and adaptive thinking' as a critical skill for graduates to survive in a quickly changing external environment and Barner and Scheepers (2017) note that encouraging students to 'view disruption and change as an opportunity and providing them with a process to adapt and change' (p100) will allow them to contribute significantly to the fast-changing media environment.

Deuze and Witschge (2017) assert that '"Beyond journalism" is an approach to journalism that considers it as a dynamic object of study' (p13). Their work points to the need to go 'beyond boundaries [being] what is needed in this time of flux' (p13). The fieldwork institutions examined go some way to addressing this through collaborative and iterative project delivery and experimentation; bold approaches to fully student-led constructivist delivery; broad canvas, blending of subject areas within modules; and in their steps to separate the handling of journalistic content from platform and delivery mode, thus preparing students for an unpredictable future.

Teaching and assessing 'the process'

As discussed above, the flexibility of the curriculum design is a significant theme in the outcomes of this research. This is also reflected in its delivery with a focus on 'the process' itself, rather than content or assessment outcome, with reflections on taking a non-prescriptive approach to tools, media or skills. Interviewee 5 identifies a deliberate focus on moving away from a specific list of outcomes to a more flexible perspective in the 'storytelling' concept, where the focus is not on teaching tools but on a range of narrative devices. The 'discovery mindset' that is advocated by Barnes and Scheepers (2017) for 're-imagining' journalism could be said to be enhanced by an education setting 'where graduates can explore the future of media without being bound by traditional normative value judgments' (Mensing and Ryfe 2013).

Barnes and Scheepers (2017) note that 'by encouraging students to view disruption and change as an opportunity and providing them with a process to adapt and change, it empowers them to respond to the volatility in the environment' (p100). This links strongly to a curriculum that is characterised by experimentation, with a focus on developing the 'discovery mindset' of the students and also adheres to Nielsen and Strovang's assertion of the importance of allowing the student to 'take the main control of the problem space' (2015, p985). Dziuban et al. (2004) also emphasise that students learn better if there is a focus on 'student-centred instructions'. Löbler (2006) notes that it is important to help students to 'develop their abilities into competencies' (p32).

This approach can also be seen as important within assessment too. Löbler (2006) asserts that students should never feel that they are being 'tested' by the lecturer. Her research reflects that if students instead are guided through the assessment process with questions, they will be led to their own answers and, having gone through the process, will be able to make their case more effectively and critically (Löbler 2006). This approach is supported by the work of Nielsen and Stovang, whose DesUni model 'works with processes of constantly turning "what is" and "what has been" upside down' (2015, p986).

The focus on teaching and assessing the process demands the academic role to be one of opening up ways of new thinking and to encourage the student to address the problem from different perspectives (Löbler 2006). This is contrary to the traditional approach of assessment strategies which 'normally assume that lecturers know what the students need to learn, and how it may be accomplished' (Penaluna and Penaluna 2009, p722).

Conclusion

In acknowledging that it is no longer possible to merely impart a skills 'toolkit' that will prepare students for future careers as journalists due to fast-changing technologies and new business models, the research shared in this chapter recognises that it is significant to journalism education that students instead 'recognise the kind of skills they might want to acquire'. It therefore concludes that it is incumbent on educators to ensure that journalism graduates enter the industry with the appropriate mindset to navigate the environment, which they will negotiate and lead, and thus contribute to the sustainability of the industry of the future.

The result is a repositioned role of the journalism educator, as a facilitator of the exchange of ideas and inspiration, allowing students to benefit from external networks and communities, the input of industry 'experts' to the curriculum as mentors and advisers, the insights of fellow team and classmates, as well as the audience and their role in not only responding to but also in helping to create news. It suggests that this new paradigm must be embraced by journalism educators in order to reshape the profession of the future and to allow graduates to help to lead the industry through moving away from traditional approaches to news gathering and reporting.

The analysis of findings gathered from field sites, semi-structured interviews and a review of literature highlights that the creation of a 'reconceptualised' journalist, as someone who can respond to the pressures in the current environment and lead the industry of the future, is realised through specific characteristics of pedagogy and curriculum that contribute to an enterprising mindset.

References

Anderson, C.W., 2011. Blowing up the newsroom: Ethnography in an age of distributed journalism. *In*: Domingo, D., and Paterson, C. (eds.), *Making Online News*. New York: Peter Lang, 151–160.

Atkins, R., 2022. *The Future of News*. Society of Editors Conference, Mary Ward House, London. 11 May 2022. Available at: www.societyofeditors.org/soe_news/newsrooms-must-constantly-innovate-to-secure-their-future-says-bbcs-ros-atkins/

Baker, T., and Nelson, R.E., 2005. Creating something from nothing: Resource construction through entrepreneurial bricolage. *Administrative Science Quarterly*, 50 (3), 329–366.

Barnes, R., and Johanna de Villiers Scheepers, M., 2017. Tackling uncertainty for journalism graduates. *Journalism Practice*, 12 (1), 94–114.

Borden, S., 2007. *Journalism as Practice: MacIntyre, Virtue Ethics and the Press*, Burlington, VT: Ashgate Publishing.

Bridgstock, R., 2012. Not a dirty word: Arts entrepreneurship and higher education. *Arts and Humanities in Higher Education*, 12 (2–3), 122–137.

Bridgstock, R., Dawson, S., and Hearn, G., 2011. Cultivating innovation through social relationships: A qualitative study of outstanding Australian innovators in science, technology and the creative industries. *In:* Mesquita, A. (ed.), *Technology for Creativity and Innovation: Tools, Techniques and Applications*. Hershey: IGI-Global, 104–120.

Caplan, J., Kanigel, R., and Tsakarestou, B., 2020. Entrepreneurial journalism: Teaching innovation and nurturing an entrepreneurial mindset. *Journalism & Mass Communication Educator*, 75 (1), 27–32.

Carey, J., 2000. Some personal notes on journalism education. *Journalism*, 1 (1), 12–23.

Carey, C., and Naudin, A., 2006. Enterprise curriculum for creative industries students: An exploration of current attitudes and issues. *Education & Training* 48 (7), 518–531.

Castells, M., 2010. *The Rise of the Network Society*. 3rd edn. Cambridge, MA; Oxford: Blackwell.

Collins, L., and Nerlich, B., 2015. Examining user comments for deliberative democracy. *Environmental Communication*, 9 (2), 189–207.

Davies, A., Fidler, D., & Gorbis. D., 2011. *Future Work Skills 2020*. Palo Alto, CA: Institute for the Future for University of Phoenix Research Institute.

Deuze, M., and Witschge, T., 2016. What journalism becomes. *In:* Peters, C., and Broersma, M. (eds.), *Rethinking Journalism Again*. London: Routledge, 115–130.

Deuze, M., and Witschge, T., 2017. Beyond journalism: Theorizing the transformation of journalism. *Journalism*, 19 (2), 1–17.

Downie, L., and Schudson, M., 2009. The reconstruction of American journalism. *Columbia Journalism Review*, 1–21. Nov–Dec 2009.

Duening, T., 2010. Five minds for the entrepreneurial future. *The Journal of Entrepreneurship*, 19 (1), 1–22.

Dziuban, C.D., Patsy, M., and Joel, L.H., 2004. Higher education, blended learning, and the generations: Knowledge is power-No more. Research Initiative for Teaching Effectiveness, University of Central Florida.

Ekdale, B., Tully, S.H., and Singer J.B., 2015. Newswork within a culture of job insecurity. *Journalism Practice*, 9 (3), 383–398.

Essig, L., 2013. Frameworks for educating the artist of the future: Teaching habits of mind for arts entrepreneurship. *Artivate: A Journal of Entrepreneurship in the Arts*, 1 (2), 65–77.

Essig, L., 2015. Means and ends: A theory framework for understanding entrepreneurship in the US arts and culture sector. *The Journal of Arts Management, Law, and Society*, 45 (2), 227–246.

Fayolle, A., and Gailly G., 2008. From craft to science: Teaching models and learning processes in entrepreneurship education. *Journal of European Training*, 32 (7), 569–593.

Fayolle, A., and Klandt H., 2006. Effect and counter-effect of entrepreneurship education: New lenses for new practical and academic questions. *In:* Fayolle, A., and Klandt, H. (eds.), *International Entrepreneurship Education*. Aldershot: Edward Elgar, 10–17.

Frost, C., 2018. Five challenges facing journalism education in the UK. *Asia Pacific Media Education*, 28, 153–163.

Gibb, A., 2005. The future of entrepreneurship education. Determining the basis for coherent policy and practice. *In:* Kyro, P., and Carrier, C. (eds.), *The Dynamics of Learning Entrepreneurship in a Cross-cultural University Context,* University of Tampere Research Centre for Vocational and Professional Education, 44–68.

Glasser, T., 2006. Journalism studies and the education of journalists. *Journalism Studies*, 7 (1), 146–149.

Kearney, G., and Harris, P., 2013. Supporting the creative industries: The rationale for an exchange of thinking between the art and business schools. *International Journal of Education Through Art*, 9 (3), 311–326.

Kerr, W.R., Nanda, R., and Rhodes-Kropf, M., 2014. Entrepreneurship as experimentation. *The Journal of Economic Perspectives*, 28 (3), 25–48.

Klerk, S., 2015. The creative industries: An entrepreneurial bricolage perspective. *Management Decision*, 53 (4), 828–842.

Kramp, L., and Loosen, W., 2018. The transformation of journalism: From changing newsroom cultures to new communicative orientation? *In*: Hepp, A. (ed.), *Communicative Figurations.* Frankfurt: Springer International.

Lewis, S.C., and Usher, N., 2013. Open source and journalism: Toward new frameworks for imagining news innovation. *Media, Culture and Society*, 15 (5), 602–619.

Löbler, H., 2006. Learning entrepreneurship from a constructivist perspective. *Technology Analysis & Strategic Management*, 18 (1), 19–38.

Loosen, W., and Schmidt, J-H., 2012. (Re) Discovering the audience: The relationship between journalism and audience in networked digital media. *Information, Communication and Society*, 15 (6), 867–887.

Love, J., and Wenger, E., 1998. *Situated Learning – Legitimate Peripheral Participation.* Cambridge: Cambridge University Press.

Mensing, D., 2010. Rethinking [again] the future of journalism. *Journalism Studies*, 11 (3), 511–523.

Mensing, D., and Ryfe, D., 2013. Blueprint for change: From the teaching hospital to the entrepreneurial model of journalism education. *The Official Research Journal of the International Symposium on Online Journalism*, 3 (2), 26–44.

Murphy, C., 2019. Changing by the click: The professional development of UK journalists. *Education Sciences*, 9, 248–249.

Neilson, S.L., and Stovang, P., 2015. DesUni: University entrepreneurship education through design thinking. *Education and Training*, 55 (8/9), 977–991.

Oakley, K. 2014. Go-od work? Rethinking cultural Entrepreneurship. *In:* Bilton C, and Cummings, S. (eds), *Handbook of Management and Creativity*, Cheltenham: Elgar, 145–159.

Pavlik, J., 2013. A vision for transformative leadership: Rethinking journalism and mass communication education for the 21st century. *Journalism & Mass Communication Educator*, 68 (3), 211–221.

Penaluna, A., and Penaluna, K., 2009. Assessing creativity: Drawing from the experience of the UK's creative design educators. *Education and Training*, 51 (8/9), 718–732.

Pollard, V., and Wilson, E., 2013. The 'entrepreneurial mindset' in creative and performing arts Higher Education in Australia. *Artivate: A Journal of Entrepreneurship in the Arts*, 3 (1), 3–22.

Rae, D., 2007. *Entrepreneurship: From Opportunity to Action.* New York: Palgrave Macmillan.

Rae, D., 2005. Entrepreneurial learning: A narrative-based conceptual model. *Journal of Small Business and Enterprise Development*, 12 (3), 323–335.

Sarasvathy, S.D., 2001. Causation and effectuation: Towards a theoretical shift from economic inevitability to entrepreneurial contingency. *Academy of Management Review*, 26 (2), 243–263.

Shank, R., and Neaman, A., 2001. Motivation and failure in educational systems design. *In:* Forbus, K., and Feltovich, P. (eds.), *Smart Machines in Education*. Cambridge, MA: MIT Press, 37–69.

Sparre, K., and Faergemann, H.M., 2016. Towards a broader concept of entrepreneurial journalism education. *Journalism Practice*, 10 (2), 266–285.

Spilsbury, M., 2018. Journalists at work. Their views on training, recruitment and conditions. London: National Council for the Training of Journalists. Retrieved from National Council for the Training of Journalists website: www. nctj. com/downloadlibrary/JaW%20Report, *202018*.

Storey, J., Salaman, G., and Platman, K., 2005. Living with enterprise in an enterprise economy: Freelance and contract workers in the media. *Human Relations*, 58 (8), 1033–1054.

Wahl-Jorgensen, K., 2009. News production, ethnography and power: On the challenges of newsroom-ethnicity. *In:* Bird, E. (ed.), *The Anthropology of News and Journalism: Global Perspectives*. Bloomington, IN: Indiana University Press, 21–35.

Willemsen, S., Witschge, T., and Sauer, S., 2021. Improvisation and entrepreneurial journalism: Reimagining innovation. *Journalism Studies*, 22 (11), 1487–1503.

Wilson, N., 2009. Learning to manage creativity: An occupational hazard for the UK's creative industries. *Creative Industries Journal*, 2 (2), 179–190.

10

MY STORY

Journalism for and by young people to prevent the recruitment of children and teenagers by non-state armed groups in Colombia

Mathew Charles

Introduction: Journalism in the Colombian context

Journalism can and does inspire change. Some forms of journalism even appeal directly for action. Such advocacy models convert the reporter from a mere bystander and communicator of information into a participant and motivator, whose task becomes to call for and foster some kind of social transformation. In Colombia, for example, the absence of effective institutions within what might be described as the country's 'alternative social order', loosely defined by entrenched corruption and the normalisation of protracted violence (Ramírez, 2010), local journalists, in particular, often become 'surrogates of the state' (Charles, 2020). It is not uncommon for a reporter to assume the role of police officer, judge and prosecutor, investigating and exposing the criminal and corrupt, while simultaneously providing assistance for their victims. Fellow citizens become 'constituents', who require support and guidance (Charles, 2019). This is described by Arroyave and Barrios (2012: 4) as 'a special type of advocacy reporting', which 'goes beyond normal news coverage' to 'taking part in solving community problems'. It seems appropriate, therefore, to use journalism as a method to prevent the recruitment of children and teenagers by non-state armed groups (NSAGs) in the country.

Since the 2016 peace agreement between the Colombian state and the leftist Revolutionary Armed Forces of Colombia (FARC) rebels, it is widely accepted and even expected that journalists carry the responsibility to promote peace (Charles, 2020). This so-called peace journalism sets out to empower the marginalised and seek common ground to 'unify rather than divide societies' (Tehranian, 2002: 80), but in the Global North, this approach has been heavily criticised, particularly by war correspondents from legacy media organisations, who argue that journalists need to preserve their neutral roles of 'observers' rather than partisan 'players' during conflict (Loyn, 2007). Within the Colombian context, however, local

DOI: 10.4324/9781003301028-13

journalism, in particular, has been charged with the construction of a community narrative, perceived as essential to reconciliation through its efforts to build or repair fractured social bonds (Ripley, 2009). It is argued that this emotionally literate style of reporting can identify conflict structures and 'patterns of conflict resolutions' (Howard, 2009: 11) through its potential to 'promote participation, foster social dialogue, and forge empathy and understanding' (Howard, 2009: 16).

My Story: journalism for and by young people (My Story) is a peacebuilding project funded by the UK Arts and Humanities Research Council (AHRC) to specifically prevent the illegal recruitment of children and teenagers by NSAGs in Colombia. Since 2016, as several resurgent armed factions seek to fill the criminal void left behind by the FARC guerrillas, children and teenagers have become targets for these armed groups seeking to replenish and expand their ranks (Charles, 2022).

Previous research has shown how many young people who join NSAGs in Colombia do so because they perceive it as the only solution within contexts of marginalisation and poverty (Charles, 2021). Life in the ranks of a NSAG is perceived as providing escape, projecting power or even guaranteeing survival. The aim of My Story is therefore to challenge and transform these misguided perceptions through the promotion of what we call Peace Skills (defined specifically as self-awareness; self-management; the effective management of interpersonal relationships; social consciousness and responsible decision-making). The project uses journalism as a means to explore and build capacity to employ these skills, transforming perceptions of the self and the future among children and teenagers considered at risk.

Transformation in this sense constitutes an experience in which alternative imaginaries are encouraged, formed and explored. For the young project participants, My Story and the transformative journalism upon which it is based develops socio-emotional competences, enhances employment opportunities and encourages a more positive outlook on life.

The Peace Skills we have established are based on and adapted from the Life Skills model formulated by the World Health Organisation (WHO), defined as 'cognitive, emotional, interpersonal and social skills that enable individuals to deal effectively with the challenges of everyday life' (WHO, 2009). Such skills teach young people how to deal effectively and non-violently with conflict. The WHO argues that the participation and performance of children and teenagers in school can be improved by developing these skills, which, in turn, will increase their chances of finding employment and ultimately protect them from violence.

The young participants in our project are children and teenagers considered at risk of recruitment by NSAGs in some of Colombia's most violent communities. The project is divided into seven regional bureaux and through the creation of a news website,[1] the young journalists report on their lives, as well as on the lives of their peers and their communities.

The young participants live with the daily threat of violence and of being recruited. Their high-risk communities are characterised by the permanent presence of NSAGs, where rebels, paramilitaries or gang members live among the population. In these places, the children and teenagers who participate in our project are likely to have relatives involved in NSAGs and to be in regular contact with guerrillas, paramilitaries or other criminals. Young people themselves may be directly involved in criminal activities. In such a climate, it is therefore not possible to talk openly about recruitment as to do so would put the lives of the participants, the researchers and those who support us at risk. Instead, the goal is to work to promote Peace Skills and transform a young person's perception of their personal circumstances and their future life chances.

For the young reporters involved, journalism therefore constitutes a tool not only to explore their community, but also their place within it. Journalism becomes a vehicle to build confidence, self-esteem and general self-efficacy, challenging and provoking reflection about protracted violence and the structures which underpin it. This transformative journalism shapes young citizens by promoting their self-awareness and social consciousness, and by strengthening their resilience and shaping their socio-emotional resistance against the illegal recruitment by NSAGs.

My Story is firmly anchored within the traditions of participatory action research (PAR), which emphasise how the research process should be experienced as transformative, based in principles of social justice, non-hierarchical relationships and reciprocal learning between participants and researchers. Participative or artistic methods, in particular, are invariably considered an important space for critical reflection and for 'imagining alternative ways forward' (Crossick and Kaszynska, 2016: 118).

This chapter explains the My Story project in detail. Subsequent sections briefly explore the importance of news and journalism for young people and outline the project's specific narrative themes, which guide our model of transformative journalism. First, however, it depicts the violent context for the tens of thousands of Colombian youths living on the country's margins.

Living with conflict and the threat of recruitment by non-state armed groups

Despite the peace process in Colombia, many marginalised communities continue to live with protracted violence as the conflict reconfigures along new localised wars over territory and access to illicit economies. The number of youngsters being recruited by NSAGs in Colombia has been rising steadily since the 2016 peace accord. Colombia's Human Rights Ombudsman issued 165 alerts between 2017 and 2020, highlighting situations in which children and teenagers have been forced or enticed to take up arms. The numbers have risen to levels not seen since before the country's peace process began in 2012 (Charles, 2022).

Colombia's sustained violence shapes 'how individuals and communities perceive themselves, construct memories and identity, and create their shared beliefs and values' (Dancey and Morrison, 2019: 34). A positive outlook among teenagers living with protracted conflict can therefore founder in these contexts of crisis and uncertainty because 'the perceived irreconcilability of intractable conflicts is conceptually tied to the lack of hope for resolution' (Leshem et al., 2016: 303). Emotions in violent settings are often dominated by pessimism and fear (Jarymowicz and Bar-Tal, 2006: 373), which can have severe and negative consequences for both the individual and the wider community. For children and teenagers, in particular, research has shown how such hopelessness, pessimism and fear has a damaging impact on a child's self-esteem and contributes to low self-efficacy (Charles, 2021).

In these contexts of marginalisation, defined largely by abject poverty, violence and a general lack of opportunities for the young, schools in particular become spaces in which shared negative outlooks develop 'a collective emotional orientation' based on distrust and hopelessness (Jarymowicz and Bar-Tal, 2006: 374). In addition to low self-efficacy, this can create negative identities, which ultimately restrict a young person's ability to imagine a different future. Such negative identities, which embody insecure or harmful relationships (among other factors), are in contrast to more positive identities, shaped by expectations of success, supportive relationships, educational and employment opportunities and positive community interactions (Johns et al., 2017).

In contexts of war, children and teenagers learn to see guns, uniforms and military vehicles as symbols of authority and sometimes even as 'cool'. For a child from a poor, rural community, joining a NSAG increases access not only to clothing, food and healthcare, but also to a sense of respect not attainable through civilian means (Wessells, 2006). The excitement associated with wielding power can be highly seductive to children and teenagers, who seek escape from the tedium of life on the margins. The interplay between these personal and situational influences creates 'conflict anxieties' (Charles, 2021), generating feelings of physical and emotional insecurity. Poverty can engender desperation, while victimisation can create hatred and vengeance. As mentioned above, there is an overwhelming sense of fear; fear that lives might be lost and homes taken. Against such a backdrop, a young person's decision to join a NSAG can be interpreted as an attempt to regain or assert control.

It is a mistake to assume all recruitment of children and teenagers by NSAGs is 'forced'. In the majority of cases, the young person exerts some form of agency, but when such agency is exerted in contexts of major influence by NSAGs or in situations of extreme socio-economic precarity, it may equally be a mistake to assume elements of volunteerism. In reality, most cases of recruitment occur in what has been called the 'grey space' between forced and voluntary (Bjørkhaug, 2010). Indeed, by questioning choice and volunteerism, Honwana (2006: 73) argues that we need to make a differentiation between the *tactical* and *strategic* agency of children, the former being employed to 'cope with and maximise the concrete, immediate circumstances of the military environment in which they have to operate', while the latter requires a position of power, including 'full consciousness of the ultimate goals of actions and an ability to anticipate long-term gains or benefits'.

This political agency of children is often ignored because the most common definitions of children and childhood are based on universal assumptions of vulnerability and innocence (Douglas, 2010; Berents, 2020). Within the context of conflict, this can lead to narratives of victimisation, in which children are perceived as nothing more than passive targets of violence. Such protectionist approaches fail to take sufficient account of the diverse experiences of those living in conflict-laden circumstances. As Charles and Fowler-Watt (2020: 2) highlight, 'to suggest that childhoods of war are somehow exceptional (meaning unusual or not typical) is therefore to victimise the millions of children in the Global South for whom conflict and violence are daily realities'.

Likewise, to label the experiences of children and young people living on the margins as simply 'traumatic' ignores the plurality of their lived experiences and their ability to carve out possibilities for themselves amidst these adverse circumstances. On the contrary, 'child owned' and 'child authored' narratives of war, in this case presented as journalism, offer a 'productive way of thinking about children's agency' and break 'the systematic and comprehensive silencing of children's voices' (Berents, 2020: 461).

Journalism, children and ethics

As Carter et al. (2021: 355) point out, arguments about the societal value of news are consistently made about news for adults, but less frequently about children's news. Such debates also tend to focus strongly on the role and consumption of news in the Global North, where notions of childhood emphasise Western concepts of innocence and protectionism, as discussed above. The in-depth literature review provided by Carter et al. (2021) shows how such research has shown the potential negative emotional effects of adult news on children (Cantor and Nathanson, 1996; Van der Molen, 2001; Van der Molen, Valkenberg and Peeters, 2002) and how it has argued that children need to be protected from exposure to 'inappropriate' violent content (Smith, Pieper and Moye Gusé, 2011). Furthermore, scholars have also suggested that adult issues like politics should be avoided because they are uninteresting or not pertinent to children and their lives (Van der Molen and Konijn, 2007).

In the Global South, and contexts of violence in particular, such arguments simply do not carry weight. In Colombia, the setting of our project, many young people become victims of violence, either directly or indirectly. Violence and the suffering it can cause shape the everyday experience of youth and is therefore not something that can be concealed, but instead needs to addressed directly. Young audiences need to understand the roots and consequences of violence in their community.

Carter et al. (2021: 355) highlight the 'censorship, sanitisation and dumbing down of children's news' as a result of 'adult assumptions about potential harm to children's emotional wellbeing'. In Colombia, it is possible to argue that the reality of life has already damaged a young person's well-being and that therefore news and participation in social debate can form part of their necessary healing through ensuring their inclusion.

Children and teenagers not only need access to information, events, issues and policies, which affect them and their communities in a way that is accessible to them, but they also need to be included in the wider public debate. Neglecting the voices and opinions of children and teenagers denies young people the opportunity to be heard, which is detrimental to the public sphere and the formation of democratic citizenship. These claims are supported by scholars who have argued that attempts to protect young people from what is happening in the world are likely to undermine their citizenship and participation in civic life (Messenger Davies, Carter, Allen and Mendes, 2014; Donders and Van den Bluck, 2020). To exclude children and teenagers from political debates about the causes of and solutions to violence in Colombia is therefore to exacerbate further their sense of marginalisation, isolation and low self-efficacy. In contexts of violence and amidst the backdrop of the threat of recruitment by NSAGs, the consequences of this can be disastrous.

In contrast to the protectionist approach, some studies have shown how children and teenagers are keenly interested in certain political issues (Clark and Marchi, 2017) and have emphasised how young people can play a key role in peacebuilding (see Altiok et al., 2020 for a review of the key literature). In March of 2021, the United Nations Committee on the Rights of the Child adopted 'General Comment No. 25 on children's rights in relation to the digital environment' requiring member states to give 'due weight' to the views of children and to provide them with the opportunity 'to be heard' (cited in Carter et al., 2021: 357). Such participation is at the heart of My Story, but this inclusion of children and teenagers brings with it significant ethical challenges. There is insufficient space within the confines of this chapter to explore these in detail, but some of the key issues are identified and briefly explored below.

Semi-covert research

Holloway (1997: 39) defines covert research as 'research processes in which researchers do not disclose their presence and identity as researcher and participants have no knowledge of their research identity'. Covert research is usually interpreted as a violation of the principle of informed consent by using deception. While the My Story research team does not conceal its identity or the fact we are implementing a research project, the overall objectives are presented to participants and the wider community as peace and education oriented, rather than as recruitment prevention specifically. In most contexts, it is only the headteacher and our partner NGO staff who are aware of the main goal of our project. This perhaps semi-covert approach is guided by the intention to uphold the welfare of the participants and the researchers. As highlighted above, to implement recruitment prevention strategies in high-risk communities poses significant danger to those involved.

Revictimisation

Inviting a young person to share their story is not necessarily to revictimise them. Revictimisation can occur if a victim is forced to relive certain facts or episodes without due consideration. Irresponsible lines of questioning that focus on 'How did that make you feel?' or 'Tell me again how they hurt you' can cause harm. This *extraction* of information for the benefit of the reporter/researcher and their publication should be contrasted against the *generation* of information, which can be achieved in partnership between the contributor (or the victim) and the researcher/journalist.

The young participants in our project construct their own stories, in their own time and without a reliance on the interview genre. They are in control of the production of their own narrative, choosing what and when to share. Such a process can even prove cathartic (Charles and Fowler-Watt, 2020).

Furthermore, to assume that all young victims are traumatised is wrong and can contribute to this sense of revictimisation. Trauma is only one element of a much larger and more complex mosaic of psychosocial impacts for victims of conflict. Indeed, for many former child soldiers, for example, the biggest challenge is not the impact of past violence, but the formidable stresses of the post-war living situation (Wessells, 2006).

Although some victims do clearly experience trauma and may manifest signs of post-traumatic stress disorder (PTSD), it is an oversimplification to lump all victims together in the single category of 'traumatised'. Using former child soldiers as a further example, this pathological emphasis, which views them as emotionally scarred and morally damaged, does not fit with evidence that indicates most former child soldiers function quite well (Blattman and Annan, 2010; Wessells, 2006). Indeed Tedeschi and Calhoun (1995) suggest a model of post-traumatic growth (PTG), which proposes that there can sometimes be positive effects of traumatic experiences (see also Charles and Fowler-Watt, 2020).

In contrast to concepts of trauma, Nussio (2012) formulates a theory of 'emotional legacies' among ex-combatants in Colombia. His study focusses specifically on emotional dimensions of ex-combatants' retrospective understanding of their experience. An ex-combatant's 'remembered war past' is depicted according to their 'reasons for joining' and 'experiences of war'. This remembered war past determines the ex-combatant's current perceptions of their involvement in conflict, which in turn underpins their emotional legacies. The aim of his research is to link an individual's perspective of their past with their present situation. In direct contrast to being 'traumatised', Nussio's research shows how individuals can continue to live and function in the present, even if it is in the shadow of their particular emotional legacy.

Exposure to sensitive content

The young participants in our project are exposed to violence and its consequences as part of their everyday experience, as explained above. This does not give us *carte blanche* to expose them to more, but it does render censorship strategies rather meaningless.

Our aim is not to shy away from sensitive issues, but to promote a deeper understanding of them, while indicating where young people might seek support if they are affected or overwhelmed. Our coverage is therefore not intended to scare or generate gossip, but to inform, educate and shape citizens-in-the-making by facilitating spaces in which their opinions can be formed and heard.

Within our project, there are both producers and consumers of news, that is to say the young journalists, who create the content, and their audience of peers who read, watch and listen to it. We have an ethical responsibility to both.

For producers, the question is always why are we covering this issue? What can we learn from it? How can we tell this story without upsetting people? Our young reporters are taught not to use over-emotive or inflammatory language and to promote compassion and empathy above all else.

For consumers, our aim is to provide them with responsible coverage, avoiding sensationalism. This involves the difficult challenge of always explaining why something has happened and placing its significance in a wider context.

All sensitive material is clearly marked with a warning and it is also accompanied with action guidelines. That is to say that we identify support groups or helplines where any young person affected by our coverage might seek help or further support.

Wider safeguarding issues

Harm or the risk of harm comes in various shapes and sizes and our research team is trained to identify a wide range of safeguarding issues, including sexual abuse, exploitation and grooming, among others. Safeguarding involves collective and individual responsibilities, as well as preventative actions, to ensure that children participating in our project are protected from deliberate or unintentional acts that may lead to harm or the risk of harm. Working in partnership with our NGO partner, we have clearly defined procedures and protocols for the reporting of safeguarding issues, which can be found on the project website.

Peace skills as narrative themes

The transformative journalism which guides our project is built upon four narrative themes (My place in the world; The people around me; The country I see; The future and the changes I'd like), each of which is directly linked to an individual Peace Skill. As described above, these Peace Skills lay the concrete foundations on which the prevention of recruitment of children and teenagers by NSAGs can be constructed.

Peace Skills constitute socio-emotional, as well as cognitive abilities to deal effectively with the specific and everyday risks that emerge from living in violent contexts. They are intended to confront the socio-emotional challenges, which previous research has linked directly to the recruitment of children and teenagers by NSAGs: low self-esteem; weak self-confidence; managing healthy relationships; controlling emotions and adequate planning for the future.

For our young reporters, the overall aim of their journalism is not solely to question the world around them, but also how this world has shaped them and their standpoint, provoking reflection and challenging dominantly held attitudes and perspectives about self and society. It is through this reflection that the transformative potential occurs as negative perspectives and postures give way to a more positive stance and expectations.

It is important to explain that each piece of multimedia content published on our website is accompanied by additional educational material for use by other professionals seeking to engage in recruitment prevention or peacebuilding more generally. The website is an effective toolkit for individuals and organisations that may also see the benefit in promoting Peace Skills and recruitment prevention.

The project also creates potential employment opportunities within the creative economy by providing a formal qualification in journalism and audiovisual production for the young participants.

My place in the world (self-awareness and self-management)

Children who grow up in war zones typically feel powerless, disaffected and unable to obtain basic necessities and improve their life circumstances. They can feel trapped and abused and experience a strong sense of humiliation. It creates a strong desire to achieve power so they can restore their lost dignity and regain a sense of personal efficacy (Wessells, 2006).

My place in the world promotes self-awareness and emotional self-management, both of which are foundations of positive self-esteem. If a young person is able to understand their strengths and weaknesses, they are more likely to feel confident in themselves and be able to construct a plan about their future. They will also be able to better identify the needs, feelings and values that influence their perspectives.

The victimisation of children and teenagers during conflict, whether it occurs inside a family or at the hands of government forces or guerrilla groups, compels many of them to take up arms (Wessells, 2006). Young people can be bereaved by conflict and many children and teenagers join NSAGs as an emotional response, often to avenge the death of their loved one. This desire for revenge is also associated with perceptions of justice, rooted in perceptions of undeserved harm. Attempts to even the score are emotionally fuelled and constitute attempts to counter what can otherwise be a powerful and debilitating impotence in the face of abject violence and grief. Self-management and being able to understand how our emotions are experienced and to be able to control them is therefore vital to building resistance against recruitment.

In his story, The Death of My Father, one young participant recounts the murder of his father by dissident factions of the FARC. He charts his grief over the course of several months and explains how with psychological support, he managed to convert his desire for revenge into strength for success:

> At first I wanted to kill the bastards. I wanted to join the rival group and use the gun they'd give me to shoot them all in the head. It was such a powerful

feeling. But talking helped me realise that this action would change nothing. My dad wanted me to study and be successful. And that's what I'm doing to honour him.

Instead of looking outwards in blame and judgment, self-awareness helps us see our role in each interaction with others. Learning to become aware of these feelings helps to respond responsibly, with compassion and understanding, instead of with aggression or in defence. A greater sense of self-awareness helps us learn about ourselves and ultimately to become better, more empathetic individuals who can engage in productive and cooperative relationships.

The people around me (the effective management of interpersonal relationships)

Relationships with others can have positive as well as negative consequences on our lives. *The people around me* is therefore about advocating for meaningful relationships and understanding how some relations may block growth or even seek to deliberately harm us.

Another young reporter tells his story of being rejected by his parents and living on the streets. His story False Friends explains how he 'got in with the wrong crowd', describing the group of gangsters that became the 'family' he was so desperate for. Alone and in need of protection, he was unaware of the dangers involved and did not realise how this pulled him deep into the criminal underworld. What is the point of his story? To show others that their friends are not always what they seem:

> With time I realised who they were and I felt a little scared because I thought they were real friends. That's what happens, you see. You become so desperate for love and attention that you don't realise these are bad people and that they don't care about you at all.

Research underscores the importance of family in children's choices to join armed groups (Delap, 2005; Wessels, 2006). The profound importance of the family in children's recruitment is most visible in regard to separated children, who are no longer under the care of their parents (Delap, 2005).

However, during long and entrenched periods of conflict, families also become a microcosm of the violence permeating the wider society, creating a highly toxic environment for young people. Many children and teenagers join armed groups to escape these negative family situations (Garbarino and Kostelny, 1996).

In a world where social bonds have been severely fractured, seeking out loved ones in an effort to find protection and support is unsurprising. Some young people also join NSAG to be with their boyfriends or girlfriends, although these relationships are often false and part of defined recruitment strategies by the various NSAGs, as explored in The Day I Saw the Light:

One day I met a guy who was 17-years-old. He was new to school and had arrived to finish his studies in the ninth grade. We started getting to know each other more. We talked a lot and he would look at me and waited for me after practice every day. We started dating. I really liked him.

We were together for six months until one day after training, when we were alone, he grabbed me and told me I had to go with him. I was surprised and sad. I was very afraid and I said no. He said if I didn't accompany him to the guerrilla, they'd kill him.

I realised that the boy I thought was my boyfriend had been trying to recruit me all that time. He wanted to gain my trust and then turn me in to the armed group.

That's what dissidents do in Meta. They use older boys and girls to seduce younger ones.

The country I see (social consciousness)

The country I see aims to enhance the social consciousness of the young reporters. It is about how we understand the lives of others and the systems within which we live. It is understanding that we have the power to change our world through the way we participate in society. It is about caring for our neighbours and those less fortunate than ourselves. It is about protecting our environment and being able to recognise that some people are often marginalised or excluded through the prejudice and fear of others. It is about promoting and protecting diversity.

Our social consciousness is based on our ability to feel empathy, our ability to build bridges to universes other than our own, and to imagine and feel what the world is like from the perspectives of others.

In a special series of our podcast In My Own Words, our young journalists explore what it is like to 'be different'. From growing up black, to being religious, bisexual or a Venezuelan migrant, these stories include tales of bullying and suffering at the hands of prejudice:

> Perhaps you have never been bullied. In that case you probably won't know what it's like to feel worthless. You just want to curl up in a ball and sleep forever. Imagine that. Imagine it. Go on. It's not nice, is it?

The young journalists are not telling their stories for the sake of it. They understand the power in communicating their experiences to a wider audience of their peers:

> It has been hard to tell my story, but I hope you have listened and that you like it. It was hard, but I know it's worth the pain if others among you listening can learn from my experiences. The most important thing to remember is that I got over the bullying and I'm a normal person so if I can do it, so can you. Remember you are not alone!

In Colombia, empathy can help rebuild social ties fractured by the conflict. By exploring our differences and the impact they have had on the country, we also build mutual understanding, which ultimately binds communities together.

The future and changes I'd like (responsible decision-making)

The future and changes I'd like intends to promote responsible decision-making. This is about how we use critical or creative thinking to imagine the life we want for ourselves. Being able to decide for ourselves means we can make things happen instead of just letting them happen to us.

To illustrate this theme, our young reporters launched a campaign to promote conscientious objection. Military service is compulsory for all men over the age of 18 in Colombia and although there are some restrictions (for only children, children registered as victims, among others) and because it is possible to pay exemption fees to avoid being drafted, in reality the vast majority of those conscripted are from the country's poorest families. The right to conscientious objection, however, is a little known concept:

> I wrote a letter saying I wanted to object conscientiously. My moral principles and ethics prevent me from carrying a weapon or learning destructive things. But they didn't understand. I entered the room where I would state the reasons why I did not want to do military service. There was a lawyer, a nurse, psychologist, the public prosecutor, the general, and of course, all from the institution.
>
> My moral principles and ethics prevent me from carrying a weapon or learning destructive things.
>
> The atmosphere changed after my presentation. It was against me indirectly. It was a debate of five professionals, who prepared rather absurd arguments and tricky questions to reduce my arguments to something that had no worth for them at all.
>
> [...]
>
> I have started a group with others in the same situation, and because there is a lot of misinformation on the subject. The goal for us is to tell the young people in our country that conscious objection is an option for those who do not want to go to war.

The young reporters are constantly encouraged to think about different possibilities like conscientious objection and their consequences. As part of their campaign, they made a recommendation that military service should be abolished. They found it contradictory to the country's peace process. In an opinion column, one young reporter wrote:

> Military service can also be considered a form of slave labour or forced recruitment in which conscripts are paid a bare minimum to risk their lives,

often against their will. In modern, peaceful and civilised societies, young people should have the basic right to deny military service. The armed forces should offer professional career options rather than relying on generations of young men for free labour.

As critical thinkers, we ask questions all the time. We reflect about the world and the people in it in order to understand ourselves and guide our own behaviour. As creative thinkers, we create solutions and move away from the normal patterns of thought or behaviour. We see problems from different perspectives which allow us to create new opportunities. We are constantly learning about ourselves and reflecting on who we are and what we need to be happy and succeed.

A transformative journalism

Through an exploration of the four narrative themes and the promotion of the Peace Skills that underpin them, the aim is to provoke individual transformation for the young reporter. Through their journalism, the young participants are given the opportunity to question, challenge and reflect. By reinforcing their socio-emotional competences, we build resistance to recruitment by NSAGs by ultimately transforming a young person's outlook on their future and their potential, leading to stronger self-efficacy and a more positive identity. The hope is that such positivity rejects life inside the ranks of an NSAG as a viable life choice.

Such transformation is achieved by creating a space in which the young reporters can be vulnerable and reflect on their situations by putting pen to paper to explore their motivations, circumstances, thoughts and feelings. It is through this process that we as researchers and they as research participants are able to discover opportunities for alternatives. It is through such deep reflection and by sharing their stories with others that research participants can begin to think about different possibilities for their lives. Within psychology, for example, the construction of narratives is perceived as a therapeutic tool, which involves reshaping the individual's life story so as to emphasise a more healthful direction.

Communicating one's narrative to an audience can also help others, in particular, those listening or watching, who may share similar experiences or vulnerabilities. That is to say that it creates 'micro-solidarities' (Richmond, 2013) in which experiences are mirrored and paths to success are shared and reinforced.

The transformative potential of this project therefore lies within a navigation of the immediate and the imagined. In this sense, transformation is not necessarily about guaranteeing lasting change, but rather about opening up the possibilities to consider new alternatives and new perspectives, which in the longer term could result in something more sustainable.

Through reporting on others and on themselves, this narrative inquiry instigates reflection not only about their actions and choices, but also about the impact of these actions on others, and the impact others' actions have had on them. Our young reporters re-orientate themselves through their process of reflection and self-recognition, conveying the dialogic exchanges within an individual's multitudinous self, as well as their attempts to find themselves and understand their lives through the prism of their relationships, and within the systems and structures of their environment.

Conclusion

There is no doubt that recruitment prevention is extremely difficult. Successful recruitment prevention relies on integral approaches, which include economic investment in infrastructure, extracurricular activities and wider education/employment opportunities in addition to grassroots interventions aimed at boosting young people's socio-emotional resistance. My Story is therefore not presented as a magic formula to confronting the illicit recruitment phenomenon, but it does provide solid foundations on which other strategies can be developed and wider opportunities can be constructed.

There are of course no guarantees that enhanced and strengthened Peace Skills will prevent recruitment by NSAGs, but there is little doubt that a confident child or teenager with a positive outlook is much less likely than one suffering from low self-esteem to perceive life inside an armed group as providing opportunities and solutions.

The extent of transformation achieved by the My Story project remains to be evaluated. As the project is ongoing at the time of writing, we are not in a position to formally assess this, but early indications have been positive. The young journalists have reported feeling safer, more confident and generally happier about their prospects. Indeed many are investigating the possibility of studying journalism at university.

At the beginning of the project, we conducted a survey to measure violence-related attitudes, behaviours and influences among the project participants. Our aim is to repeat this survey once the project draws to a close. The hope is to show measurable change in behavioural patterns or change in some of the mediating or moderating factors associated with aggression and violence. The survey will allow us to quantify if and how we have been able to transform a young person's outlook on their life and their future.

Note

1 https://mihistoria.co

References

Altiok, A., Berents, H., Grizelj, I. and McEvoy-Levy, S. (2020). Yout, peace and security. In Hampson, F.O., Özerdam, A. and Kent, J. (Eds.). *Routledge Handbook of Peace, Security and Development*. London: Routledge, pp. 433–447.

Berents, H. (2020). This is my story: Children's war memoirs and challenging protectionist discourses. *International Review of the Red Cross*. doi:10.1017/S1816383120000120

Bjørkhaug, I. (2010). Child soldiers in Colombia: The recruitment of children into non-state armed groups. MICROCON Research Working Paper 27.
Blattman, C. and Annan, J. (2010). The consequences of child soldiering. *The Review of Economics and Statistics* 92(4), pp. 882–898.
Cantor, J. and Nathanson, A.I. (1996). Children's fright reactions to news. *Journal of Communication* 46(4), pp. 139–152.
Carter, C., Steemers, J. and Messenger Davies, M. (2021). Why children's news matters: The case of *Newsround* in the UK. *Communications* 46(3), pp. 352–372.
Charles, M. (2019). Beyond 'bearing witness'. Journalists resisting violence in Colombia's 'after war'. In I. Shaw and S. Sentham (Eds.). *Reporting Human Rights, Conflicts and Peacebuilding: Global Perspectives*. London: Palgrave.
Charles, M. (2020). Understanding trauma for reconciliation and peace-building journalism in Colombia. *Journalism Practice* 15(2), pp. 259–270. https://doi.org/10.1080/17512786.2020.1713857
Charles, M. (2021). *La niñez que peleó la guerra en Colombia*. Bogotá: Universidad del Rosario.
Charles, M. (2022). Recruited childhood. The participation of children and teenagers in organised crime and conflict after the peace agreement. *Documentos OCCO*. The Colombian Observatory of Organized Crime Working Paper Series Number 4. Bogotá: Universidad del Rosario.
Charles, M. and Fowler-Watt, K. (2020). The Tree of Love: Life writing and 'seasons of self' among former child soldiers in Colombia. *Life Writing*. https://doi.org/10.1080/14484528.2020.1805652
Clark, L.S. and Marchi, R. (2017). *Young People and the Future of News*. Cambridge: Cambridge University Press.
Crossick, G. and Kaszynska, P. (2016). *Understanding the Value of Arts & Culture: The AHRC Cultural Value Project*. Swindon: Arts and Humanities Research Council.
Dancey, S.T. and Morrison, E. (2019). Colombia Critical Review: The future is unwritten. *Changing the Story*. Retrieved 16 January 2020 from https://changingthestory.leeds.ac.uk/colombia-critical-review/
Delap, E. (2005). *Fighting Back*. London: Save the Children.
Donders, K. and Van den Bulck, H. (2020). Universality of public service media and pre-school audiences. In P. Savage, M. Medina and G.F. Lowe (Eds.). *Universalism in Public Service Media*. GÖteborg: Nordicom, pp. 49–67.
Douglas, K. (2010). *Contesting Childhood*. Rutgers University Press. Kindle Edition.
Garbarino, J. and Kostelny, K. (1996). The effects of political violence in Palestinian children's behavioural problems. *Child Development* 67(1), pp. 33–45.
Holloway, I. (1997). *Basic Concepts for Qualitative Research*. London: Blackwell.
Honwana, A. (2006). *Child Soldiers in Africa*. Philadelphia: University of Pennsylvania Press.
Howard, R. (2009). *Conflict-Sensitive Reporting: State of the Art. A Course for Journalists and Journalism Educators*. Paris: UNESCO.
Jaromowicz, M. and Bar-Tal, D. (2006). The dominance of fear over hope in the life of individuals and collectives. *European Journal of Social Psychology* 36(3), pp. 367–392.
Johns, D.F., Williams, K. and Haines, K. (2017). Ecological youth justice: Understanding the social ecology of young people's prolific offending. *Youth Justice* 17(1), pp. 3–21.
Leshem, O., Klar, Y. and Flores, T. (2016). Instilling hope for peace during intractable conflicts. *Social, Psychological and Personality Science*, 7(4), pp. 303–311.
Loyn, D. (2007). Good journalism or peace journalism? *Conflict and Communication Online* 6(2). Available online: www.cco.regener-online.de/2007_2/pdf/loyn.pdf

Messenger Davues, M., Carter, C., Allan, S. and Medes, K. (2014). News, children and citizenship. In H. Thornha and S. Popple (Eds.). *Content Cultures*. London: IB Taurus, pp. 15–36.

Nussio, E. (2012). Emotional legacies of war among former Colombian paramilitaries. *Peace and Conflict: Journal of Peace Psychology* 18(4), pp. 369–383.

Ramírez, M.C. (2010). Maintaining democracy in Colombia through political exclusion, states of exception, counterinsurgency, and dirty war. In D.E. Arias and D.M. Goldstein (Eds.). *Violent Democracies in Latin America*. Durham and New York: Duke University Press.

Richmond, O.P. (2013). Failed state-building versus peace formation. *Cooperation and Conflict* 48(3), pp. 378–400.

Ripley, A. (2009). *The Unthinkable. Who Survives When Disaster Strikes – and Why*. New York: Three Rovers Press.

Smith, S.L., Pieper, K.M. and Moyer Gusé, E.J. (2011). News, reality shows and children's fears. In S.L. Calvert and B.J. Wilson (Eds.). *The Handbook of Children, Media and Development*. Oxford: Blackwell, pp. 214–234.

Tedeschi, R.G. and Calhoun, L.G. (1995). *Trauma and Transformation: Growing in the Aftermath of Suffering*. Newbury Park, CA: Sage.

Tehranian, M. (2002). Peace journalism. Negotiating global media ethics. *The International Journal of Press/Politics* 7(2), pp. 58–83.

Van der Molen, J.W. (2001). Violence and suffering in televisión news: Toward a broader conception of harmful television content for children. *Paediatrics* 112(6), pp. 1771–1775.

Van de Molen, J.W. and Konijn, E.A. (2007). Dutch children's emotions reactions to news about war in Iraq. In D. Lemish and M. Götz (Eds.). *Children and Media in Times of War and Conflict*. Creskill: Hampton Press, pp. 75–98.

Van de Molen, J.W., Vakkenberg, P. and Peeters, A. (2002). Television news and fear: A child survey. *Communications* 27(3), pp. 3030–3317.

Wessells, M. (2006). *Child Soldiers. From Violence to Protection*. Cambridge, MA: Harvard University Press.

WHO. (2009). *Preventing Violence by Developing Life Skills in Children*. Malta: WHO.

11

BETTER SAFE THAN SORRY

Preparing journalism students for a dangerous world

Jaron Murphy

This chapter calls for the introduction of dedicated and mandatory safety training for students on journalism courses internationally, to properly prepare new generations of journalists for working in a dangerous digital-age world where the distinction between everyday 'virtual' (or online) and 'real' (or physical) threats has dissolved. To help bring about such change, this chapter has two interrelated aims: (1) to convey in some detail why safety is an extremely challenging but essential future direction for journalism education in the digital age and (2) to support journalism educators in both institutional and industry contexts with up-to-date safety advice and resources from leading experts which could assist the formulation and delivery of appropriate safety training for students. The unique challenges in diverse national and local contexts, as well as the multiplicity of threats contingent on individual circumstances, obviously preclude a 'one size fits all' approach to safety training internationally. Nevertheless, based on the evidence of copious research by international organisations at the forefront of highlighting the scale of online and physical attacks on journalists, action by journalism educators worldwide is clearly needed as a matter of urgency to both protect emerging journalists and future-proof the profession as a viable career choice.

For instance, the latest Reporters Without Borders World Press Freedom Index (2022) describes, by way of fact files on the 180 countries and territories covered, a wide range of perilous conditions and recorded violations impacting the global rankings. As the colour-coded map on the index website vividly illustrates, much of the world's population does not enjoy anything close to resembling press freedom which is defined as "the effective possibility for journalists, as individuals and as groups, to select, produce and disseminate news and information in the public interest, independently from political, economic, legal and social interference, and without threats to their physical and mental safety". The generally bleak situation globally is categorised as "very bad" in a record number of countries – 28.

DOI: 10.4324/9781003301028-14

Significantly, the index identifies the "globalised and unregulated online information space" as a key factor contributing to "a two-fold increase in polarisation amplified by information chaos – that is, media polarisation fuelling divisions within countries, as well as polarisation between countries at the international level". Alarmingly for supporters of the Fourth Estate, while major safety risks under repressive autocratic regimes and in war zones are to be expected, journalists are also being caught in the crossfire of divisions within democratic societies and in the onslaught of "propaganda wars against democracies" (RSF 2022).

The war waged by Russia (ranked 155th) in Ukraine (106th) since the end of February 2022 is cited as an example of a physical conflict preceded by a media and online propaganda offensive; while China (175th), also among the world's most authoritarian regimes, is reported to be utilising its legislative powers to restrict and isolate its population from the rest of the world – with Hong Kong tumbling down the rankings (from 80th in 2021 to 148th). The ten worst-ranked countries for press freedom include Syria (171st), Iraq (172nd), Cuba (173rd), Vietnam (174th), Myanmar (176th), Turkmenistan (177th), Iran (178th), Eritrea (179th) and North Korea (180th). Owing to the latter's "desire for complete isolation from the world", journalists have been "arrested, deported, sent to forced labour camps, and killed for deviating from the party's narrative"; and yet at the other end of the spectrum, although only "a few rare cases of physical violence have been reported" in the top-ranked country, Norway, "threats are commonplace: according to one study, one in four journalists received threats in one way or another" (RSF 2022).

Notably, too, a number of countries which consider themselves to be democratic bastions of press freedom, like the US and UK (42nd and 24th respectively), are beset with considerable safety issues for journalists and therefore ranked lower than might be expected. The index points out that the US government has been persisting in its pursuit of the extradition of Wikileaks founder Julian Assange "to face trial on charges related to the publication of leaked classified documents in 2010" and that Assange "remains detained on remand in the UK", impacting both countries' standings. In the US, online harassment, "particularly towards women and minorities, is also a serious issue for journalists and can impact their quality of life and safety". Moreover, owing to political polarisation and low public trust in the mainstream media, there is "a troubling trend of journalists experiencing harassment, intimidation and assault in the field". Journalists have been subjected to "dangerous conditions and have faced an unprecedented climate of animosity and aggression during protests", with "unprovoked physical attacks … on clearly identified reporters" (RSF 2022).

In the UK, while the publication in March 2021 of a government-backed National Action Plan for the Safety of Journalists to tackle threats to personal safety – including online abuse – "was a welcome step", troubling issues include the resurrection "of an alarming proposal for reforms to official secrets laws that could see journalists jailed for 'espionage'"; secretive and "extensive freedom of information restrictions"; an escalation of Strategic Lawsuits Against Public Participation (or SLAPPs) against UK and international journalists which has seen London become the "defamation capital of the world"; and threats against journalists in Northern Ireland, with claims of insufficient police response, "for reporting on organised crime and paramilitary activities". On the latter point, the index reminds readers that a "shadow remains cast by lingering impunity for the 2001 murder of *Sunday World* journalist Martin O'Hagan" and that no one "has yet been brought to trial for the murder of Lyra McKee in Derry in April 2019, although further arrests were made in 2021" (RSF 2022). Since the release of the index, a man has been jailed for possession of the gun used to kill McKee.[1]

The extent to which occupational hazards have multiplied for journalists internationally can also be gauged in part from UNESCO's *World Trends in Freedom of Expression and Media Development: Global Report 2021/22* (2022) which confirms that "85 percent of the world's population experienced a decline in press freedom in their country over the past five years". Among its key findings is that journalists have been under vicious attack: "From 2016 to the end of 2021, UNESCO recorded the killings of 455 journalists, who either died for their work or while on the job. At the same time, imprisonment of journalists has reached record highs" (UNESCO 2022). Under the heading "Safety of Journalists", UNESCO calculates that, on average, every five days a journalist is killed for bringing information to the public. It adds:

> Attacks on media professionals are often perpetrated in non-conflict situations by organised crime groups, militia, security personnel, and even local police, making local journalists among the most vulnerable. These attacks include murder, abductions, harassment, intimidation, illegal arrest, and arbitrary detention.
>
> *(UNESCO 2022a)*

This can be compared to data compiled by the international Committee to Protect Journalists, which shows 2,170 journalists and media workers have been killed in the period 1992–2022. The total number includes those "Murdered" or who died "In Crossfire/Combat" situations and "On Dangerous Assignment" (CPJ 2022). The CPJ's database also records 65 journalists and media workers killed so far in 2022 (CPJ 2022a). The CPJ's last prison census, for 2021, found the number of journalists jailed for their work "hit a new global record of 293, up from a revised total of 280 in 2020" (CPJ 2021).

The release of these statistics followed UNESCO's research discussion paper *The Chilling: Global trends in online violence against women journalists* (2021) which garnered input from hundreds of journalists from more than 120 countries (including understudied developing countries) and resulted in 28 "recommendations for action" (see UNESCO 2021: 91–93). Opening the paper, which contains detailed information and graphic accounts illustrating the gravity and extremity of the experiences of women reporters targeted online, the authors explain succinctly:

> There is nothing virtual about online violence. It has become the new frontline in journalism safety – and women journalists sit at the epicentre

of risk. Networked misogyny and gaslighting intersect with racism, religious bigotry, homophobia and other forms of discrimination to threaten women journalists – severely and disproportionately. Threats of sexual violence and murder are frequent and sometimes extended to their families. This phenomenon is also bound up with the rise of viral disinformation, digital conspiracy networks and political polarisation [exacerbated by the COVID-19 pandemic]. The psychological, physical, professional, and digital safety and security impacts associated with this escalating freedom of expression and gender equality crisis are overlapping, converging and frequently inseparable. They are also increasingly spilling offline, sometimes with devastating consequences.

(UNESCO 2021: 5)

Indeed, as the paper highlights, terrifying parallels have been drawn between the relentless persecution in the Philippines of Rappler founder and Nobel Peace Prize co-winner, Maria Ressa, under the regime of President Rodrigo Duterte (who stepped down at the end of June 2022 after reaching his six-year term limit) and prominent journalist Daphne Caruana Galizia who was assassinated via a car bomb in Malta in October 2017. There have been other shocking assassinations of journalists in recent years – for example, the Slovakian investigative reporter Ján Kuciak, who was shot dead along with his fiancée, Martina Kušnírová, in February 2018; Saudi journalist Jamal Khashoggi, who was murdered at the Saudi consulate in Istanbul and dismembered in October 2018; and the Mexican reporter Antonio de la Cruz, who was shot dead in June 2022 (the 12th journalist killed there that year, amid an 85% increase in attacks since President Andrés Manuel López Obrador came to power three years ago). However, the misogynistic nature of the online attacks on Ressa (who also suffers racist abuse) and Galizia, combined with the clear link established between online and physical violence, should also prompt journalism educators into concerted action to help protect female students. The report quotes Caoilfhionn Gallagher QC (now KC), who represents Galizia's bereaved family, underlining the appalling "similarities between Maria and Daphne's cases, including a long period … in which they both experienced a combination of attacks, from multiple different sources, online and offline – State-facilitated and State-fuelled" (UNESCO 2021: 64). At the time of writing, Galizia's family are still awaiting justice.

Advice from experts

By and large, although there have been notable initiatives offering support for the well-being of journalists (such as the Dart Center for Journalism and Trauma in the US and Europe and the Headlines Network in the UK), journalism course providers and industry bosses have tended historically to be unsystematic, even a bit blasé, about equipping fledgeling reporters with the knowledge to anticipate potential safety threats and the practical skills to minimise risk, respond if necessary in an effective manner, and ultimately safeguard themselves and the stories they are bringing to light. Instead, with growing experience, journalists have often strategised and countered risks for themselves – for example, investigative journalists sharing confidential information and collaborating internationally so that if any of them were to be killed, the story being worked on would not die too. The widespread paucity of dedicated safety training on journalism courses and in newsrooms historically could be explained in part, perhaps, by the fact that some educators might be (1) reticent about sharing their own triggering past experiences of being threatened or worse and (2) reluctant to potentially discourage or even scare off trainee reporters by referring not just to such incidents but also to the grisly details of the murders of journalists which represent the 'worst-case scenario' in an industry they are preparing to enter in the near future. Nevertheless, a basic premise of this chapter is that it is dangerous, in itself, to leave it to the School of Hard Knocks and therefore growing experience in industry to compensate for poor or non-existent safety training on journalism courses that purport to qualify their graduates for the 'real' working world.

What, then, should journalism educators consider and do to prepare students to stay safe while serving the public interest and holding power to account? To help, four experts in the field of journalism safety share their advice and recommended resources.

John Bosco Mayiga – programme specialist, freedom of expression and safety of journalists, UNESCO

Mayiga is responsible for implementation of UNESCO's safety of journalists programmes, including monitoring and reporting the killing of journalists, maintaining UNESCO's Observatory of Killed Journalists (see UNESCO 2022b) and organising the International Day to End Impunity for Crimes against Journalists (see UNESCO 2022c).

UNESCO is the United Nations lead agency responsible for promoting freedom of expression and safety of journalists. This mandate is implemented within the framework of the UN Plan of Action on the Safety of Journalists and the Issue of Impunity (see UNESCO 2016), which is a multi-stakeholder normative instrument for tackling the problem of impunity for crimes against journalists. The implementation of this plan is anchored on six pillars: awareness-raising, standard setting and policy making, monitoring and reporting, capacity-building, academic research, and coalition-building.

What journalism students should be learning, in Mayiga's view, about personal safety in the online environment:

1. **Digital security:** This should be the first step for everyone engaging with digital technologies. It is more important for journalists because of the nature of their work, particularly the professional ideology of the confidentiality of sources.

2. **Media and information literacy:** This is the ability to critically engage with digital technologies, leveraging the potential of technology, cognisant of the potential harms that the same technologies can engender. UNESCO implements the Media and Information Literacy Programme which seeks to enhance the capacities of policy makers, educators, information and media professionals, youth organisations and disadvantaged groups through provision of various competences and tools to help people to maximise advantages and minimise harm in the digital information ecosystem.
3. **Digital rights:** Knowledge of digital rights is not only essential for purposes of journalists guaranteeing their own rights but also ensuring that they promote the digital rights of citizens as a whole. Given the opacity that is usually associated with digital technologies, rights like privacy, protection of personal data, encryption and decryption are essential parts of a rights framework that journalists should learn and be conversant with. In this realm, UNESCO has led several initiatives mainly at the normative and policy level, including a policy brief on transparency and accountability in the digital age (see UNESCO 2021a) as well as a global initiative to enhance the transparency of internet companies, which resulted in the development of High-Level Principles on Transparency (see UNESCO 2021b) that has received broad support from companies, regulators and civil society.

Mayiga's list of recommended resources which could support teaching/learning of students in this regard. Some of the resources are referenced in-text above. The others are:

- World trends in freedom of expression and media development: global report 2021/22 (also referenced in-text earlier in this chapter – see UNESCO 2022)
- Media and information literate citizens: think critically, click wisely! (see UNESCO 2021c)
- Survey on privacy in media and information literacy with youth perspectives (see UNESCO 2017)
- Steering AI and advanced ICTs for knowledge societies: a Rights, Openness, Access, and Multi-stakeholder Perspective (see UNESCO 2019).

What journalism students should be learning, in Mayiga's view, about personal safety in the physical environment:

1. **Newsroom safety:** Since the newsroom is the primary working space of journalists, it is important for journalism students to learn about the safety mechanisms at the organisational level.
2. **Safety of women journalists:** Journalism students need to learn that women journalists are disproportionately targeted and their physical safety is threatened more than their male counterparts. UNESCO is promoting the safety of

women journalists through a number of initiatives (see UNESCO 2021d) such as research on good practices, capacity-building, and awareness-raising.
3. **Emotional well-being:** Trauma, particularly for journalists covering conflict and highly emotional events, is one of the marginalised safety issues. Journalism students learning about trauma would enable them to understand the connection between the physical environment and their mental well-being.

Mayiga's list of recommended resources which could support teaching/learning of students in this regard:

- *Safety of journalists covering trauma and distress "Do no harm"* (see UNESCO 2022d)
- *Safety of journalists covering protests: preserving freedom of the press during times of turmoil* (see UNESCO 2020)
- *Freedom of expression and the safety of foreign correspondents: trends, challenges and responses* (see UNESCO 2021e)

Nikolia Apostolou, Resource Centre Director, Global Investigative Journalism Network (GIJN)

For the past 15 years, Apostolou has been writing and producing documentaries from Greece, Cyprus and Turkey for more than 100 media outlets, including the BBC and the Associated Press. She covered extensively Greece's economic crisis which started in 2010 and the European migrant crisis. Her documentaries have been screened in festivals around the world and have won multiple awards in various competitions. She's also a Dart and a Fulbright fellow. Apostolou is currently teaching digital journalism and on the Master's programme in Media and Refugee/Migration Flows at the University of Athens. Previously, she's also taught at Panteion University.

The GIJN serves as the international hub for the world's investigative reporters. Its core mission is to support and strengthen investigative journalism around the world – with special attention to those under repressive regimes and from marginalised communities.

What journalism students should be learning, in Apostolou's view, about personal safety in the online environment:

Journalism students should be learning first off how, as consumers, their personal data is collected. As they're young, their digital footprint is still small. They need to learn how to protect themselves from this data collection because it may be used against them when they become important journalists breaking scandals.

They'll also need to learn how to protect their communication in order to protect their sources. Simple steps like getting two-factor log-in passwords, buying paid versions of VPNs and antivirus software and using encrypted services like Proton Mail and Signal.

Apostolou's list of recommended resources which could support teaching/learning of students in this regard:

- *Digital security basics* (see Shelton 2016)
- *Steps to take for your digital security, along with great tools and links to other tip sheets* (see GIJN 2022)

What journalism students should be learning, in Apostolou's view, about personal safety in the physical environment:

Students should be learning about harassment from sources, as they might often find themselves alone with them. The year 2021 was one of the deadliest years for journalists. Therefore, they should learn how to stay safe: never go alone to a location or a country that's dangerous and you don't have experience of, work with other local journalists, learn how to blend in a country and not stand out like a tourist, remember you're just human, always get advice from experienced journalists/friends/professors, follow your gut. Don't be a hero.

Apostolou's list of recommended resources which could support teaching/learning of students in this regard:

- *Tip sheet on what to do when you need to flee your city/country (see GIJN 2022a)*
- *A list of guides on journalists' security and a list of journalism safety and security groups (see GIJN 2022b)*
- *A great tool for journalists and organisations that need to do a risk assessment on a particular situation or story (see GIJN 2022c)*
- *Covering street protests tip sheet (see GIJN 2022d)*
- *Presentation by the Organized Crime and Corruption Reporting Project (see OCCRP 2021)*

Apostolou's closing comments

What you're doing is important. This should be a fundamental class for all journalism students. I was never taught in school about any of this and it only made me feel more vulnerable. Information is power and your students need to know how to protect themselves. Also, this is an ever-changing topic, so we all need to continue learning about it.

Gideon Sarpong, Co-founder and currently Policy and News Director at iWatch Africa

As it states on the website of the University of Oxford's Reuters Institute for the Study of Journalism, where Sarpong's fellowship paper "Keeping journalists safe online: a guide for newsrooms in West Africa and beyond" was published in April 2022:

> Gideon is a policy analyst and media practitioner with nearly a decade of experience in policy, data and investigative journalism. He is an alumnus of the Young African Leaders Initiative (YALI), Thomson Reuters Foundation,

Free Press Unlimited and Bloomberg Data for Health Initiative. Gideon is a 2020/21 Policy Leader Fellow at the European University Institute, School of Transnational Governance in Florence, Italy and a Ghana Hub Lead for the Sustainable Ocean Alliance. He is also a 2020/21 Open Internet for Democracy Leader at the Center for International Media Assistance and the National Democratic Institute in Washington, DC and believes in promoting a safe, secure and inclusive digital ecosystem.

(Sarpong 2022)

In his paper, Sarpong presents "gender-inclusive guidelines and protocols to counter online abuse and harassment of journalists in West Africa" which could potentially be applied or adapted to newsrooms elsewhere. Published around the time of international headlines on the targeting of Indian journalist Rana Ayyub, Sarpong's paper provides a practical 'roadmap' consisting of five action points (Sarpong 2022):

1. Build digital rights literacy
2. Establish safety practices
3. Conduct risk assessments
4. Implement support mechanisms
5. Assign roles and tasks

While his views on journalism safety online are summed up in his introductory write-up for his downloadable paper on the Reuters Institute website, Sarpong provided these additional comments specifically in relation to teaching journalism students:

> Journalism educators may assist students better appreciate the evolving power struggle over the online ecosystem between undemocratic leaders around the world today and platform owners. Students must be equipped to navigate the new landmine of internet shutdowns, legal restrictions and arrests increasingly being deployed by autocrats to stifle independent journalism and critical commentary. I believe that students must be prepared to use newer technologies (e.g., VPNs) to help circumvent internet and platform restrictions by state actors as we witnessed in Nigeria last year. For student journalists, they should first of all understand that journalists, particularly female journalists today, are very susceptible to online attacks.
>
> They should be aware of the political nature of such attacks and must be prepared to report it when abused. Student journalists must also be aware that their work will be vigorously scrutinised by groups who may seek avenues to undermine their credibility and undermine press freedom generally. Student journalists should establish professional relationships with experienced [journalists] who may guide them very early in their careers to avoid some mistakes that may put their safety at risk. Journalists must also be adequately prepared in dealing with adversarial governments.

Rebecca Whittington, online safety editor, Reach PLC

Whittington is the online safety editor for Reach plc, publisher of more than 130 national and regional titles in the UK (including the *Daily Mirror*, *Daily Express* and *Manchester Evening News*). She joined Reach in 2021, in a newly created role – the first of its kind – to tackle the growing problem of journalists coming under attack online. She has previously worked in a number of journalism roles and was course leader for undergraduate journalism at Leeds Trinity University in the UK. Her PhD from the University of Leeds analysed digital impacts on news production and brand and journalistic identity at local newspapers in the UK.

What journalism students should be learning, in Whittington's view, about personal safety in the online environment:

1. We all have a role to play in making online spaces safe – we can take personal responsibility by ensuring our accounts are secure, we can use online tools responsibly and we can treat people in the way we would like to be treated. Check your privacy settings regularly and make sure you are happy with the information you share about yourself online; think about what pictures, comments and personal information you are happy to have connected to you and consider what social media you may have used in the past and check you are happy for it to remain online. Personal protection and awareness of risk and how to prevent it is vital – while in no way can online harm, harassment or abuse be justified, taking these steps can help minimise the risk of becoming a victim of doxxing, harassment and invasion of personal online space.
2. Don't shoulder online abuse or harms alone. Talk to a colleague or manager or someone you trust about what you have experienced. Online abuse can make an individual feel incredibly isolated, exposed and vulnerable, but talking about it will help take the first steps to regaining control. Many colleagues may have faced something similar and may be able to advise on the steps they took. If there is a support network such as an established person within your sphere who helps manage online safety then get in touch with them. If you are working alone or working as a freelancer, then make use of the services and resources provided by your union or online networks such as the Coalition Against Online Violence.[2]
3. Don't feed the trolls. It can be tempting to respond to hateful comments, but a response will often give oxygen to the haters. Instead, stifle them by blocking, reporting and ignoring. Your lack of interaction makes you a much less interesting target.
4. Stalking, hate crime and sexual harassment are a crime in the UK. If you are a victim of this kind of abuse online it should be taken seriously by your employers and the police if you wish to report it. Again, make sure you tell someone if this happens to you.
5. Take time out. It's important to give yourself a break from social media and online work. Try to separate work and personal social accounts so you have

the breathing space you need. It can be hard to maintain a physical space from work when so much of it is conducted from our homes or mobile devices that come into our homes. Shut the laptop, put the work phone in a drawer, mute notifications and take a break.

Whittington's list of recommended resources which could support teaching/learning of students in this regard:

- *Coalition against online violence* (in-text link above; also see www.iwmf.org/coalition-against-online-violence/#members)
- *Center for countering digital hate* (https://counterhate.com/)
- *Meta safety for journalists* (www.facebook.com/formedia/mjp/journalist-safety-online)
- *HeartMob* (https://iheartmob.org/resources)
- *#DontTakeTheFlak* (on Twitter)

What journalism students should be learning, in Whittington's view, about personal safety in the physical environment:

1. Planning ahead – even in a breaking news scenario, planning ahead can protect your safety. Think about what environment you are going to and what the risks might be – discuss these with your manager. For example, if you are covering a crowd event, the atmosphere can depend on a number of factors, including the event itself, alcohol consumption and emotion of the crowd.
2. Make sure your managers know where you are going and what you are doing. Check in with them when you return. Make sure you discuss the risks of the job and establish together how you plan for those – see point 1.
3. Make sure you use the right kit for the job – using a tripod and mic can improve film quality and reduce the number of critical comments online about production problems. It also means you don't have to stand too close to crowds, interviewees or scenes to capture the right shot. Check your phone has battery power! Make sure, if you are covering a crime scene or a high-tension situation, that you plan your positioning so that you stay within eyesight of police or security, so that if you run into problems you have support nearby. Whatever the story, it's never worth more than your personal safety, so stay out of the crowds and instead find a viewpoint that captures the scene without putting you at risk.
4. Think about your travel to and from a job. If driving, park on a busy road and stay within public places wherever possible when walking to the job, particularly if you are covering breaking news, a crowd or an emotive story or if you are working out of hours or when it is dark. If you are meeting a contact, try to arrange a meeting place in a public place. If that is not possible, make sure your managers have the exact address of where you are going and the timings, so they can check in with you.

5. Trust your gut. If something doesn't feel or look right, then don't be afraid to move away and tell your managers. Never put getting the story before your own welfare.

Whittington's closing comments

There are clear links between online and physical safety and we should not silo the two elements. As these areas of knowledge and understanding develop, it is important trainee and student journalists learn about safety and risks to help manage these challenges when they emerge. The chilling effect of threats to journalism safety is a significant threat to democracy; together we need to continue to support, report and challenge platforms for abuse and hate.

Promising developments in the UK

As the creation of Whittington's pioneering online safety editor role at Reach plc indicates, there has been a growing conversation in the journalism industry in the UK about how to address rampant online abuse, the danger of related physical threats, and support for staff. Correspondingly, a conversation has also been ongoing in journalism education in the UK, gaining momentum after the main course accrediting body, the National Council for the Training of Journalists (NCTJ), received feedback concerning some candidates who felt 'triggered' or traumatised by scenarios presented in reporting assessments which tutors considered to be quite challenging topics but typical of situations that working journalists must contend with. On 6 September 2022, the NCTJ announced via its website that students on "accredited courses must be given resilience training to cope with the demands of real-world journalism". By then, the NCTJ had updated its performance standards for accredited courses "to ensure students are adequately supported to deal with challenging scenarios in training and assessments, and to prepare them for what they may encounter in the newsroom". At the end of the announcement, without elaboration, the NCTJ stated that a "new course in journalism safety will also be launched on the NCTJ's Journalism Skills Academy by autumn 2022" (NCTJ 2022). At the time of writing, details of the new course content are yet to be revealed.

However, an article on the *journalism.co.uk* website clarified (1) that training providers would have the onus on them as well as the discretion to deliver the resilience training "in any way that works for them, including content, delivery and timetabling within their course structure", subject to annual review and (2) that the new safety course "is designed for any current or prospective journalist who would like to gain more skills and support about staying safe in different contexts" and "will include advice on how to protect yourself and others online, including dealing with privacy and online abuse, and how to manage reporting on sensitive subjects" (Granger 2022). Within the 2022/23 Programme of Study for the mandatory Essential Journalism module of the Level 5 Diploma in Journalism, the NCTJ's position is explicit in several places. In the Social Media study unit section, for instance, it states that candidates must understand "the nature of online abuse and what actions they can take to ensure digital safety" as well as how to go about "moderating reader comments" (NCTJ 2022a: 15). Later, in the Mobile Journalism section, it is stipulated that candidates must "understand the importance of health and safety when working as a mobile journalist and how to assess risks to themselves and others" (NCTJ 2022a: 17).

The NCTJ's position is also apparent in the 'Health and Safety' section, which is among the non-examined topics. Forming part of a holistic bundle of items including employee and employer responsibilities in terms of legislation, avoiding injury in using equipment and in the workplace generally and integrating into newsrooms (whether in the office or working from home), there are objectives for candidates to "understand how to minimise risk when working alone" and "learn strategies to minimise risk if a situation becomes threatening". It is also flagged that journalists "may, in the course of their duties, be present at events which are dangerous and possibly horrific" and therefore candidates

> must be aware of these possibilities including: staying safe during an unfolding incident when lives are at risk, the possibility of seeing people who are dead and/or badly injured, and distressing images and video arriving into a newsroom from the scene, including via social media [this should be related to the ethical studies about publication of such material].
>
> *(2020a: 18)*

Overall, then, in the UK, the NCTJ's 'direction of travel' towards increased safety and resilience support for students, to bolster their readiness for industry, is promising. The expert advice and recommended resources incorporated into this chapter could assist tutors on NCTJ-accredited courses to formulate and deliver appropriate training. Innovative and exemplary practice could, in turn, help to spur the spread of such training for journalism students internationally.

Notes

1 Lyra McKee was a journalist from Northern Ireland who wrote about the legacy of the Troubles for several publications. She was shot dead on 18 April 2019.
2 https://onlineviolenceresponsehub.org/about-the-coalition-against-online-violence

References

CPJ 2021 [online]. "Number of journalists behind bars reaches global high", 9 December. Available from: https://cpj.org/reports/2021/12/number-of-journalists-behind-bars-reaches-global-high/, accessed 17 September 2022.
CPJ 2022 [online]. "2170 journalists and media workers killed". Available from: https://cpj.org/data/killed/?status=Killed&motiveConfirmed%5B%5D=Confirmed&motiveUnconfirmed%5B%5D=Unconfirmed&type%5B%5D=Journalist&type%5B%5D=Media%20Worker&start_year=1992&end_year=2022&group_by=year, accessed 17 September 2022.

CPJ 2022a [online]. "51 journalists and media workers killed". Available from: https://cpj.org/data/killed/2022/?status=Killed&motiveConfirmed%5B%5D=Confirmed&motiveUnconfirmed%5B%5D=Unconfirmed&type%5B%5D=Journalist&type%5B%5D=Media%20Worker&start_year=2022&end_year=2022&group_by=location, accessed 17 September 2022.

GIJN 2022 [online]. "Digital security". Available from: https://gijn.org/digital-security/, accessed 18 September 2022.

GIJN 2022a [online]. "Essential steps for journalists in emergency situations", 31 January. Available from: https://gijn.org/2022/01/31/essential-steps-in-emergency-situations/, accessed 18 September 2022.

GIJN 2022b [online]. "Safety and security", March. Available from: https://gijn.org/safety-and-security-organizations/, accessed 18 September 2022.

GIJN 2022c [online]. "The journalist security assessment tool". Available from: https://advisory.gijn.org/cybersecurity-assessment/, accessed 18 September 2022.

GIJN 2022d [online]. "Abraji's security manual for covering street protests". Available from: https://gijn.org/abrajis-security-manual-for-covering-street-protests/, accessed 18 September 2022.

Granger, Jacob 2022 [online]. "NCTJ makes resilience training mandatory for its journalism courses", 12 September. Available from: www.journalism.co.uk/news/nctj-rolls-out-resilience-training-on-journalism-courses-in-a-sign-of-the-times/s2/a964200/, accessed 19 September 2022.

NCTJ 2022 [online]. "Resilience training to be delivered to students on all NCTJ-accredited courses", 6 September. Available from: www.nctj.com/news/resilience-training-to-be-delivered-to-students-on-all-nctj-accredited-courses/, accessed 19 September 2022.

NCTJ 2022a. "Essential journalism programme of study 2022–2023", pp. 1–28, September 2022. Available to NCTJ tutors via www.nctj.com/qualifications-courses/qualifications/national-qualification-in-journalism

OCCRP 2021 [online]. *"Newsroom safety" presentation*, November. Available from: https://docs.google.com/presentation/d/13iSBtB__z772Zk3S4Vj2NN72KLKCLpYJ/edit#slide=id.p1, accessed 18 September 2022.

RSF [Reporters Without Borders] 2022 [online]. "RSF's 2022 World Press Freedom Index: a new era of polarisation", 3 May. Available from: https://rsf.org/en/rsf-s-2022-world-press-freedom-index-new-era-polarisation-0, accessed 17 September 2022.

Sarpong, Gideon 2022. "Protecting journalists from online abuse: a guide for newsrooms", 4 April. Available from: https://reutersinstitute.politics.ox.ac.uk/protecting-journalists-online-abuse-guide-newsrooms, accessed 18 September 2022.

Shelton, Martin 2016. "Digital self-defense for journalists: an introduction", 12 August. Available from: https://gijn.org/2016/08/12/digital-self-defense-for-journalists-an-introduction/, accessed 18 September 2022.

UNESCO 2016 [online]. "UN plan of action on the safety of journalists and the issue of impunity". Available from: https://en.unesco.org/un-plan-action-safety-journalists, accessed 18 September 2022.

UNESCO 2017. *Survey on privacy in media and information literacy with youth perspectives*. Available from: https://unesdoc.unesco.org/ark:/48223/pf0000258993, accessed 18 September 2022.

UNESCO 2019. *Steering AI and advanced ICTs for knowledge societies: a Rights, Openness, Access, and Multi-stakeholder Perspective*. Available from: https://unesdoc.unesco.org/ark:/48223/pf0000372132, accessed 18 September 2022.

UNESCO 2020. *Safety of journalists covering protests: preserving freedom of the press during times of turmoil*. Available from: https://unesdoc.unesco.org/ark:/48223/pf0000374206, accessed 18 September 2022.

UNESCO 2021 [online]. *The chilling: global trends in online violence against women journalists*, April. Posetti, Julie; Shabbir, Nabeelah; Maynard, Diana; Bontcheva, Kalina; Aboulez, Nermine (authors). Available from: https://en.unesco.org/sites/default/files/the-chilling.pdf, accessed 17 September 2022.

UNESCO 2021a [online]. "Letting the sun shine in: transparency and accountability in the digital age". Puddephatt, Andrew (author). Available from: https://unesdoc.unesco.org/ark:/48223/pf0000377231, accessed 18 September 2022.

UNESCO 2021b [online]. "UNESCO initiates global dialogue to enhance the transparency of internet companies, with release of illustrative high-level principles", 3 May. Available from: https://en.unesco.org/news/unesco-initiates-global-dialogue-enhance-transparency-internet-companies-release-illustrative, accessed 18 September 2022.

UNESCO 2021c [online]. *Media and information literate citizens: think critically, click wisely!* Available from: https://unesdoc.unesco.org/ark:/48223/pf0000377068, accessed 18 September 2022.

UNESCO 2021d [online]. "Safety of women journalists". Available from: https://en.unesco.org/themes/safety-journalists/women-journalists, accessed 18 September 2022.

UNESCO 2021e [online]. *Freedom of expression and the safety of foreign correspondents: trends, challenges and responses.* Available from: https://unesdoc.unesco.org/ark:/48223/pf0000378300, accessed 18 September 2022.

UNESCO 2022 [online]. *World trends in freedom of expression and media development: global report 2021/22.* Available from: www.unesco.org/reports/world-media-trends/2021/en, accessed 17 September 2022.

UNESCO 2022a [online]. "Safety of journalists". Available from: https://en.unesco.org/themes/safety-journalists#:~:text=On%20average%2C%20every%20five%20days,journalists%20among%20the%20most%20vulnerable, accessed 17 September 2022.

UNESCO 2022b [online]. "UNESCO observatory of killed journalists". Available from: https://en.unesco.org/themes/safety-journalists/observatory, accessed 18 September 2022.

UNESCO 2022c [online]. "International day to end impunity for crimes against journalists". Available from: www.unesco.org/en/days/end-impunity, accessed 18 September 2022.

UNESCO 2022d [online]. *Safety of journalists covering trauma and distress "Do no harm".* Available from: https://unesdoc.unesco.org/ark:/48223/pf0000381200, accessed 18 September 2022.

REFLECTIONS

Space to reflect

This chapter aims to capture the reflections of a group of the contributing authors as they met to discuss the evolution of their individual chapters and to locate them in the wider context within which they had produced their work. The conversation was facilitated and written up by me as the editor. I also extrapolated the manifesto for change from the key themes of our discussion. We hope that this closing section of the book provides some food for thought for our fellow journalism educators and that the conversation continues!

Setting the conversation

As the philosopher and critical pedagogue Paolo Freire (1989: 13) reminds us, 'Dialogue is a moment where humans meet to reflect on their reality as they make and remake it'. There is transformative potential inherent within this process. We started our conversation by briefly stating where we are each coming from, our own situatedness within our writing, next moving onto a group discussion to consider the challenging landscape within which the book was produced and how this had shaped our thinking. It gave us a moment to reflect on the context within which we are working and also to share these thoughts together, before expanding on the emergent themes that we had discerned as individual perspectives. This was followed by an interactive discussion on collective reflections to finally draw some tentative conclusions about the challenges that we detect and possible routes through – future directions for journalism education, presented as a manifesto for change.

Facilitator: Karen Fowler-Watt, Editor.

Lived experiences and situatedness

David Brine: I spent about 25 years working in local and regional newspapers where I covered lots of local government, education, health service type stories. I have a degree in politics and I have always been engaged with politics and media. I started teaching the subject of Public Affairs about five years ago for news company training schemes, and now I'm involved with the Facebook (now Meta) Community News Project, working with professional journalists in newsrooms. I train them one day a week for the UK industry-standard NCTJ[1] diploma, including a Public Affairs module. In recent years, I have become aware of a drop-off in political engagement and I think there is a real disconnect between younger people and political institutions. The other trigger for my chapter (Chapter 5) was the pandemic when, as a news junkie, I consumed so much content and I was struck by the fact that every story had a public affairs element to it. So these intersecting themes urged me to write the chapter, and the challenge that I am trying to unlock is how we can use some of the examples from public interest journalism to inspire students to engage. Also, how we can make space within the curriculum to have a dialogue with students about why public interest journalism is important.

Fiona Cownie: The pandemic provided energy for some of the moves to engage with the sustainability agenda through the two case studies that we used to inform our analysis (see Chapter 8). Bringing people together out of necessity in an online manner suddenly moved the story from the local to the genuinely global, and the access to online content that underpinned teaching delivery in the pandemic is shown as important in our second case study about showing the interconnectedness of the sustainability agenda.

Biographically, I feel that I have moved full circle over the past 40 years, from studying a human geography degree and writing my dissertation about the challenges of energy and refuse to bringing my interest in sustainability to the book. I now have a university-wide role of promoting the sustainability agenda and I do believe that the United Nations Sustainable Development Goals (SDGs) offer a very useful tool to move us towards a more sustainable future. Of course, not everyone will agree, but my personal view is that they are as good as we've got. Sure, they could be used quite instrumentally, but I still feel that they pull people's thinking together to define what sustainability might mean.

Max Mauro: I came into sports media, on the one hand, because I have always had this passion for sport since I was a child, and on the other I see the role that sport plays in contemporary politics and on the global stage. This passion for sports is evident in politics and the economy, with football clubs being acquired by investment funds, mostly based in the US. So I am intrigued by a number of aspects and I tried to bring these into the conversation about how to better educate young people who want to work in sports media or journalism, so that we can equip them with the critical understanding that I think is necessary not only to make sense of what is going on, but, even more importantly, for the credibility of sport itself. If you are not ready to investigate issues like corruption and doping as a sports reporter, how can sport survive and be trusted? So this is the background and the kind of message that inspired me to write the chapter (see Chapter 4).

Andy Bissell (author, Chapter 2): I was a journalist for 30 years and back in the day I inherited this world of getting the best angle or getting exclusives and dealing with individuals and families in tragic circumstances and I think one tends to become increasingly reflective as one gets older. I have always been a little bit troubled by the formulas that all the standard 'how to' journalism textbooks advocate – the focus on asking the *who, why, what, where* – the sort of journalism that if you're not careful can tend to de-humanise people. I would like to think that my later time in journalism was hallmarked by striving to obtain a deeper understanding of people and, hence, better quality journalism. Then, when I had the privilege of entering HE and doing an educational doctorate, I could explore that in a lot more detail. I think that has shaped me and supported my personal crusade against 'joining the dots' journalism. It has also enthused me in working with young people to get them, wherever possible, to behave ethically and morally and to think about themselves and building good relationships, listening to others, building empathy.

Graham Majin (author, Chapter 3): I did a degree in philosophy and literature, so I had a bit of a background, to think about truth and epistemology, and then I trained as a teacher. After a few years, I moved into broadcast journalism radio, TV and then, at the BBC, documentary filmmaking. I ran my own business for a while and then I did a PhD and came into academia. It was really in that space that there was a kind of a collision at that point, I think, between the *praxis* of working journalist and working teacher and the different ways people think about things in academia compared to out in industry. So, these issues about truth and what is truth and how it is thought of in academic contexts, compared with in a working newsroom, fascinate me. It is quite a privilege to work on this book project and to contribute and discuss these things with you all; it brings together education, truth, journalism, and teaching all these things seem to be related somehow.

Jo Royle: My interest in entrepreneurship and its relationship with journalism comes from my professional background as an academic in the creative field of journalism/media in a faculty of management at my university in Scotland. When the university restructured in 2016, I became Head of School and recently Dean of the independent School of Creative and Cultural Business. I named the school personally (with consultation!) to represent the interface of creativity and business that had been at the centre of my academic life – and I am interested in that kind of interface that poses challenges as well as a lot of opportunities. The same has been the case for the enterprise/journalism mix that interfaces fully with communities and that could be essential to bringing unheard voices to the fore and underpinning a more democratic media. There has still not been much research conducted in this area, so it was the focus of my doctorate and this book chapter (see Chapter 9) gave me an opportunity to think about its application further.

Julian McDougall: I think what I have realised, now reflecting, is that I have always been in between spaces: my degree was in communications and critical theory, then I became an English and media teacher and then I did my doctorate in education in the cultural studies school at Birmingham between those two spaces. Then I came to Centre for Excellence in Media Practice (CEMP), a research centre in a university. In schools I was always the person interested in media and now working in a media faculty and running a doctorate in education, I am the person interested in education! I don't occupy a fixed position or have certain loyalties and I think that not being in any particular space was helpful when writing my chapter (see Chapter 6), which is asking questions about how we work with an organisation like BBC Media Action and various stakeholders trying to make it more of a reciprocal thing between spaces. Currently, many of my intellectual and political positions are more in tension than ever before: I would usually be sceptical about professional journalism as being in a hierarchical position of privilege over randomers on social media, because I come at this more from a post-structuralist position. So working with Media Action for this chapter, my academic instinct is to be sceptical about their intentions, because, even if unintentionally, we have a global north mainstream media player using a top down development paradigm to help vulnerable people in fragile major ecosystems, and all of that is problematic, But that has to be better than just fiddling while Rome burns, doing well-intentioned post-structuralist post-truth academic work whilst media ecosystems become increasingly populist. The personal and the political collide in the chapter in that respect and as I get older, I feel a little bit lost in the chaos.

A challenging landscape

In this section of the conversation we reflected on the context within which we produced the book and how this shaped our individual chapters. We also drew out individual perspectives on things that surprised us, hunches that were confirmed, themes that emerged.

Andrew Bissell: I am speaking personally here, but as I was thinking about the context within which I wrote my chapter (Chapter 2), I was reflecting on the fact that every generation has its own unique set of technological, social and cultural challenges. With the accelerated change that we have seen over the past 50 years, I think we can feel connected and yet oddly unconnected and that's a very confusing landscape. Within that era of confusion, I was struck by philosopher Charles Taylor's[2] belief, that despite the technological focus of the current age, the greatest challenge facing the 21st century is how to attain a better understanding of the 'other', of different cultures and ethnicities. I agree with that observation and believe that it is the challenge facing us all – not just in social science research – but it is very pertinent for journalism in an increasingly complex and connected world, but a world in which understanding remains elusive. We need to get more involved in understanding people better – certainly in terms of education – and that was the starting point for me. I see journalists as purveyors of interpretation and so I gravitated towards philosophers who perhaps give us insights into how we can, as educators, encourage our students to interpret and understand other people in a better way. So, I'm interested in the work of mid-20th century philosophers, like Hans-Georg Gadamer,[3] and his concept of horizons. To pick up on the idea of dialogue, he says that it's through dialogue and, crucially, finding space for dialogue that both interviewer and interviewee can arrive at what he calls a 'fused understanding', i.e., a deeper understanding as opposed to a superficial one, so that's where I am coming from. I am thoughtful – as I know many of us are – about the maelstrom of changes that are going on around us, but I went back to the roots, where journalism is about how we better interpret and understand each other. I drew on this early to mid-20th- century philosophy to develop ideas on how we can move away steadily from an exclusive skills focus in journalism education to create spaces where we can together broaden our horizons and deepen our understanding of each other, So, the understanding starts with, I think, students and staff understanding each other better, and hopefully when the students leave us to go out and become journalists, they have a more reflective approach to better understand the people they meet and report on.

Karen Fowler-Watt: You talked at the beginning about the lack of connectivity. I wondered whether you feel that it was something that was particularly pertinent at this point in time, 'post-Covid'?

Andy Bissell: Personally, I think we can talk casually about reaching the unreached but that can be quite disingenuous if we are all approaching from our own prejudiced viewpoint. It's not just a question of reaching people, it is what you do when you reach them. If we are not careful, we become seduced into a sense that we are connected and somehow create around ourselves a supportive technological framework, but personally I don't feel like that. The students I spoke to were also concerned about different aspects of being connected – not just the echo chambers and problems of seeking media that reinforce their own views – and the connections that they could not trust whether among friends or within the media itself. They also voiced concerns about being shut down – cancel culture came up quite a lot.

Max Mauro: The possibility to truly connect with the real world is not only, as you said, about echo chambers, it's also about the way human beings relate with each other and because very often we tend to forget that at this moment in time, one-third of the world has never been online. So my issue is that, growing up and living in the West, which is giving young people that wrong perspective of what is going on, never more than today, we need to work together in order to survive, when you think of climate crisis, for example. I think young people need to understand that their own world is not the only one, and that the fact that you are always in contact and in touch through social media and digital devices is not the only way that you can live, so this is something that worries me and I don't know if it's exactly what you had in mind, with regard to connectivity, Andy?

Andy Bissell: It is. It is that, and as another facet of being connected, I started exploring with the students questions about journalistic norms, for example, like objective truth and they, like us, recognise the limitations of objective truth in terms of all the biases and prejudices that we bring with us in life. They live in an 'opinion world', this post-truth world, so they were talking about their various interpretations of the world, and what interpretations can be deemed better than other interpretations if we are moving away (in a connected world) from objective truth? So, philosophically rather than lapse into some sort of relativism, there is a debate about how we can prioritise some interpretations over others, so connectivity has given them a platform to voice their own interpretations and opinions.

Max Mauro: Well, if I may, I'm not sure that something like objective truth ever existed! Or is it even possible? The online environment brings a multiplicity of perspectives and technically everyone can express their own views, which complicates things. Then there are the implications of people feeling threatened, despite being in powerful positions. This is the way I tend to see cancel culture. I have always been a bit doubtful about objective truth, even when I worked as a journalist, I always had the feeling that it's just me bringing some evidence of what I have witnessed. I would still question this idea of objective truth, even though, as a journalist, you need to believe that you are bringing this to the public.

Andy Bissell: In Gadamer's world, it's through dialogue and finding space in the curriculum to have these sorts of conversations so you can explore respectfully each other's perspectives and both parties emerge more reflective and have a mutual and deeper understanding of each other. I think the creation of these reflective spaces is going to be increasingly more important [in journalism education], rather than a focus on skills.

Karen Fowler-Watt: We have started to scope out the landscape, weaving a tapestry of challenges – social media, cancel culture, connectivity and notions of belonging.

David Brine: I wanted to build on the conversation about connectivity. I am grappling with this feeling, based on my observations over the past four or five years, that students are becoming less connected with politics with a capital 'P' – and with political institutions. It is so vital for our students going into news journalism that they understand how these institutions work, because you are coming up against them all the time, even when you don't think a story is a public affairs type of story or public interest journalism. A lack of understanding about how political institutions work can reduce the impact of the journalism produced. So I am exploring how we can engage, what is it predominantly an apolitical group of people with politics when many students say 'it's politics and it's boring'. Obviously, I see that as a challenge, rather than something to get depressed about!

Graham Majin: I think what everyone is saying is absolutely fascinating. You just cannot hide from epistemology, it's the central issue, it's the elephant in the room! I mean, Max states that there's no such thing as objective truth and he is suggesting that his statement is objectively true! His statement puts very neatly the orthodox mainstream view of epistemology that you will encounter when people like us sit down and start talking and I am asking, where does that come from historically in terms of intellectual history? How did that view became the mainstream view? It was introduced, effectively by the baby boomer generation, in the last third of the 20th century, and that is the way we see the world, through their eyes, the changes in values and the epistemic changes that they wrought. And they changed everything: They changed music, fashion, absolutely everything – including education and journalism – and my chapter brings these two things together: It looks at how the things we take for granted – our assumptions about truth, our assumptions about the value of education and about journalism – were constructed for us by the baby boomer generation. Now the world is changing, the tectonic plates are starting to rip, and I think it's going to get quite brutal and unpleasant. So, the question for me is: are our assumptions – both in education and journalism – fit for purpose? Discuss! I have tried to be provocative – hopefully not too provocative! – but I've tried to encourage people to see what is invisible because we can't see our assumptions and our prejudices.

Max Mauro: May I jump in? We are talking about the importance of conversation and I have in front of me a little book by Michel de Montaigne, who was considered the founder of the essay. In 1571, he wrote 'The Art of Conversation' in which he says that 'in conversation the most painful quality is perfect harmony'. So, I think we are perfectly in step with this quote, because I totally disagree with Graham! First of all, I want to be optimistic and to believe in the younger generation, because as much as I try to challenge my own pessimism, I feel that amongst people aged 20–25 or even younger there is a will to learn and to move forward, so I cannot agree with you. Obviously there has been a seismic change in culture and also the cultural industries that is undeniable, but I don't know if what was before was any more linear or more logical. Things are constantly changing, but I want to be optimistic about looking forward! Also, with regard to journalism, we have great examples of journalism, though these days they are not always coming from the big media, but from small independent news companies, so I don't know where this conversation leads us but I felt there was an element of pessimism in what you said. I agree that possibly my view, if presented superficially, might seem to be in line with the prevalent belief about post-truth I would like to think it is a bit more complex than that and it's situated in an understanding of historical and epistemological changes, but I want to be a bit more positive and optimistic.

Graham Majin: Perhaps the word is realism, rather than pessimism or optimism. Again, I think the dominant discourse, as it were, which came from the Boomer generation I would describe as *utopian*. So, anything that is less than utopian is frowned upon in the current orthodoxy. That would be my provocative view. I will just rewind if I can, to refer again to what Andy said, citing Taylor and this idea of understanding people or really how do we do that, how do we understand them? Is it through trying to have dialogue, which we have also mentioned? Increasingly the views of other people are labelled as 'misinformation' or 'disinformation' or 'fake news' and attempt to censor or silence them, because they are seen as hateful. I don't see how the direction in which we seem to be heading is possible – that we need to understand each other more – because we seem to be understanding each other <u>less</u> with every day that passes. That's not pessimistic; I'm just trying to observe the reality and not be blind to it. How do we understand each other more if we're not prepared to listen to things that are uncomfortable and difficult? I don't know.

Jo Royle: The old certainties are definitely not there anymore; this became clear in the research I share in my chapter, where I consider how journalists can be more entrepreneurial – because they need to be self-sufficient and independent. Entrepreneurship is so often seen as synonymous with capitalist, start-up culture – yet at its core so much more. I think it's interesting to examine how embedding an exchange of thinking between entrepreneurial and journalism disciplines can address the rapidly changing, unpredictable needs of the industry. This has led me to the idea of a 're-conceptualised journalist', and a re-developed approach for journalism curriculum and pedagogy that produces graduates who embody independent, flexible and adaptable practice – as well as having a strong skill set, they have an 'entrepreneurial mindset',

Julian McDougall: To go back to the quote from Freire that started this conversation, it is useful, but slightly out of context, because he writes about the pedagogy of the oppressed – about who gets to start dialogue and on what terms. I am working with Global South partners (see Chapter 6) and of course the idea of 'giving voice' to people in the Global South is deeply problematic, so the dialogue that Freire speaks of, if you are working with, for example, BBC Media Action, as I was, then you are working in countries where people are especially vulnerable to misinformation, in fragile societies lacking any kind of purchase on the civic structure of democracy. In this context, the idea of BBC Media Action appointing me as a Western academic to create a media literacy solution for these problems is on one level absurd, but at the same time really well-intentioned, so the whole chapter is about how I worked with them to try to create what we call a 'third space', which is kind of Freirean as an idea, and that's where you have this dialogue, which is a genuine, reciprocal, semi-porous membrane between bottom-up, organic – often indigenous – lived experiences of journalism, of dealing with information and dealing with fragile societies and risk. There is a paradox, what I call an 'oxymoronic neutrality', because the premise you start out from embarking on this kind of work is that you will be the solution to the problem. The lack of media literacy is the problem, but clearly the people that are creating the problem are highly media literate! So we developed a theory of change, adding two questions to the notion that media literacy is a solution:

1. How can it develop your capabilities in the world to do things differently? It's okay to just sit in your house being media literate and critical, but unless you do anything with that the media ecosystem is not going to change very much.
2. What do you want the positive consequences of that more capable citizenry to be?

Otherwise, going back to the conversation about post-truth and relativism, the problem is that all of those theoretical ideas have been seized upon by the alt-right, by conspiracy theorists and the left and the liberal, centrist-liberal academic world is left watching as post-truth develops in a bad way. Probably many of us thought it would develop in a good way, so in terms of Karen's question about the wider context and the collective, I am a bit of an outlier because I'm not coming to this as a journalist or journalism educator.

Karen Fowler-Watt: We like that – bringing different perspectives!

Julian McDougall: I come from a cultural studies perspective where you would see in a way all news is fake news – I will probably upset some of the journalists in the virtual room here – but if you come from this from a kind Stuart Hall paradigm, then you will look at *The Guardian* newspaper story and a Facebook post about vaccines or 5G, with the same healthy scepticism: it's not a purely relativist approach, but nevertheless the starting point is the same: how has this information been selected and constructed, how is it representing things? Of course, now, the problem is that as Graham said, things are getting worse, we are in a bad state where to have that kind of detached relativist complacency is dangerous as well, so in my chapter I am oscillating between these various positions and confusion.

Fiona Cownie: I found this project quite difficult, as I have never taught a journalism student and I am not embedded within journalism in the way that most of you are, but I take from this conversation so far the fundamental point about not replicating people in your own image. I think the sustainability agenda comes in there, in that we all hope that in engaging with sustainability in all its forms, the student journalists will re-evaluate their priorities and will be able to see excitement, interest, value in some of the things that perhaps ten years ago they might have thought were a little turgid. So I am able to contribute that to the idea of not reincarnating ourselves in the future. I would argue that sustainability is one of those points of distinct mission and that some – not all – students already see as being a distinctive aspect of who they are, because they're interested in that, whereas only some of our own age group display that interest.

Through the process of researching and writing the chapter (Chapter 8), I have tried to build some kind of framework for a map but I am keenly aware of *greenwashing* or of painting a picture that is not necessarily representative, as there are few modules on the journalism programme that I am writing about where the SDGs are embedded in the teaching materials. So I have tried to present case studies which show how sustainability can be engaged with, but not many people appear interested in it, or certainly aren't taking the time to declare that interest. That struck me as being a challenge; when you're trying to promote something, how can you do so in a way that you are not misrepresenting what's going on? How can you reflect on good practice to build a model for the future, but knowing that good practice is really a small island amongst something that doesn't really demonstrate much interest in sustainability?

Max Mauro: I am also working from a niche which is not very popular within journalism and media studies research – sport, but I take into account that the study of sports journalism IS very popular as we see from the number of students enrolling in sports journalism courses. In my chapter I try to reflect on the meaning of this popularity of sport, the power of sport, the complexity of sport in terms of media spectacle for political, ethical, moral, financial implications and what young students can make of this when their reasons for joining sports journalism courses are often because they are excited about the game, performances, statistics of what happened on the pitch that can be shared on social media. So how can we teach them? We constantly see proof that there is a sports element to everything. Even with the war in Ukraine one of the first things that people started to talk about when they wanted to put pressure on Russia was 'Why is UEFA[4] not banning Russian teams?' 'Why is FIFA[5] not doing something?' It was like it was the most important thing – it wasn't obviously – but the fact that Putin had hosted all the major sporting events over the last ten years said something in terms of *sportswashing*. So my chapter is about this, it is about trying to complicate things (probably!) in terms of how sports journalism is perceived and to bring different perspectives, including from working sports journalists.

Julian McDougall: The point that's just been made takes us to another – a big – elephant in the room, if you're talking about the landscape and you're writing from the UK, until relatively recently, if you wanted a case study on the dangers of misinformation you would be looking at Putin's Russia and the old mantra 'nothing is true, everything is possible'. You would be looking at perhaps China and then of course Trump, but I would argue, now that it's here [in the UK] and I think it's probably fair to say, whatever your politics that we're living through an unprecedented period of state level misinformation in our own country, so what resistance is there? Also what resistance is there from within journalism, which is much more complex than it used to be? I no longer believe that we can say that we live in a country where we enjoy a healthy relationship between free press, democracy and politics. I would observe that the UK is no longer as distinct from Russia and other countries as we might have thought or may have enjoyed believing up until Brexit and that's got to complicate things, for a book like this.

Andy Bissell: One of the themes that came through from speaking to students was a genuine concern about the future, fear and anxiety – fear of where their own personal lives were heading where our country was heading, where the world was heading. One consistent theme was this sense of a genuine and disturbing distancing of the public from government that came through loud and clear. It was interesting in that in an increasingly complex world, they felt insecure about engaging with people who were very different from them. I was left with a mixture of excitement – we've got a great opportunity here to create circumstances in which we can empower them – but also a degree of sadness that these young people had such concern about their own futures. I am very much with Max in the optimism camp, and I still feel that we can work harder to create a learning environment, to empower them to ask the big questions of those in authority and to encourage them to reflect on how they can become better listeners so they can get a deeper understanding of others.

Collective reflections

Julian McDougall: I would like to make an observation which is not based on any experience of mine, but just through listening to what you have all been saying and from my reading: I have a sense, looking at it from the outside, of a kind of confused state. There has always been this weird tension in media education between training people to work in the thing that you're at the same time critiquing, so students can have a very confused experience. They want to work in media, but they are at the same time being compelled to critique it in an almost hostile way at times. That has always been there, but it seems to me that in journalism education you are now at once training and advocating for the thing at the same time because the thing [journalism] is under threat (hence the premise of this book) – that must be very difficult pedagogically.

David Brine: I think it is three things: I think it is the skills, the advocating that media is really important and also the critiquing how it is done in practical terms. These are three things that don't always sit easily together, but I think it is important to have those three tracks running in order for students to get a well-rounded perspective – even when those three tracks collide. I am definitely aware of that tension.

Karen Fowler-Watt: And that has shifted a lot, hasn't it? We have discussed the challenges that we see facing journalism in the current 'post-pandemic' context, but the issue of trust has been a long-running issue to the point where we are all aware that a real suspicion and lack of trust has developed over time around journalists, including – and at times especially – 'mainstream' news organisations.

Andrew Bissell: I think a key challenge is how, alongside the skills and the training we encourage young people to reflect more deeply on their own perspectives. I think that's really important, the more they can get in touch with how they view the world, the more they can then appreciate alternative worlds.

Max Mauro: I think the main challenge is definitely trying to make sense of where students are coming from. So the student-centred perspective is crucial, but it's complicated in the contemporary context by social media. Social media is used by older generations in a different way from those growing up in it; their minds work differently, so I think this presents a crucial challenge. If we want to centre higher education around student perspectives, we need to understand where they are coming from. That is not so easy.

Karen Fowler-Watt: One example of the complexities we face might be that generation Z tends to see opinion and comment as the same as 'balanced' news reporting.

Max Mauro: Exactly. This is why, as I have said, particularly with something apparently as simple as sport, students need to be helped to develop a perspective and an understanding of how their subject is received by the audiences and how they should try to detach themselves from their own personal views – I think this is a big challenge, but I always want to be positive!

Andrew Bissell: We use the term the 'storytellers of the future', but I think we are saying that we need to understand the mindset of the storytellers of the future a little more because how they view the world does not necessarily equate with the way that we do, or people who are currently in industry.

Karen Fowler-Watt: So things to reflect on for journalism educators as well as for students. To Julian's point about tensions at the heart of journalism education, I think there has always been a difficulty for journalism educators, as well as practising journalists, that there is barely any time to reflect on your own practice – it's tomorrow's fish and chip wrapper and for broadcasters it is on to the next bulletin – so skills training has often been dominant, because it is about churning stuff out. As you were saying, Andy, perhaps that works when you are teaching according to the normative formulas, but now it has become more complex. The media literacy thread runs through this: how media literate are we as journalists, how media literate are audiences, how media literate are our student journalists?

Julian McDougall: There is a tension, though, that you cannot sidestep in this project – which I am sure everyone is aware of – that once you introduce media literacy to this then one of the first things we do is talk about this notion of an ecosystem, then we talk about whose voices are dominant within that ecosystem and it is indisputably the case that most journalists are from a very narrow demographic. Obviously there's a certain absurdity to me saying this because I'm probably now very squarely within that demographic, I'm very much in the power-holding group, so the logical conclusion is not to be the person that does it as a Western academic, but I guess the same thing must be true for journalism education where there must be an impulse to deconstruct where the voice is. Returning to the Paolo Freire quote: how do you use education? Is there a social mobility trajectory or diversity? At the same time, you're dealing with students who are paying fees and that presents another challenge. So, I don't know what the answer is, but I wonder if one of the challenges is at the same time as training the students, that you have in front of you, trying to advocate for change, for social justice dimensions and that's partly about representation and who actually gets to be a journalist, right? But it's difficult to do that when you are part of the problem.

Graham Majin: I think we are presenting ourselves with a circular argument: we're asking: 'What should journalism education be like?' and then we ask, 'What is journalism like?' and 'What is the requirement for journalism?' 'What is tomorrow's journalism going to be like?' We don't know so it's unanswerable – that is the whole point of the book! That is our dilemma! However, I do feel that it's like someone in the 19th century saying what sort of horse-drawn wagons will they be using in the late 20th century or what sort of steam engines will they be using? We are imprisoned, in our worldview, and all our assumptions and prejudices and the world is changing. Returning to the collapse of trust in official journalism and the massive rise of unofficial journalism – are we training journalists to work in official media, as Julian has said, the 'state-sanctioned' official voice or are we training them to work on the other side, as sceptical voices online, because these are two incompatible worlds that are fragmenting and flying apart. It is very difficult – there are no simple answers.

Andrew Bissell: I think it helps if we get away from the discourse of training, yes, people need skills, but I think that language is redundant in light of the complexities of the world that students are going to be entering and if we're talking about a more holistic reflective practitioner, I think we need to reassess terminology.

Jo Royle: Yes, I think the need for a new paradigm is really evident. The next generation of journalists need to be able to recognise very clearly and then negotiate the changes in the environment, rather than forge on trying to make an old model of news creation fit an altered marketplace. Creativity and innovation are required more than ever, as shifts in the newsroom and business models underline the precarity in the industry – and there is also the changing dynamic between journalists and audiences. I think this is key, because it has inevitably led to a more diverse and dynamic means of interaction which provides a space where new 'deliberative democratic potential' can occur. A 'linear approach' to processes in the newsroom actually restricts the potential for all voices to be heard and prevents a fully democratic media, so I would suggest that journalism must be fully publicly engaged, have new technologies embedded in processes and characterised by an entrepreneurial approach – then we might discover a new vision. This means developing a new approach to defining the role of the journalist at an ontological level – journalism requires a perspective of 'becoming' rather than 'being' as journalists' roles are constantly evolving and expanding.

Julian McDougall: This is a bit of a tangent but just bear with me for a minute! We are always worried about where we're going to go next, but you can never judge what's happening next outside of the logic of the present moment you're in. I remember when Wikipedia was part of this whole Web 2.0 big moment, and it was the democratisation of knowledge and citizen journalism, but I have recently become aware of how Wikimedia is positioning itself as a really big presence in sub-Saharan Africa in terms of media literacy and factual information. I don't know how I feel about that, because on the one level it's a good thing because it's democratisation of journalism, but there's an absence in that space of any professional journalism and so it has shifted from being a slightly subversive citizen journalists space to having hegemony as an establishment professional journalism outfit. Except it's not – it effectively gatekeeps so called factual information. They are owning a citizen journalism space.

Graham Majin: I think that's a historical process that we see with every type of journalism, that every time there is a new type of communication – typically printing – it is usually used for anti-hegemonic, subversive activity and then it is quickly taken over by the rich and powerful.

Julian McDougall: Perhaps there is something in our manifesto about being in the space and being agents of change in the space because if you – that is, those being educated – are not in the space, other agents will be.

Andrew Bissell: That will be the way forward, though, eventually, because it's getting away from just viewing journalism as a skills agenda but, equally, I wonder whether the term journalism itself is too exclusive and not universal.

Jo Royle: This is where an extended curriculum could help within journalism education aligned to an extended definition of the role of the journalist. The breaking of barriers in a range of ways could be seen as being key to the 're-imagined' journalism curriculum – that also occupies a different space, as we have already discussed, through creating different types of newsroom, allowing for experimentation and integrating with the community, to ensure that related practice becomes participative, open and iterative. So, in terms of the physical space, the newsroom should not be viewed as a solid entity in today's post-industrial journalism and this extended, non-linear, inclusive newsroom can be seen as more inclusive, residing at the heart of a democratic media that allows all voices to be heard.

Towards a manifesto for change

Our reflections led us to conclude that, as journalism educators we need to occupy the space where change can take place, but we are doing so in a context of confusion and chaos. Whilst we do not presume to have clear answers to the important questions raised in this dialogic forum – such as what journalism should we teach? – as a small collective we perceive a series of threats that could provide opportunities. To engage with these journalism educators globally may need to become agents of change.

Build resilience

Challenges	New directions
Connected but disconnected	Space for dialogue and reflection
Skills focus	Re-conceptualise mindset
Lower levels of civic engagement	Encourage understanding of others
Norms are disrupted	Interrogation of assumptions
Tensions: best practice vs. critique	Inculcate healthy scepticism
Narrow set of dominant voices in ecosystem	Agitate for change/social justice
Journalism is part of the problem	Avoid producing in own image
Solutionism	Broader canvas and interdisciplinarity

Notes

1 Founded in 1951, National Council for the Training of Journalists (NCTJ) is the main provider of accredited journalism training in the UK.
2 See Taylor, C. (1992). *The Making of the Modern Identity*. Cambridge, MA: Harvard University Press.
3 Hans-Georg Gadamer (1900–2002) was a German philosopher best known for *Truth and Method* (1960) on hermeneutics.
4 Union of European Football Associations (UEFA) is the governing body of football in Europe
5 International Federation of Association Football (FIFA) governs football worldwide.

INDEX

Note: Page numbers in *italics* refer to figures. Page numbers in **bold** refer to tables.

access 74–75, **76**, 78–82, 84
accreditation 15, 54, 118
accredited courses, real-world journalism 157
adaptability 15, 57, 120–121
advice from experts 149–150
advocacy: models 130; reporting 130; storytelling and 79
Algerian social media 79–80
alternative social order 130
American journalism 40
Anderson, C.W. 117, 123
anxiety 16, 32, 170
Apostolou, N. 152–153
Armitage, S. 1
Arts and Humanities Research Council (AHRC) 131
Associate Dean of Innovation 118
Atkins, R. 118
autonomy 102
awareness 75, **77**, 78–84
Ayyub, R. 154

Balada Yayang Bebeb in Indonesia 80
"bank-clerk" education 27
Barnes, R. 116–117, 120, 124–125
baseline skills, entrepreneurial skills 120
BBC Media Action 70, 73–74, 164, 168; interventions 78; media and digital literacy 75; mixed methods and multi-stakeholder 75

BBC Newsround 89
BBC Radio 5 Live 90
behavioural outcomes 103
Bell, A. 92
Bell, M. 41
Birt, J. 37
Bissell, A. 4, 16, 163–166, 170–173
Black Lives Matter 1, 5, 11, 89
Bloomberg Data for Health Initiative 154
Blue Peter 90
Boomer Epistemology 44
Boomer generation 37–40, 44–45, 167
Boomer Journalism 4, 41–42
both-side-ism 63
Boyle, R. 52
Bradshaw, T. 58
Bridgstock, R. 125
Brine, D. 162, 166, 171
Brit Awards 97
British universities, marketisation 53
Broadcast Journalism Training Council (BJTC) 54
Brown, D. 38–39
Buchan, G. D. 104
Buckingham, D. 71
bullying 140

Calhoun, L. G. 136
capability 74–75, **77**, 78–81, 84–85
capacity and resilience, media literacy 72
capital and labour 117
Caplan, B. 39, 123

Care Quality Commission (CQC) 62
Carey, C. 120
Carter, J. 45, 134
Castells, M. 117
Centre for Excellence in Media Practice (CEMP) 2, 6, 164
Charles, M. 134
children and ethics: emotional wellbeing 134; re-victimisation 135–136; safeguarding issues 137; semi-covert research 135; sensitive content, exposure to 136–137
civic engagement 71
civil society organisations (CSOs) 83
class diversity 95
climate change 42–43
climate-friendly practices 103
Clinical Commissioning Groups (CCG) 62
cluster analysis, media literacy 78–81
Coalition Against Online Violence 155
collaborative bricolage 119
collaborative ecosystem approach 70
comfort zone 74
communication 68; degrees 54; resilience 74
community: -centred collaboration 117; mobilisation 79; -oriented model 118; of practice 52
confidence 132
conflict anxieties 133
consequences, media literacy 75, **77**, 78–82, 85
contemporary media landscape 57
contemporary newsroom 116
continuous mediatization 116
corruption 49, 54
counter-script media work 71
covert research 135
Covid-19 misinformation 80
Cownie, F. 5, 162, 169
credentialism 38–40
Cudlipp, H. 36
culture/cultural: of job insecurity 116; lag 37; representation 55
Cummings, D. 62
Cup Diaries in Myanmar 80

Davies, A. 125
Davies, S. 40
Dawe, G. 102
decision making 102–103, 131, 141–142
Denzin, N. 59
design thinking 73

DesUni model 121–122, 126
DesUni teacher 124
detachment journalism 41
Deuze, M. 115, 117, 123–125
dialogue 161
digital and media literacy levels 78
digital communities 14
digital conspiracy networks 149
digital divide 52
digital media and social media 52
digital revolution 51
digital rights 151
digital security 150
Diploma of Journalism (NCTJ) 66
discourses of truth 76
discovery mindset 121–122, 125
discursive polarisation 71
distrust 133
diversity 95
Domeneghetti, R. 56
doping 49
Drayson, R. 102
Duening, T. 122–124
Dziuban, C. D. 125

economic restructuring 116
ecosystem hygiene 71
Edinburgh International Television Festival 63
Educational Signaling Theory 39
Education for Sustainable Development (ESD) 100
'Effectuation Theory' 122, 124
Ekdale, B. 116
El Kul project in Libya 80
embedding attitudes 120
embedding entrepreneurial skills and mindset: co-curricular approaches 120–121; curriculum design 121–122; risk-taking 122–123; significance 120
emotions/emotional 133; legacies 136; scepticism 70–71; self-management 138; well-being 134, 152
empathy 90–91, 141
employability 5
employment contracts 116
empowerment 27
enthusiasts 52
entrepreneurial constructivist approach: external engagement and community networking 123–124; student-led delivery 124–125; teaching and assessing process 125–126

entrepreneurialism 115; attitudes 119; bricolage 119; education 119; problem-solving approach 121–122; self-efficacy 123; skills 5; spirit in students 120
entrepreneurial journalism: defining 118–119; embedding entrepreneurial skills and mindset 120–123; emergent new models 116–117; entrepreneurial constructivist approach 123–126; journalism educators, skills from 117–118; journalism industry and marketplace, characteristics 116–118; journalist role, extension 117; sense of precariousness 116
environmental degradation 54
Esports and Sports Media, degrees in 54
Essential Media Law 66
Essig, L. 119, 124
ethical-political journalism 40
ethical-political narratives 42
ethical-political responsibilities 45
ethnic and racial diversity 58
European migrant crisis 152
ex-combatants in Colombia 136
experimentation 117

Faergemann, H. M. 116
'Failures of State' series 68
fake news 19, 26, 28, 167–169
false equivalence 63
Farrington, N. 53
Fayolle, A. 119
Fidler, D. 125
FIFA World Cup 49–50, 170
Floyd, G. 1, 94
Football Journalism, degrees in 54
Fowler-Watt, K. 134, 165–166, 169, 171–172
Freedom of Information Act 67
freelancing careers 120–121
Free Press Unlimited 154
Freire, P. 161
Frost, C. 120–121
fusion of horizons 31

Gadamer, H-G. 4, 165
Gailly, G 119
Galizia, D. C. 149
gamification 71
gender: empowerment 79; equality crisis 149; and ethnic diversity 57–58; inequality 79
Generational Cohort Theory 37
genocide 1, 101

getting it right mindset 121–122
Giro d'Italia 49
Global Current Affairs 107
Global Investigative Journalism Network (GIJN) 152–153
Global South 101
Gomes, E. 68
Gorbis, D. 125
"Greener Broadcasting" strategy 43
'green pen' model of journalism 104
grey space 133
Grimes, D. R. 44
Guardian, The 48, 55, 169
Guenee, P. 16
Gustafsson, M. 11

Hale, B. B. 68
Hanitzsch, T. 37
Harrabin, R. 42
hate crime 155
Henry, D. 5
hermeneutics 24, 33; attentiveness 31; self-reflection 29; storytellers 25
Higher Education (HE) 100; *see also* journalism education
Holloway, I. 135
hopelessness 133
Horizon Journalism 33–34
Human Capital Theory 39
human-caused global warming 43
humanist education 28
human trafficking 49
Hutchins, B. 52
hybridity 14

"If You Don't Know" podcast 89
immersive storytelling 34
impunity 150
inclusivity 5; future 98–99; newsroom environments and 92–97; role models 97–98
incoherent journalisms 45
Independent, The 90–91
Indian Institute of Journalism 14
industry-accredited television journalism teaching 14
industry-conceived model 118
inequalities 102–103
information disorder 71, 76
in-house sports reporters 53
inoculation strategy 71
in-stadium spectators 50
Instagram 99

International Center for Journalists (ICFJ) 12–13
international sport competitions 49
international sports journalism 54
interpersonal relationships 131, 139–140
intersectionality 95
iWatch Africa 153–154

jobs: losses, media environment realities 116; skills and intellectual education 120–121
Johnson, B. 68
journalism 90; in Colombian context 130–132; educators 1–2, 13–14, 59, 63, 154, 174; pedagogy 2; practice 11; students in dangerous digital-age world 146
journalism education 2, 11, 96, 98–99; advised 33; challenges 3–5; future directions 17–18; new directions in 5–6; and practice 32; 'red flags' 12–18; re-imagining 11–12; relationship with industry 15–16; teaching and assessment methods 13–15; well-being and duty of care 16–17; WJEC panel recommendations **18**; *see also* media literacy (ML)
Journalism Education and Trauma Research Group (JETREG) 17
Journalism Education Research Group (JERG) 2
journalistic identity 119
'Journalists at Work' survey (2018) 118
J-Schools 14, 16

Kemp, S 101
Keniston, K. 38
Ketter, S. 57
Khashoggi, J. 149
Klahan 9 78–79
Klerk, S. 119
Kolandai-Matchett, K. 104
Kramp, L. 116
Kuciak, J. 149
Kunti, S. 55

Laucella, P. 52
learning from good practice 103–105
Leone, S. 30
Level 5 Journalism Apprenticeship 65
libraries of knowledge 19
Liew, J. 57
listening 2–3
load shedding 13–14
Löbler, H. 125–126

Loch Ness Monster 67
Loosen, W. 116
Love, J. 124

'mainstream media' organisation 85
Maitlis, E. 62–63
Majin, G. 4, 44, 163, 166–167, 172–173
Major League Baseball 49
marketisation 53
mask-wearing 13
Mass, C. 43
mass media and professional sports 49
Mauro, M. 4, 162–163, 165–167, 169–171
Mayiga, J. B. 150–152
McCurdy, C. 11
McDougall, J. 4–5, 163–164, 168–173
media: artivism 72; development paradigm 83; and digital literacy 70; ecosystem 83; and information, critical evaluation 82–83; and information literacy 151; polarisation 147; practitioners 83; professionals, attacks on 148; theorists 25
Media and Information Literacy 71
media literacy (ML) 4–5, 71; awareness 84; capabilities 83–85; cluster analysis 78–81; collective 74; complex and contested 72–73; consequences 85; fact-checking and verification 85; information disorder 71; as inoculation against misinformation 80; levels 4–5; mainstream media organisation 85; publics' 71; spirit of "solutionism" 71; in their own lives 82; theory of change 73–76, **76–77**; toolkit and training 81–84
Mensah, D-G. 5, 89–99
mental well-being 152
Meta Community News Project 62, 65
micro-solidarities 142
Middle East and North Africa (MENA) region 83–84
military service 141–142
Mill, J. S. 44
Miller, T. 57
Minogue, D. 58
misinformation 97
Mott, F. 40
multimedia artefacts 110
multimedia journalists 121
Multimedia Sports Journalism, degrees in 54
multimedia teaching artefacts 108
Murdoch, R. 51
Murphy, C. 120
My Story 131–132

National Action Plan for the Safety of Journalists 147
National Council for the Training of Journalists (NCTJ) 4, 15, 54, 66, 118, 157
Naudin, A. 120
networked media sport 51
networked misogyny 149
newsroom: -centricity of journalism education 123; environments and inclusivity 92–97; safety 151
Newsround 98
newsworthiness 28
non-government organisations (NGOs) 83
non-hierarchical relationships 132
non-predictive learning mindset 120
non-predictive mindset 121–122
"non-sporting" issues 49
non-state armed groups (NSAGs) 130–132
Nussio, E. 136

Oakley, K. 117
Oates, T. P. 55
Obrador, A. M. L. 149
Olympia 57
Olympic Games 49–50
'one size fits all' approach 146
online abuse 147, 154
online and physical violence 149
online content, strengthening 105–106
online harassment 147
online spaces, safety in 155
online threats 146
online violence 148–149
on-the-ground journalism 66
Open Jirga 79
opportunistic narratives 1–2

Paris, S. 90
participatory action research (PAR) 132
partisanship and nationalism 57
Pauly, J. 55
Pavlik, J. 118
peace journalism 130
Peace Skills as narrative themes 131–132; decision-making 141–142; interpersonal relationships 139–140; and recruitment prevention 138; self-awareness and self-management 138–139; social consciousness 140–141
pedagogical guidance 100
personalisation 110
personal protection and awareness 155
Personal Protective Equipment (PPE) 62

personal safety in physical environment 151–152
pessimism 133, 167
physical conflict 147
physical threats 146
podcast listening 82
political polarisation 149
politics and public affairs: challenges 63–65; journalism student 65–66; as key knowledge 65; NCTJ public affairs 66–67; theory into practice 67–69
portable digital devices 51
post-pandemic era 1, 171
post-pandemic journalism education 3–4
post-traumatic growth (PTG) 136
post-traumatic stress disorder (PTSD) 136
poverty 133
power of shares 80
Practical Journalism 12
pre-bunking 71
press freedom 147
pressures, sports journalism 52
Price, J. 58
privacy settings 155
problem-solving approach 120
professionalisation of football 49
prolongation of education 38
pseudo-youthful 38
psycho-social approach 16
public affairs, multimedia journalism course 64
public service journalism 56

Qatar Foundation 17
Quality Assurance Agency (QAA) 100
quality press 50
quality sports journalism 56

race/racism 54, 97; diversity 95; and ethnic minorities 58; and social justice 1
radio co-presenting 79
Radio Television Afghanistan 79
Ramirez, R. 42
Rao, S. 104
real-life journalism 67
real-world journalism 157
rebelliousness 38
reciprocal learning 132
re-conceptualised journalist 168
recruitment by non-state armed groups 132–134
reductionism 101
Reflective Sustainability Mind Map 108
're-imagining' journalism 125

Index

Reporters Without Borders World Press Freedom Index (2022) 146
resilience 124, 174
resilient communities, media literacy 72–73
resistance to learning 64
Resolution Foundation 11
Ressa, M. 149
revictimisation 135–136
Revolutionary Armed Forces of Colombia (FARC) rebels 130
rich media environment 51
risk-managing mind 122–123
Rowe, D. 50, 56
Royle, J 5–6, 163, 168, 172–174
Russia–Ukraine war 147

safeguarding issues, children and ethics 137
Salzburg Academy for Media and Global Change 19
Salzburg Global Seminar 17
Sarasvathy, S. D. 122–123
Sarasvathy's Effectuation Theory 119
Sarpong, G. 153–154
scheduled media content 50
Scheepers, M. 116–117, 120, 124–125
Scottish Daily Mail 66
'self-audit' group awareness 83
self-awareness 131–132, 138–139
self-censorship 45, 56
self-determination 102
self-education 34
self-efficacy 5–6, 132, 135, 142
self-esteem 132, 138
self-exfoliation 33
self-management 131, 138–139
self-openness 33
self-sufficiency 115, 118
semi-covert approach 135
semi-professionals 52
sensitive content, exposure to 136–137
sexual harassment 155
sexual violence and murder, threats 149
Shenker, J. 68
skills-focused journalism education 33
smartphones 51
social consciousness 131, 140–141
social discontent 39
social distancing 13
social interaction 16
social literacies research 72
social media 56–57, 98
social networking capacity 124
social stress 37

societal problems, students' perceptions of 26–27
socio-economic inequity 14
socio-emotional competences 131
solutionism 71
Sparre, K. 116
special advisors (SPADs) 62
spectatorship, social dimension of 51
Spellerberg, I. 104
sponsored content, purveyors of 52
sports broadcasting 54
sports communication 54
sports journalism 64; challenges and opportunities 55–58; circulation and advertising revenue 51; education 53–55; in-house sports reporters 53; journalistic profession 50; mass media and journalism 49–50; in media industry 51; media landscape 49–53; as new media producers and bloggers 52; professional boundaries 57; professional sport leagues 49; professional sports, commercialisation and commodification 51
"sports/media complex" 49–50
sportswashing 4, 48–49, 170
stalking 155
Stephenson, R. 90
Storey, J. 118
storytelling 23–24, 79
Strategic Lawsuits Against Public Participation (SLAPPs) 147–148
strengthening, media ecosystem 78
student-centred perspective 171
student-led delivery 124–125
Sunday Times, The 68
Sunderland, M. 5
Super Bowl 51
sustainability: authentic engagement with 111; -informed content 110; -informed curriculum 109; -informed stories 104
sustainability in journalism education: education for 101–102; framework development 109, *112*; Higher Education (HE) 101–102; integrating 103–105; interdependence 108; journalism educators' approaches to 109–110; outcomes 111; recommendations for action 111–113; student learning experience related to 110–111; tools for 110
Sustainable Development Goals (SDGs) 5, 101, 162; UNESCO learning outcomes 102–103
Sydney Morning Herald 55

tacit knowledge 121
Talo iyo Tacab in Somalia 79
Taylor, C. 164
Taylor, D. 44
technological developments, media environment realities 116
Tedeschi, R. G. 136
television sets in Western societies 50
terrestrial TV stations 50–51
theory of change 74; access 74–75, **76**; awareness 75, **77**; BBC Media Action' 73–74; capability 75, **77**; comfort zone 74; communicative resilience 74; consequences 75, **77**; information disorder 76; mapping organisational strategy **76–77**; mixed methods and multi-stakeholder 75; Sen's capability approach 74
Thomson Reuters Foundation 153–154
Tik Tok 96–97, 99
Times of India, The 55
Tour de France 49, 57
traditional media 51
transformative journalism 142–143
trust and mistrust 76
Truth and Method 25, 32
Tunisian media ecosystem 74
Turchin, P. 39
Twitter 99

UK, developments in 157–158
undergraduate journalism 54
UNESCO 150–152; information disorder era 71; learning outcomes 100, 102–103
unit curriculum 107–108
university-educated journocrats 37
university journalism departments 40
Unofficial Journalism 42, 44

unprovoked physical attacks 147
Utopian radicalism 38

victimisation 133–134
victims of conflict 136
Victorian Liberal Journalism 40–41, 44
violence 6, 73, 132–136, 138–139, 147, 149
viral disinformation 149
'voice-giving' work 73
volunteerism 133
Vukić, T. 104

Wae Gyal Pikin Tinap 79
Wahl-Jorgensen, K. 123
Weedon, G. 54–56
well-being of journalists 149–150
Wenger, E. 124
White, N. 93
Whittington, R. 155–157
Willemsen, S. 120
Wilson, B. 54–55, 122–123
Witschge, T. 115, 117, 123–125
women: empowerment 79; journalists, safety of 149, 151–152; reporters 148; social capital 76
World Economic Forum report 14
World Health Organisation (WHO) 13, 131
World Journalism Education Congress (WJEC) 12–13
World Journalism Education Council 11–12
World Weather Attribution network 42
writing ability, news reporters 57

Young African Leaders Initiative (YALI) 153–154
youth-led NGO partnerships 71
youth media empowerment 79

For Product Safety Concerns and Information please contact our EU
representative GPSR@taylorandfrancis.com
Taylor & Francis Verlag GmbH, Kaufingerstraße 24, 80331 München, Germany

www.ingramcontent.com/pod-product-compliance
Lightning Source LLC
Chambersburg PA
CBHW051359290426
44108CB00015B/2079